Lessons for Implementing Human Rights from COVID-19

This book explores the effect of the pandemic on human rights; civil and political rights (CPR); economic, social, and cultural rights (ESCR); and freedoms around the world.

The COVID-19 pandemic radically changed many aspects of the lives of individuals and entire societies. This crisis and the unprecedented experience required extraordinary solutions, regulations, and rapid responses from decision-makers to limit the spread of the disease and protect societies. To this end, during this period, many countries chose to impose states of emergency, resulting in the granting of extraordinary powers to the executive. This has sometimes been a very convenient pretext for introducing various types of restrictions, oppressive surveillance, and other legal arrangements that can be qualified as human rights violations. The authors make a scholarly summary of this period, identifying possible rights violations – but above all – recommendations for the future. This crisis has shown how important it is to have universal, equitable health and social protection systems that cover all community members equally and without discrimination, and the authors remodel the concept of "human rights" and "human needs". The book covers varied examples from lockdowns to vaccination to information control, across Spain, Poland, South Africa and Uganda, the Czech Republic, Belarus and Ukraine, and Russia.

This book will appeal to higher-level students and scholars of law, political science, and international relations and will also be helpful for public policymakers at national and international levels.

Jędrzej Skrzypczak is an Associate Professor and the Head of the Department of Media Systems and Press Law in the Faculty of Political Science and Journalism at Adam Mickiewicz University in Poznan, Poland. Additionally, he serves as the Chair of the Research Committee 26 on Human Rights of the International Political Science Association and Vice President of the Polish Press Law Association.

Oscar Pérez de la Fuente is an Associate Professor of Philosophy of Law and Political Philosophy in the Department of International and Ecclesiastical Law and Philosophy of Law and in the "Gregorio Peces-Barba" Human Rights Institute at Carlos III University of Madrid, Spain. He has written on cultural pluralism, free speech, and legal interpretation. He is Coordinator of the "Cultural pluralism and rights of minorities" workshop and is currently Vice-Chair of the Research Committee 26 on Human Rights of the International Political Science Association.

Innovations in International Affairs
Series Editor: Raffaele Marchetti,
LUISS Guido Carli, Italy

Innovations in International Affairs aims to provide cutting-edge analyses of controversial trends in international affairs with the intent to innovate our understanding of global politics. Hosting mainstream as well as alternative stances, the series promotes both the re-assessment of traditional topics and the exploration of new aspects.

The series invites both engaged scholars and reflective practitioners and is committed to bringing non-western voices into current debates.

Innovations in International Affairs is keen to consider new book proposals in the following key areas:

- **Innovative topics**: related to aspects that have remained marginal in scholarly and public debates
- **International crises**: related to the most urgent contemporary phenomena and how to interpret and tackle them
- **World perspectives**: related mostly to non-western points of view

Titles in this series include:

World War Aid
Interventionist Aid and War in Ukraine
Igor Pellicciari

Activism in Hard Times in Central and Eastern Europe
People Power
Edited by Patrice C. McMahon, Paula M. Pickering and Dorota Pietrzyk-Reeves

Lessons for Implementing Human Rights from COVID-19
How the Pandemic Has Changed the World
Edited by Jędrzej Skrzypczak and Oscar Pérez de la Fuente

For more information about this series, please visit: https://www.routledge.com/Innovations-in-International-Affairs/book-series/IIA

Lessons for Implementing Human Rights from COVID-19

How the Pandemic Has Changed the World

Edited by Jędrzej Skrzypczak and Oscar Pérez de la Fuente

Routledge
Taylor & Francis Group
LONDON AND NEW YORK

First published 2025
by Routledge
4 Park Square, Milton Park, Abingdon, Oxon OX14 4RN

and by Routledge
605 Third Avenue, New York, NY 10158

Routledge is an imprint of the Taylor & Francis Group, an informa business

British Library Cataloguing-in-Publication Data
A catalogue record for this book is available from the British Library

ISBN: 978-1-032-76560-0 (hbk)
ISBN: 978-1-032-77368-1 (pbk)
ISBN: 978-1-003-48271-0 (ebk)

DOI: 10.4324/9781003482710

Typeset in Times New Roman
by KnowledgeWorks Global Ltd.

Contents

Notes on Contributors

Editors

Oscar Pérez de la Fuente is Associate Professor of Philosophy of Law and Political Philosophy in the Department of International and Ecclesiastical Law and Philosophy of Law and in the "Gregorio Peces-Barba" Human Rights Institute at Carlos III University of Madrid, Spain. He has written on cultural pluralism, free speech and legal interpretation. He is Coordinator of the "Cultural pluralism and rights of minorities" workshop, and is currently Vice-Chair of the Research Committee 26 on Human Rights of the International Political Science Association.

Jędrzej Skrzypczak is Head of the Department of Media Systems and Press Law in the Faculty of Political Science and Journalism at Adam Mickiewicz University, Poznań, Poland. In 2016 and 2022, he was nominated as an official candidate for the National Broadcasting Board by the coalition of opposition parties. He is Chair of the Research Committee 26 on Human Rights of the International Political Science Association and Vice President of the Polish Press Law Association.

Contributors

Wojciech Adamczyk is Associate Professor of AMU, in the Department of Journalism in the Faculty of Political Sciences and Journalism at Adam Mickiewicz University, Poznań, Poland.

Roman Bäcker is Professor of Political Sciences at Nicolaus Copernicus University, Torun, Poland. He was the former President of Polish Political Association (2012–2016).

Krzysztof Duda is Assistant Professor in the Department of Political Culture in the Faculty of Political Science and Journalism at Adam Mickiewicz University, Poznań, Poland. He is a member of the Political Science Committee of the Polish Academy of Sciences, where he serves as secretary.

Anna Jach is a historian, and Assistant Professor in the Chair of Eurasian Area Studies in the Institute of Russian and East European Studies in the Faculty of International and Political Studies at Jagiellonian University, Kraków, Poland.

Tomasz Litwin is Associate Professor at Jesuit University Ignatianum, Cracow, Poland.

Tomasz Maksymiuk is Chair of Social Medicine at Poznań University of Medical Sciences, Poznań, Poland.

Hannah Muzee works as a Lecturer at Kyambogo University, Uganda.

Joanna Rak is Professor of Political Sciences at Adam Mickiewicz University, Poznań, Poland.

Marianne Séverin is a Researcher at the Center for African Studies, Les Afriques dans le Monde (LAM) at Sciences Po Bordeaux, France.

Maciej Skrzypek is a PhD student at Adam Mickiewicz University, Poznań, Poland.

A. Yu. Sungurov is Professor and Head of Department of Applied Political Science at the National Research University Higher School of Economics, St. Petersburg, Russia.

Vladyslav Zinichenko is a PhD student at Adam Mickiewicz University, Poznań, Poland.

Introduction

How Has the COVID-19 Pandemic Changed the World from the Human Rights Perspective?

Jędrzej Skrzypczak and Oscar Pérez de la Fuente

Diseases, particularly infectious diseases, have had a massive impact on the lives of human populations. For centuries, they have decimated them, hampered the progress of humanity, and led to the collapse of countries or even entire civilisations. Paradoxically, their role, significance, and influence on the fate of people, countries, and continents grew with social development, including mobility development. They became increasingly dangerous, and their impact on the world's future accelerated in a particular way. Their deadly toll became greater and greater since humankind began to move significant distances in an ever shorter time to create ever larger habitats and establish cities (Krajewska, 2020)

The word epidemic derives from the Greek, *epi* meaning after, and *demos* – people. It is a disease situation involving many persons in a given area (e.g. region, country, or continent). According to the Cambridge English Dictionary, the word means "an outbreak of a disease that spreads rapidly and attacks many people" (Cambridge Dictionary, 2023). Pandemic also originates in Greek (*pan* – everyone and *demos* – people) and is defined as "an epidemic that's spread over multiple countries or continents" (Intermountain Healthcare, 2020).

According to another classical epidemiological definition, "an epidemic occurring worldwide, or over a vast area, crossing international boundaries and usually affecting a large number of people" (Bonneux & Van Damme, 2010), and pandemic is "an epidemic occurring worldwide or over a vast area, crossing international borders and usually affecting many people" (Ibid.). According to this definition, it can be argued that pandemics occur annually, given that seasonal epidemics cross international borders and affect large numbers of individuals. However, as is rightly pointed out, seasonal epidemics are not considered pandemics (Kelly, 2011),

Infectious diseases became more and more threatening as human populations grew. Thus, such illnesses decimated ancient Greece and Rome's city populations in ancient times. In 430 BC, the so-called Athenian Plague (probably the bubonic plague, typhoid, or Ebola/Marburg viruses) killed one-quarter of the population of Athens. In contrast, the so-called Antonine Plague of 166–189 AD also claimed many lives (whether it was typhoid, measles, or smallpox is still unknown). In ancient times, the natural vector for the spread of infectious diseases was human migration, whether in connection with trade, wars, conquests, or military movements. In the Middle Ages, there were many reports of pestilence harassing

DOI: 10.4324/9781003482710-1

humanity. Naturally, this can also be traced to poor hygiene, low-grade nutrition and, consequently, a lack of immunity. At the time, all such cases were called pestilence, miasma, or the Black Death, although different pathogens probably caused the individual waves. Their true causes were not known at the time. However, attempts were always made to explain it somehow, such as by the gods' revenge, punishment for sins, or even the alignment of the stars. Numerous conspiracy theories were also created, pointing to not only representatives of various minorities, such as Jews, vagabonds, beggars, and foreigners but also representatives of certain professions, such as persons with a specific smell, such as furriers or tanners, as responsible for the outbreak. This usually resulted in pogroms against these groups or at least in spreading hatred (Krajewska, 2020; Sampath et al., 2021).

For centuries, no effective remedy was known either. Preventive and curative measures, therefore, included prayers (e.g. to St Roch, patron saint of the plagued) and penitential rituals (e.g. whippings), sprinkling vinegar on letters and objects, lighting fires on street corners, bloodletting, laxatives, preparations of unicorn's horn, goat's liver, fish scales, toad hearts (Ibid.).

On the other hand, it was discovered quite quickly that an effective way of combating contagious diseases, which also deserves recognition from today's perspective of medical knowledge, was quarantined. The name derives from the Latin *quarantine* and means 40 days of isolation. This was also sometimes used as a prophylactic measure against new arrivals. As early as the Middle Ages, medics fighting epidemics also tried to protect themselves, for example by wearing very characteristic masks in the shape of a bird's beak in which various herbs were placed (Głąb & Kępa, 2010).

In the history of humankind, several pathogens have had a "tremendous worldwide career" in killing millions of persons. These include, firstly, the plague. The plague pandemic in the Middle Ages, like SARS-CoV-2, also started in China, but in Yunnan Province. Afterwards, it was "brought" to Europe along the Silk Road or with the Mongolian armies along trade routes across the continent. The disease, caused by the plague bacillus bacteria, was scientifically described as late in the 19th century (in 1894, by Alexandre Yersin). A vaccine for the illness was invented in 1890, and later, with the discovery of antibiotics, the disease was no longer dangerous. Another affliction reaping a bloody harvest was cholera, an acute gastrointestinal affliction transmitted through contaminated water. Seven pandemics of this type have been recorded over the centuries. In the case of the most severe of these in 1817, the disease spread from India to the rest of the world. It was not until 1880 that Robert Koch described the cholera bacillus, and later, a vaccine was also invented, but above all, the need for hygiene and clean water was recognised (Głąb & Kępa, 2010; Krajewska, 2020; Sampath et al., 2021).

Another pathogen responsible for the pandemic was typhoid fever, categorised as a so-called "dirty hands" disease and transmitted by food. It spread mainly during wars as camp fever, on ships or in prisons and was usually associated with hunger, poverty, and filth. Smallpox has taken a huge death toll over the centuries; it is a viral infectious disease. The largest smallpox epidemics were seen in South and North America in the 16th century, brought by white colonisers. The illness is estimated to have killed about 75% of the Indian population. The last of the great epidemics was the famous "Spanish flu" of 1918–1920, caused by the group A influenza virus, subtype H1N1. It was brought to Europe by American soldiers headed to the Western Front of the First World War, and then, with the end of the war and the return of the soldiers home after the fighting armies were disbanded, it spread throughout Europe and America. During the 20th century, several other severe influenza epidemic waves were observed, such as in 1957–1958 (Asian influenza caused by the H2N2 virus), followed by the 1968–1969 Hong Kong influenza for which the H3N2 virus was responsible. There are many other examples in this list of pathogens that caused outbreaks and pandemics. To name but a few: the HIV/AIDS virus, which was described in the 1980s and estimated to have claimed nearly 100 million lives; the Ebola virus; malaria, tuberculosis, and many others (Krajewska, 2020; Sampath et al., 2021).

It is estimated that human struggles against pathogens in the form of bacteria or viruses over the centuries have claimed more lives than all wars combined. Successive epidemics and pandemics have had an enormous impact on humanity. Firstly, they took many lives. Secondly, they usually caused significant social, economic, and political changes. Thirdly, they tended to drive scientific research and, consequently, the development of medical science and health care.

The pathogen SARS-CoV-2 coronavirus was officially diagnosed for the first time in November 2019 in Wuhan, Hubei Province, People's Republic of China, and had rapidly spread virtually worldwide by 11 March 2020. The World Health Organisation (WHO) declared the COVID-19 pandemic or Coronavirus Disease-19 (WHO, 2020). The number 19, in this case, stands for 2019, the year in which the first cases of the disease were reported in Hubei province in China. It was caused by SARS-CoV-2 or Severe Acute Respiratory Syndrome-Coronavirus-2. In this case, the "2" indicates that this is the second coronavirus discovered to cause severe acute respiratory syndromes. SARS-CoV-1 was identified in 2003, although cases of the illness were observed as early as 2002 in Guangdong province in southern China. This group of viruses originated in animals (bats), which eventually "jumped" to humans via other animals. Its particular threat and the reason for its "worldwide career" lay, on the one hand, in its ease of spread by the droplet route and its high infectiousness. Secondly, the disease symptoms do not appear until a few days after infection, so infected individuals could unknowingly transmit the virus over a distance. Thirdly, it was a relatively new virus about which very little was known, either about ways of infection, diagnosis, or treatment. Another reason was the lack of natural population immunity – finally, the high capacity for mutation (Krajewska, 2020).

According to data from the WHO, by 5 July 2023, 767,726,861 individuals had been infected with the pathogen, and 6,948,764 had died from SARS worldwide (WHO, 2023b). The situation by the WHO region is as follows: Europe: 275,710,979, Western Pacific: 204,787,106, Americas: 193,111,732, South-East Asia: 61,191,036, Eastern Mediterranean: 23,384,115, and Africa: 9,541,129 (WHO, 2023b). In turn, the pandemic situation in individual countries is as follows: the United States: 103,436,829 cases of infection, China: 99,292,081,

India: 44,994,351, France: 38,989,382, Germany: 38,435,774, Brazil: 37,671,420, Japan: 33,803,572, Republic of Korea: 32,256,154, Italy: 25,897,801. Interestingly, the only country where, at least officially, no case of infection, let alone death, has been reported in Turkmenistan (WHO, 2023b).

It is worth recalling here that human rights are defined as a set of legal norms to which all human beings, regardless of race, gender, nationality, ethnic origin, language, religion, or any other status, are entitled to protect human dignity (UN, 2023a; Marks, 2016). Many different classifications of this legal category can be indicated in the doctrine. One of the most important is the division into civil and political rights (CPR) on the one hand and economic, social, and cultural rights (ESCR) on the other (UNIC, 2018). The Universal Declaration of Human Rights of 1948 (UN, 1948) did not distinguish between the rights of individuals. At that time, it was planned to regulate both categories in one document.

Ultimately, they were included in two different documents, that is the International Covenant on Civil and Political Rights (UN, 1966a) and the International Covenant on Economic, Social, and Cultural Rights (UN, 1966b), which was caused by Cold War tensions between the East and the West. Western democratic countries emphasised the importance of CPR, while the Soviet bloc countries referred to economic, social, and cultural ones.

As mentioned above, two separate pacts were adopted within the UN in 1966 due to this dispute. After eliminating the Iron Curtain, it was pointed out that such a division was anachronistic and completely unnecessary. Some differences are indeed emphasised, namely that ESCR usually involve the obligation of states to a high level of investment to fulfil their responsibilities towards their citizens. In contrast, CPR require the state only to refrain from interference with individual freedoms (OHCHR, 2024c).

It is not feasible to describe all the issues and threads concerning the phenomenon described here in a monograph such as this. It was also not possible to describe the situation in each country or even region of the world. In 11 chapters, the authors of individual parts analyse the impact of the COVID-19 pandemic on selected human rights such as personal freedom, freedom of movement, freedom of speech, access to information, CPR, equality of citizens before the law, right to health, prohibition of forced labour, prohibition of subjecting to forced medical experiments, and the right to consent to medical procedures. As you can see, in this book, you can find categories of human rights as well as CPR or ESCR.

Therefore, the question arises whether, after the COVID-19 pandemic, it is necessary to remodel the concept of traditionally defined human rights, for example towards the idea of these categories understood as human needs. Although this is not a new concept (Gasper, 2005; Goldewijk & Fortman, 1999; Hamilton, 2003; Pogge, 2007), it may be instrumental in the context of the issues discussed here. However, regardless of the theoretical concepts, there is no doubt today, based on the experience related to the COVID-19 pandemic, that it is necessary to give a completely new position and meaning to the right to health as fundamental in the 21st century – as the experience of recent years has shown – the need to ensure an appropriate level of physical and mental well-being. We should, therefore, have no doubts that this category should be included in human rights in the sense referred to above.

Many dimensions of this right have been identified, in particular, equal and easy access to healthcare, prevention of illness, protection against health risks, and maternal and child care. It was first reaffirmed in the 1946 Constitution of the WHO. The preamble emphasises that "the enjoyment of the highest attainable standard of health is one of the fundamental rights of every human being without distinction of race, religion, political opinion, economic or social condition" (WHO, 1946).

Health is defined as "a state of complete physical, mental and social well-being and not merely the absence of disease or infirmity" (Ibid.). In the 1948 Universal Declaration of Human Rights, Article 25 postulates the right to a standard of living that ensures, among other things, health (UN, 1948). The 1966 International Covenant on Economic, Social and Cultural Rights in Article 12 guarantees the right of everyone to the enjoyment of the highest attainable standard of physical and mental health (UN, 1966b). At the same time, it obliges States Parties to take all possible measures to achieve the full realisation of this privilege, in particular, to prevent, treat, and combat epidemic, endemic, occupational, and other diseases and to create conditions that would ensure medical assistance and care for all in the event of illness. At the turn of the 20th and 21st centuries, the right to the highest attainable standard of health began to be emphasised. Consequently, the Office of the Special Rapporteur for the privilege of everyone to the highest possible standard of physical and mental health was created in 2002 (OHCHR, 2008).

The impact of the COVID-19 pandemic on cases of threats to, even violations of, human rights and CPRs or ESCRs, remains a highly controversial issue. This crisis required unusual solutions, regulations, and a solid response to limit the spread of the disease and protect societies. The dramatic health situation often made it relatively easy to justify even the most restrictive solutions and constraints. Often, however, it was a convenient pretext to introduce oppressive surveillance of individuals and entire communities and to undermine the violation of human rights, such as political, social, and cultural rights (especially freedom of speech) and the right to privacy. Civil liberties and political rights were constantly interfered with to save lives and health. It was not only in authoritarian states that there were various temptations to pursue, under the pretext of fighting the pandemic, private interests, intentions and political and legal actions in a non-transparent manner (Club de Madrid, 2021).

As was the case centuries ago, during this pandemic, numerous conspiracy theories, albeit on an unprecedented scale, have emerged to explain the reasons for the emergence and spread of the pathogen, which have absolutely no support in facts or scientific research. According to one such "theory", 5G cellular networks were responsible for spreading the virus and were created to increase the coverage of 5G networks. According to another theory, the virus was said to have leaked from a laboratory in Wuhan, China, prepared as a bio-weapon. Other concepts claim that COVID-19 vaccines are part of a conspiracy to control the population or implant microchips in human bodies to control them. Still, diverse factoids reported several drugs effective in treating infected individuals, such as hydroxychloroquine or ivermectin. According to yet another theory famous on social media, the pandemic was invented by pharmaceutical companies to profit from the sale of vaccines. According to proponents of this view, any news journalistic footage showing hospitals besieged by critically ill patients was just a staged fabrication invented to deceive the public. It seems that never before in history has there been so much disinformation. This is why the term infodemia was used as a metaphor for infecting with factoids (WHO, 2023). Indeed, the extraordinary popularity of social media has contributed to all these negative phenomena (Ibid.).

It will be argued that, as never before, a so-called medical populism has developed. Here, this term refers to political or social behaviour and strategies of downplaying the dangerous effects of a disease, proposing easy solutions to a crisis or scientifically unproven treatments, and raising pseudo-scientific objections to medical knowledge to demonstrate assumed populist theses (Lasco, 2020). According to another definition, medical populism is a "political style based on performances of public health crises that pit 'the people' against 'the establishment'. While some health emergencies lead to technocratic responses that soothe the anxieties of a panicked public, medical populism thrives by politicising, simplifying, and spectacularising complex public health issues". (Lasco & Curato, 2019).

When vaccines for the coronavirus were developed in record time as virtually the only panacea in the fight against the disease, and it seemed that the COVID-19 pandemic would finally crush all sorts of flat-earthers, including adherents of the anti-vaccine movements, it paradoxically turned out that these movements were strengthened. Even their arguments were taken up by some populist political actors.

After several successive waves of infections reported in various regions of the world, it can reasonably be considered that the pandemic died down due to multiple factors, such as administering over 13.5 billion doses of vaccines, obtaining herd immunity, and mutations of the virus itself. Even the People's Republic of China announced at the turn of December 2022 and January 2023 the lifting of all restrictive measures. On 5 May 2023, the Director of the UN World Health Organisation, Tedros Adhanom Ghebreyesus, declared "the end of the COVID-19 pandemic as a public health emergency". At the same time, he stressed that this did not mean the disease was no longer a global threat (UN, 2023). Hence, it can be accepted that the current time perspective allows for a scientific summary of this period, indicating possible cases of related human rights violations – but most importantly – recommendations for the future.

It is also essential to reflect on the role the treaty bodies of international organisations, particularly the United Nations (UN), have played in global pandemic management. At the time, a variety of actions were taken in response to the COVID-19 pandemic, articulating concerns about the protection of human rights, the social inequalities associated with the application of emergency measures during this period, emphasising, in particular, the need to respect the principle of non-discrimination and equality. At the same time, the need for international cooperation was emphasised. These actors also played a crucial role in monitoring human rights violations. In addition, UN bodies have consistently called, as they grapple with the impact of the spell, for international solidarity, the sharing of resources and knowledge, and the need for a human rights-based approach in dealing with the pandemic and its aftermath to ensure that emergency measures are lawful, necessary, proportionate, non-discriminatory, and temporary and that they are closely reviewed and, where necessary, adjusted to ensure compliance with international human rights standards (OHCHR, 2020).

Numerous guidelines and statements were issued at the time, calling on States to ensure that measures taken in response to the pandemic complied with international human rights standards. In doing so, they wished to draw attention to the disproportionate impact of the phenomenon on population groups particularly vulnerable to the harmful effects of such measures. These include representatives of such groups, including migrants, refugees, prisoners, and persons living in poverty, the elderly, individuals with disabilities and those in precarious living situations, particularly in the crisis of homelessness, and various minorities, that is including racial and ethnic ones.

Another issue of interest and concern to UN treaty bodies during the pandemic, quite understandably, was the right to health. This highlighted the obligation of UN member states to ensure equal access to healthcare and to provide health services in a timely, respectful and non-discriminatory manner.

Another issue highlighted by the UN in the context of the pandemic was the need to preserve the freedom of professional media and access to reliable and legal information and to combat disinformation. It was emphasised that during the COVID-19 onrush, there was a need to provide accurate, accessible and timely information on the virus and related health measures (OHCHR, 2024a).

The activities undertaken within the framework of the so-called Special Procedures of the UN Human Rights Council, that is involving the activities of special thematic rapporteurs, working groups, and independent experts, should also be noted. The actions of these actors in this area addressed various aspects of the pandemic, including ESCR. This mode called for specific legal solutions to limit its adverse impact on work, education, housing, and food security. In addition, social protection measures were called for to support those affected by the contagion. Concerning freedom of expression and assembly, it was warned against using the pandemic as a pretext to suppress dissent and limit freedom of expression or access to information. On the other hand, regarding the protection of the rights of certain vulnerable groups of the population, the rights of indigenous peoples, children, persons with disabilities, and others were called. In addition, with some anti-pandemic measures, potential environmental risks were also seen in this context (OHCHR, 2024b).

It is essential to highlight the role of the WHO in the global fight against the COVID-19 pandemic. As the coordinating body for international public health, the WHO's activities and responsibilities cover several vital areas to instruct and support member countries in detecting, preventing, and responding to the phenomenon. The Organisation's tasks during the COVID-19 surge included but were not limited to monitoring and assessing the development of the latter; providing expert and reliable information on the pandemic situation; supporting related guidance; coordinating global mitigation efforts; facilitating international cooperation among member states; supporting research and innovation in the field, in particular by coordinating research and making a significant contribution to accelerating vaccine development; promoting equitable access to resources; and countering misinformation. The WHO provided comprehensive guidance on managing a viral outburst, including strategies for testing, treatment, prevention, and control of infection and necessary public health measures. In addition, the WHO offered technical assistance to member countries to strengthen their health systems, improve surveillance, and implement effective public health measures. It should also not be overlooked that, through regular press briefings and reports, the WHO has played a crucial role in informing the global community about the dynamics of the onslaught, research findings and efforts to respond to the global public health threat, contributing significantly to the fight against misinformation, on 30 January 2020. The WHO announced a Public Health Emergency International Condition (PHEIC) and, on 11 March 2020, declared COVID-19 a pandemic. These statements were intended to mobilise international efforts to respond to this dangerous emergency. The WHO has also worked to foster collaboration between countries, forensic researchers, and healthcare providers to share knowledge, experiences, and resources in the fight against the upsurge. The Organisation's efforts to accelerate work on SARS-CoV-2 vaccines are particularly appreciated. Through initiatives such as the COVID-19 Accelerator for Access to Tools (ACT, WHO, 2024) and COVAX (WHO, 2023), the Institution has played a vital role in developing, producing and equitably distributing COVID-19 vaccines, diagnostics, and therapies. The WHO has also coordinated global research efforts, including the Solidarity Trial, to find effective COVID-19 treatments and has issued guidance on ethical standards in research. However, it should also be noted that throughout the pandemic, the WHO has faced robust criticism for some of its actions, particularly regarding the timeliness and speed of its declarations and responses and communication with the global community and member states. It should also not be forgotten that the Organisation was operating under enormous political pressure. Despite these challenges, its role was crucial in managing this unprecedented public health crisis globally. Significantly, the WHO has always stressed the importance of international cooperation and solidarity in addressing global health crises (WHO, 2021).

It is worth recalling that Article 19 of the WHO Constitution (WHO, 1946) empowers the Health Assembly to negotiate and agree "conventions and agreements on any matter within the competence of WHO". Therefore, at the WHO initiative, steps have been taken to develop a global agreement to ensure better preparedness and response to future pandemics. This is the so-called "Pandemic Treaty". The experience of the COVID-19 avalanche led to the recognition of the need for enhanced international cooperation in the face of global health crises. The goals of the Pandemic Treaty include improving surveillance, sharing data and pathogen samples, ensuring equitable access to vaccines, treatments, and diagnostics, and strengthening health systems worldwide. The treaty aims to provide a legal framework that will bind countries to specific commitments, thereby improving the world's ability to prevent, prepare for, and respond to future such phenomena. Negotiations and discussions on the treaty involve various stakeholders, including governments, international organisations, civil society, and the private sector. The treaty is still being negotiated. Given the complexity of the issues involved and the need for consensus among WHO member states, the current negotiations on this draft do not inspire optimism about the chances of reaching a final agreement (Furlong, 2024).

It is essential to note the role played by regional human rights bodies, including the European Court of Human Rights (ECHR), the Inter-American Court of Human Rights (IACHR), and the African Court on Human and Peoples' Rights (AfCHPR) – during the COVID-19 pandemic. These bodies have dealt with various cases highlighting the impact of the spell on rights such as the right to health, freedom of movement, the right to life, the right to information, and freedom from discrimination. Their decisions and advisory opinions have helped shape State responses to ensure they are consistent with human rights obligations (Braithwaite et al., 2020).

Concerning the measures taken by States in response to the pandemic, the European Court of Human Rights has examined complaints concerning violations of several provisions of the European Convention on Human Rights, including the right to life (Art. 2) and the prohibition of torture and inhuman or degrading treatment (Art. 3, Feilazoo v. Malta, 11 March 2021; Ünsal and Timtik v. Turkey, 8 June 2021 Fenech v. Malta, No. 19090/20 1 March 2022; Chamber judgment; Faia v. Italy, decision (Committee) on the admissibility of 29 August 2023; Hafeez v. the United Kingdom, 28 March 2023; Rus v. Romania 9 May 2023; Riela v. Italy, 9 November 2023; Grgičin v. Croatia, 12 December 2023; Maratsis and Others v. Greece, No. 30335/20; Vasilakis and Others v. Greece, No. 30379/20; Vlamis and Others v. Greece No. 29655/20) and four other applications Nos. 29689/20, 30240/20, 30418/20 and 30574/20; Krstić v. Serbia (no. 35246/21) and six other applications; Gözütok v. Turkey, No. 41412/21; the right to liberty and security of person (Art. 5 - Fenech v. Malta, 23 March 2021; Perstner v. Luxembourg, judgment of 16 February 2023; Terheş v. Romania, 20 May 2021; Bah v. the Netherlands, 22 June 2021; Khokhlov v. Cyprus, 13 June 2023; Ait Oufella v. France, No. 51860/20) and three other applications (EB v. Serbia and AA v. Serbia, Nos. 50086/20 and 50898/20), the right to a fair trial (Art. 6 – Makovetskyy v. Ukraine; Q and R v. Slovenia, No. 19938/20, 8 February 2022; Rybár and Veselská v. Slovakia; Lini SRO v. Slovakia); the right to respect for private and family life (art. 8 DC v. Italy, no. 17289/20; Narbutas v. Lithuania); Freedom of thought, conscience and religion (Art. 9); Freedom of expression, of assembly and association (Art. 10 – CGAS v. Switzerland), freedom of assembly and association (Art. 11 Constantin-Lucian Spînu v. Romania), Protection of property (Scheffer v. Slovakia No. 16627/21); Right to education MCK and M.H.K.-B. v. Germany, No. 26657/22); Freedom of movement (Pešić and Others v. Serbia, Nos. 48973/20, 54565/20 and 54676/20); the requirements for admissibility of a complaint to the ECtHR (Art. 35 – victim status and admissibility criteria, Feilazoo v. Malta, 11 March 2021; Ünsal and Timtik v. Turkey, 8 June 2021; Fenech v. Malta (no. 19090/20), 1 March 2022 (Chamber judgment); Faia v. Italy, decision (Committee) on the admissibility of 29 August 2023; Hafeez v. the United Kingdom, 28 March 2023;

Rus v. Romania, 9 May 2023; Riela v. Italy, 9 November 2023; Grgičin v. Croatia, 12 December 2023; Maratsis and Others v. Greece, No. 30335/20); Vasilakis and Others v. Greece, No. 30379/20; Vlamis and Others v. Greece, No. 29655/20 and four other applications, Nos. 29689/20, 30240/20, 30418/20 and 30574/20); Krstić v. Serbia, No. 35246/2). The Court emphasised the importance of States' obligations to protect the health and well-being of individuals, particularly in places of detention, and the need for lawful, necessary, and proportionate measures (ECHR, 2024). In Le Mailloux v. France, the Court recalled that although the right to health as such is not among the rights guaranteed by the European Convention on Human Rights and its Protocols, States have a positive obligation to take appropriate measures to protect the life and physical integrity of individuals, including in the field of public health (Le Mailloux v. France).

The Inter-American Commission on Human Rights (IACHR) has issued resolutions and recommendations to ensure the rights of vulnerable groups, including indigenous peoples, Afro-descendants, persons deprived of their liberty and migrants, in regulations to combat the contagion (IACHR, 2022). It also urged States to consider their obligations under the American Convention on Human Rights when designing and implementing pandemic response measures and to ensure that any restrictions on rights are consistent with international standards (IACHR, 2023).

The African Court on Human and Peoples' Rights has only ruled on isolated cases related to the COVID-19 pandemic (ACHPR, 2020c). At the same time, the African Commission on Human and Peoples' Rights has issued guidelines to state parties on actions and measures to respect human rights during such a spell, including, in particular, the need to ensure the safety of health workers, access to information and health care, the protection of vulnerable groups, and the importance of respecting judicial guarantees and the rule of law during a crisis (ACHPR, 2020b, 2020c; ACHPR, 2022a).

In democratic societies, accountability is a cornerstone of political responsibility and varies across political cultures. It manifests in three levels: responsiveness, answerability, and enforceability.

Responsiveness is about politicians considering the electorate's mandate through free, regular elections, effectively allowing citizens to reward or punish leaders based on their performance. Answerability demands politicians to provide information and justifications for their actions, involving both the right to receive explanations and the obligation to offer them. This level emphasizes rulers' need to respond to questions about their conduct and management.

Enforceability, or enforcement accountability, involves imposing consequences for the actions of those in public office, which includes formal or informal rewards and sanctions. It insists that officeholders explain their actions and accept the repercussions, ranging from negative publicity to legal sanctions.

Political, fiscal, and administrative accountabilities are identified as different domains where these principles apply, with political accountability central to democratic representation and political responsibility. It's also noted that accountability can be seen as a virtue, implying transparency and fairness in governance.

There are vertical, horizontal, and diagonal types of accountability. Vertical accountability allows citizens to hold policymakers accountable through elections and is supported by freedoms of opinion, association, and access to information. Horizontal accountability involves state agencies monitoring and possibly sanctioning other state agencies or officials for wrongful acts. Diagonal accountability is a newer concept where civil society actors engage in both vertical and horizontal accountability, often via direct participation in government oversight.

The interplay of these types of accountability and the roles of various actors, including the media, opposition parties, and civil society organizations, shape the democratic process. Ultimately, accountability in a democracy involves a complex web of mechanisms and relationships that aim to ensure that those in power are held responsible for their actions and are responsive to the citizens they serve.

In their texts, the book's authors took up diverse threads and cases from the political practices of many countries on different continents. The central hypothesis of the volume is that the years 2020–2022 and, thus, the period of the COVID-19 pandemic have changed the world, political systems, democracies, societies, and economies in unprecedented ways. A similar reflection also applies to human rights. The authors of the following chapters of this book focus on the issue of violations of selected human rights (HRs), or CPR, as well as ESCRs – because all these categories aim at protecting individual freedoms and ensuring justice. Although they differ in scope, origin, and application, they all relate to fundamental human rights.

As it seems, nothing will ever again be the same as before the emergence of the SARS-CoV-2 coronavirus. It is impossible, within the framework of a single study, to cover all these issues. Hence, it was decided to select some of them. Thus, firstly, the focus was on selected CPR that suffered during this period. Secondly, an attempt was made to emphasise the importance of the right to health as a human right in the new reality. Another aspect of human rights focused on was personal liberty in its various approaches. A considerable amount of space was also devoted to freedom of expression, including freedom of the media and, finally, freedom of association and the functioning of citizens' movements under pandemic conditions. In Chapter 1 by Oscar Pérez de la Fuente ("Accountability and COVID-19. The Spanish perspective"), an analysis of the COVID-19 pandemic was undertaken from the point of view of possible accountability and legal responsibility of political decision-makers, exemplified by Spain. In Chapter 2, Roman Bäcker and Joanna Rak consider the enforcement of equality before the law in Poland during the coronavirus pandemic. In Chapter 3, Marianne Séverin and Hannah Muzee address the issue of entrepreneurs' rights during the COVID-19 surge in the example of South Africa and Uganda, in the context of such negative phenomena as corruption and violation of the rights to health and development. The magnitude of the effects of the COVID-19 onslaught and international experience means that in Chapter 4, A.Yu. Sungurov (New World Order After the Pandemic: Can "New Political Thinking" Be Reinvented) will propose considerations on the need to introduce a new global political order. One should make a reservation here that, firstly, this is the voice of a researcher from Russia who refers to the experience of his country in the Gorbachev era. Secondly, it was submitted before 24 February 2022, that is before the Russian Federation unleashed a war in Ukraine. The following three fragments of the proposed work will focus on the broadly understood right to health protection issues in this challenging situation, presented in assorted aspects. The authors have attempted to answer several pertinent questions relating to the critical elements of the healthcare system in each country, that is the legal situation and protection of the rights of medical workers (Chapter 5: Models of Human Resource Management in Healthcare Systems During a Pandemic on the Example of Poland by Jędrzej Skrzypczak and Tomasz Maksymiuk) as well as possible models of organisational solutions in the fight against the phenomenon (smart quarantine vs strict lockdown) and their impact on the political rights of citizens, as exemplified by of the experience of the Czech Republic (Chapter 6: Smart Quarantine vs Strict Lockdown. Restrictions on Political Rights in Anti-Pandemic Strategies in the Czech Republic by Maciej Skrzypek). The assessment of the mandatory vaccination against COVID-19 introduced in many parts of the globe from the point of view of personal freedoms and human rights is also mentioned (Chapter 7: Is Obligatory Vaccination Against COVID-19 Acceptable from the Human Rights Perspective? By Tomasz Litwin). The subsequent three chapters address the influence of the pandemic on freedom of expression and media markets (Chapter 8: Freedom of Speech During the Time of COVID-19 Pandemic by Jędrzej Skrzypczak and Krzysztof Duda; Chapter 9: The Impact of the COVID-19 Pandemic on Changes in the Media Market and Information Pluralism by Wojciech Adamczyk; Chapter 10: The COVID-19 Pandemic as Another Pretext for Information Control. Case Studies of Belarus and Ukraine). The last fragment of the work touches on diverse aspects of grassroots activity of citizens in response to worsening pandemic-related crisis (Chapter 11: Grassroots Activity of Russian Citizens in Response to Deteriorating Pandemic-Related Crisis of the State by Anna Jach). In the end, in addition to summarising the essential individual chapters, postulates and recommendations for the future in the field of protection of human rights in the conditions of a pandemic will be presented. It cannot be ruled out that humanity will face similar challenges again in the foreseeable future.

The scientific achievements presented in this volume, thanks to authors from many world research centres, offer a wealth of topics on the described phenomena. Paradoxically, therefore, varied perspectives, accounts, approaches, and scientific methods used by the authors of individual chapters from different parts of the planet, representing diverse fields of social sciences (political science, law, philosophy) are united by the same foundation, in the form of the influence of the COVID-19 onrush on the state of respect for human rights and CPR or ESCR, speaking in favour of the uniqueness and success of this scientific project. As mentioned above, assorted scientific research methods, characteristic of legal, political, and other social sciences, were used in creating subsequent fragments of the work, such as the institutional method, legal text exegesis, the process of philosophical and ethical analysis, and case studies. Certainly, however, due to the work's framework, it was impossible to exhaust all possible themes.

Therefore, it was not realistic to describe the situation in each country or even region of the world. The authors of individual chapters, although they often referred –

which is entirely understandable due to their own experiences and participant observation – to the situation in their countries or continents (Uganda, South Africa, Spain, Poland, Ukraine, and Russia), tried on this basis to make appropriate generalisations and draw conclusions for the whole international community. Moreover, in many parts of the book, there is a comparative analysis of various political, legal, and health systems. It seems, therefore, that all these puzzles can be put together to create a picture of the essential threats resulting from pandemic restrictions on the legal situation and freedom of individuals at every longitude and latitude, regardless of the prevailing political regime in a given country.

However, thanks to this, the conclusions and arguments presented here remain fully valid and can meet with appreciable interest. Moreover, based on the analysis of cases from different parts of the world, recommendations for the future will be presented at the end.

Bibliography

ACHPR. (2020a). *African commission on human and peoples' rights. 449 resolution on human and peoples' rights as central pillar of successful response to COVID-19 and recovery from its socio-political impacts - ACHPR/Res. 449 (LXVI) 2020.* https://disasterlaw.ifrc.org/sites/default/files/media/disaster_law/2021-06/ACHR_449%202020.pdf

ACHPR. (2020b). *The African commission's response to the COVID-19 pandemic.* https://gchumanrights.org/gc-preparedness/equality-and-non-discrimination/article-detail/the-african-commissions-response-to-the-covid-19-pandemic.html

ACHPR. (2020c). *Advisory opinion no 001/2020, on the right to participate in the government of one's country in the context of an election held during a public health emergency or a pandemic, such as the Covid-19 crisis, requested by Pan African Lawyers Union (PALU).* https://www.african-court.org/cpmt/storage/app/uploads/public/60f/574/3a6/60f5743a61e75369142990.pdf

Bonneux, L., & Van Damme, W. (2010). Preventing iatrogenic pandemics of panic. Do it in a NICE way. *BMJ (Clinical research ed.)*, *9*(340), c3065. https://pubmed.ncbi.nlm.nih.gov/20534667/

Braithwaite, B., Harby, C., & Miletić, G. (2020). *Covid-19 and the impact on human rights, an overview of relevant jurisprudence of the European Court of Human Rights, AIRE Centre.*

Cambridge Dictionary. (2023). https://dictionary.cambridge.org/pl/dictionary/english-spanish/pandemic

Club de Madrid. (2021, December). *Democracy & emergencies. Lessons from the COVID-19 pandemic for democratic resilience. Final report of the Global Commission on Democracy and Emergencies.* https://clubmadrid.org/wp-content/uploads/2022/04/Global-Commission_Report_DIGITAL.pdf

ECHR. (2024). *European court of human rights. Factsheet - Covid-19 health crisis.* https://www.echr.coe.int/documents/d/echr/FS_Covid_ENG

Furlong, J. (2024, January 4). *Why the world's first pandemic treaty may never happened. With less than six months to go, countries are still not really negotiating, say diplomats.* https://www.politico.eu/article/pandemic-treaty-negotiations-countries-risking-failure-covid-who-sharing-mechanism/

Gasper, D. (2005). Needs and human rights. In R. Smith, & C. van den Anker (Eds.), *The essentials of human rights* (pp. 269–272). Hodder & Stoughton.

Głąb, H., & Kępa, M. (2010). *Wielkie epidemie na przestrzeni wieków. Wszechświat, 111*(4–6), 137–140. https://wszechswiat.ptpk.org/index.php/wszechswiat/article/view/328

Goldewijk, B. K., & Fortman, B. G. (1999). *Where needs meet rights*. WCC Publications.
Hamilton, L. (2003). *The political philosophy of needs*. Cambridge University Press.
IACHR. (2023, April 17). *Inter-American Commission on Human Rights Issues Report on the Pandemic and Human Rights*. https://www.oas.org/en/iachr/jsForm/?File=/en/iachr/media_center/preleases/2023/066.asp
IACHR. (2022). *Inter-American Commission on Human Rights. Pandemic and Human Rights*. https://www.oas.org/en/iachr/reports/pdfs/2023/PandemiaDDHH_EN.pdf
Intermountain Healthcare. (2020, April 2). *What's the difference between a pandemic, an epidemic, an endemic, and an outbreak? By Intermountain Healthcare*. https://intermountainhealthcare.org/blogs/whats-the-difference-between-a-pandemic-an-epidemic-endemic-and-an-outbreak
Kelly, H. (2011). The classical definition of a pandemic is not elusive. *Bulletin of the World Health Organization*, *89*(7), 540–541. World Health. https://apps.who.int/iris/bitstream/handle/10665/270942/PMC3127276.pdf?sequence=1&isAllowed=y·
Krajewska, H. (2020). Pandemie w historii świata. *Wieś i Rolnictwo*, *3*(188). https://kwartalnik.irwirpan.waw.pl/wir/article/view/751
Lasco, G. (2020). Medical populism and the COVID-19 pandemic. *Global Public Health*, *15*(10), 1417–1429. https://doi.org/10.1080/17441692.2020.1807581.
Lasco, G., & Curato, N. (2019). Medical populism. *Social Science & Medicine*, *221*, 1–8.
Marks, S. P. (2016). *Human rights: A brief introduction*. Harvard University.
OHCHR. (2008). *The right to health. Fact sheet no. 31*. https://www.ohchr.org/sites/default/files/Documents/Publications/Factsheet31.pdf
OHCHR. (2020). *The Office of the United Nations High Commissioner for Human Rights. Human Rights Treaties Branch, Compilation of statements by human rights treaty bodies in the context of the COVID-19 pandemic*. https://www.ohchr.org/sites/default/files/External_TB_statements_COVID19.pdf
OHCHR. (2024a). *The Office of the United Nations High Commissioner for Human Rights. COVID-19 and Human Rights Treaty Bodies*. https://www.ohchr.org/en/treaty-bodies/covid-19-and-human-rights-treaty-bodies
OHCHR. (2024b). *The Office of the United Nations High Commissioner for Human Rights. COVID-19 and Special Procedures*. https://www.ohchr.org/en/special-procedures-human-rights-council/covid-19-and-special-procedures
OHCHR. (2024c). *Key concepts on ESCRs - Are economic, social and cultural rights fundamentally different from civil and political rights?* https://www.ohchr.org/en/human-rights/economic-social-cultural-rights/escr-vs-civil-political-rights
Pogge, T. (2007). *Poverty and human rights*. https://www2.ohchr.org/english/issues/poverty/expert/docs/Thomas_Pogge_Summary.pdf
Sampath, S., Khedr, A., Qamar, S., Tekin, A., Singh, R., Green, R., & Kashyap, R. (2021). Pandemics throughout the history. *Cureus*, *13*(9), 18136. https://doi.org/10.7759/cureus.18136. PMID: 34692344; PMCID: PMC8525686
UN. (1948). *Universal declaration of human rights*. https://www.un.org/en/about-us/universal-declaration-of-human-rights
UN. (1966a). *International covenant on civil and political rights (ICCPR) adopted 16 December 1966 by general assembly resolution 2200A (XXI)*. https://www.ohchr.org/sites/default/files/Documents/ProfessionalInterest/ccpr.pdf
UN. (1966b). *International covenant on economic, social and cultural rights, (ICESCR), adopted 16 December 1966 by general assembly resolution 2200A (XXI)*. https://www.ohchr.org/en/instruments-mechanisms/instruments/international-covenant-economic-social-and-cultural-rights
UN. (2023a). *Human rights*. https://www.un.org/en/global-issues/human-rights)
UN. (2023b). *WHO chief declares end to COVID-19 as a global health emergency*. https://news.un.org/en/story/2023/05/1136367
UNIC. (2018). Kategorie praw człowieka, Warsaw. https://www.unic.un.org.pl/prawa-czlowieka/kategorie-praw-czlowieka/3131

WHO. (1946). *The World Health Organization. Constitution of the World Health Organization adopted by International Health Conference held in New York, signed on 22 July 1946*. https://apps.who.int/gb/bd/PDF/bd47/EN/constitution-en.pdf?ua=1
WHO. (2020). *Responding to the COVID-19 pandemic: WHO's action in countries, territories and areas: World Health Organisation. https://www.who.int/publications/i/item/9789240019225*
WHO. (2021). *The World Health Organisation. Responding to the COVID-19 pandemic: WHO's action in countries, territories and areas, 2020. 1 March*. https://www.who.int/publications/i/item/9789240019225
WHO. (2023a). *Infodemic management*. https://www.who.int/teams/risk-communication/infodemic-management
WHO. (2023b). *World Health Organisation, overview*. https://covid19.who.int
WHO. (2023c). *The World Health Organisation. COVAX. Working for global equitable access to COVID-19, vaccines*. https://www.who.int/initiatives/act-accelerator/covax#:~:text=COVAX%20was%20the%20vaccines%20pillar,tests%2C%20treatments%2C%20and%20vaccines
WHO. (2024). *The World Health Organisation. The access to COVID-19 tools (ACT) accelerator*. https://www.who.int/initiatives/act-accelerator

ECHR Cases

Ait Oufella v. France (no. 51860/20) and three other applications. https://hudoc.echr.coe.int/eng#{%22itemid%22:[%22002-13405%22]}
ÁRUS v. Roumanie, No 39647/21, 30/05/2023. https://hudoc.echr.coe.int/#{%22itemid%22:[%22001-225641%22]}
Bah v. the Netherlands 22 June 2021. https://www.google.com/url?sa=t&rct=j&q=&esrc=s&source=web&cd=&ved=2ahUKEwiZgNqtxaCEAxXIQPEDHVQBDtgQFnoECBEQAQ&url=https%3A%2F%2Fhudoc.echr.coe.int%2Fapp%2Fconversion%2Fdocx%2Fpdf%3Flibrary%3DECHR%26id%3D001-82625%26filename%3DBAH%2520v.%2520THE%2520NETHERLANDS.pdf%26logEvent%3DFalse&usg=AOvVaw36mbJda_NrbU9VXrswaW67&opi=89978449
Communauté genevoise d'action syndicale (CGAS) v. Switzerland 27 November 2023. https://hudoc.echr.coe.int/eng#{%22itemid%22:[%22001-229376%22]}
Constantin-Lucian Spînu v. Romania 11 October 2022. https://hudoc.echr.coe.int/fre#%7B%22tabview%22:[%22document%22],%22itemid%22:[%22002-13820%22]%7D
D.C. v. Italy (no. 17289/20) 15 October 2020
EB v. Serbia and AA v. Serbia (nos. 50086/20 and 50898/20)
Faia v. Italy, decision (Committee) on the admissibility of 29 August 2023
Feilazoo v. Malta 11 March 2021
Fenech v. Malta (no. 19090/20) 1 March 2022 (Chamber judgment)
Gözütok v. Türkiye (no. 41412/21)
Grgičin v. Croatia 12 December 2023
Hafeez v. the United Kingdom 28 March 2023
Khokhlov v. Cyprus 13 June 2023
Krstić v. Serbia (no. 35246/21) and six other applications
Le Mailloux v. France (application no. 18108/20), https://hudoc.echr.coe.int/eng#{%22itemid%22:[%22001-211715%22]}
Lini SRO v. Slovakia, decision (Committee) on the admissibility of 9 November 2023
M.C.K. and M.H.K.-B. (no. 26657/22) v. Germany and three other applications
Magdić v. Croatia 5 July 2022
Makovetskyy v. Ukraine 19 May 2022
Maratsis and Others v. Greece (no. 30335/20)
Mittendorfer v. Austria 4 July 2023

Narbutas v. Lithuania 19 December 2023
Pernechele and Others v. Italy 31 October 2023
Perstner v. Luxembourg, judgment of 16 February 2023
Pešić and Others v. Serbia (nos. 48973/20, 54565/20 and 54676/20)
Piperea v. Romania, 5 July 2022, application no. 24183/21)
Q and R v. Slovenia (no. 19938/20) 8 February 2022
Riela v. Italy 9 November 2023
Rus v. Romania 9 May 2023
Rybár and Veselská v. Slovakia, decision on the admissibility of 31 August 2023
Saakashvili v. Georgia (nos. 6232/20 and 22394/20), decision on the admissibility of 1 March 2022
Scheffer v. Slovakia (no. 16627/21) and 47 other applications communicated to the Slovakian Government on 24 January 2023; Terheş v. Romania 20 May 2021 (decision on the admissibility)
Terheş v. Romania 20 May 2021
Toromag, s.r.o. v. Slovakia
Ünsal and Timtik v. Turkey 8 June 2021
Vasilakis and Others v. Greece (no. 30379/20)
Vlamis and Others v. Greece (no. 29655/20) and four other applications (nos. 29689/20, 30240/20, 30418/20 and 30574/20)
Zambrano v. France 7 October 2021 (decision on the admissibility), 41994/21, https://hudoc.echr.coe.int/fre#%7B%22tabview%22:[%22document%22],%22itemid%22:[%22002-13421%22]%7D

1 Accountability and COVID-19

The Spanish Perspective[1]

Oscar Pérez de la Fuente

Democracy and elements of accountability

Accountability is a key element in understanding the exercise of political responsibility in democratic societies. Each political culture has its own conception of how this public servant accountability is to be specifically produced, sometimes limited to purely administrative issues, sometimes with an essentially political component. Free and pluralistic elections are one of the most common and effective mechanisms by which politicians are held accountable.

It should be noted that there are three levels of accountability: (a) firstly, there is accountability as *responsiveness*, which consists in the fact that, through periodic elections, senior members of government are obliged to take into account the mandate of the electorate (World Bank, 2004, p. 8); (b) secondly, there is accountability in the sense of giving explanations or justifications for their actions – *answerability*; and (c) thirdly, there is accountability – *enforceability* (Schelder, 1999, pp. 14–16). As we will see, sometimes, in practice, all the elements are not always present together, and there are various conflicting views on what accountability should consist of.

The first level of accountability – responsiveness – is often linked to *vertical electoral accountability*. Citizens, through their vote in periodic and pluralistic elections, can reward good rulers and punish evil rulers for their performance. Political leaders who work for the common good are supposed to be re-elected, and leaders who use their public office for private ends are supposed to be removed from office (World Bank, 2004, p. 8).

The second level of accountability relates to *answerability* and consists of providing information, explanations, or justifications for actions taken while in public office (World Bank, 2004, p. 8). The ruler can be asked for reliable facts (*informational dimension of accountability*) or valid reasons (*argumentative dimension of accountability*). Accountability implies the right to receive information and the corresponding obligation to provide all necessary details, as well as the right to receive an explanation and the corresponding duty to justify one's conduct (Schelder, 1999, pp. 14–15). Bustos Gispert proposes distinguishing the informative dimension of accountability as *to be answerable*, whose noun would be *answerability* – in the strict sense – where to be accountable means, in the first place, to be obliged to respond;

DOI: 10.4324/9781003482710-2

to answer the questions that may eventually be asked about the management of the affairs entrusted to any ruler. The argumentative dimension, such as *to be accountable* (the noun here would be *accountability*, in the strict sense), where to be accountable also means the obligation not only to answer but also to explain, justify, and even make amends; that is, to be accountable for one's own actions (Bustos Gispert, 2017, pp. 99–100).

The notion of *answerability* means that if someone is accountable, it implies an obligation to answer unpleasant questions and, *vice versa*, holding someone accountable implies the opportunity to ask uncomfortable questions (Schelder, 1999, p. 14). Therefore, rulers who do not give enough information or do not allow questions at press conferences are not being held accountable.

The third level is accountability as *enforcement.* This involves rewarding good behaviour and punishing misbehaviour by those in public office. This means that the actors involved in accountability not only 'question' but 'eventually punish' inappropriate behaviour and, consequently, those who are accountable must not only explain what they have done and why but also bear the consequences of this, which may include negative sanctions (Schelder, 1999, p. 15). Bustos Gispert proposes the concept of *liability*, where being responsible implies assuming the sanctions that may ultimately derive from the ruler's failure to fulfil the duties of their mandate (Bustos Gispert, 2017, pp. 99–100).

Bovens considers whether the possibility of sanctions is a constitutive element of accountability as a mechanism. The possibility of sanctions – irrespective of their nature – is a constitutive element of accountability as a mechanism and should be included in the definition. However, the term "sanction" has more of a formal, legal connotation. It would exclude accountability forums, such as ombudsmen. The perpetrator must face the consequences of their actions. These consequences can be highly formalised, such as fines, disciplinary measures, civil remedies, or even criminal sanctions. Still, they can also be based on unwritten rules, as in the case of political accountability of a minister in Parliament, where the consequences can extend to calling for the minister's resignation or dismissal. Sometimes, the adverse effects will only be implicit or informal, such as being held accountable in front of TV cameras or the deterioration of public image and career due to the negative publicity generated by the process (Bovens, 2010, p. 952). An interesting case to analyse is if an elected governor, allegedly accused of some unlawful act – political or else legal – goes to an election, that is, submits to *vertical electoral accountability* and obtains a sufficient majority to govern, can it be said that with this victory, he recovers political trust/accountability for that unlawful act?

In accountability, three main areas can be distinguished: *political accountability*, which is ensured through the functioning of the Parliament where there is effective opposition and well-functioning oversight committees. *Fiscal* accountability is more narrowly defined than other types of accountability, as it is simply based on formal financial accounting for the use of public resources. *Administrative accountability* may be more weakly institutionalised than other forms and tends to be the most insulated from social and political pressures (Goetz & Jenkins, 2001, p. 366).

In specific uses of the concept, accountability, or more precisely "being accountable", is seen as a virtue, a positive characteristic of organisations or officials, as Bovens explains. In this broad sense, accountability is used to positively qualify a state of affairs or a olitician's performance. It is close to the concept of responsiveness and "a sense of responsibility", a willingness to act transparently, fairly, and justly. Accountability, used in this more active sense of virtue, refers to *substantive standards for the behaviour of rulers* (Bovens, 2010, p. 949).

Historically and semantically, the word accountability is closely related to accounting/accounting in its literal sense of keeping accounts or books/bookkeeping (Bovens, 2010, p. 950). Staying close to its etymological and historical roots, accountability can also be approached as a specific social relation or mechanism involving the obligation to explain and justify conduct. Explanations and justifications are not made in the abstract but by a significant other. This usually involves not only the provision of information about performance but also the possibility of debate, questions from the forum and answers from the ruler and, eventually, a judgement of the ruler by the forum. The judgement also implies imposing formal or informal sanctions on the ruler in case of poor performance or rewards in case of good performance (Bovens, 2010, p. 951).

Political accountability may be a general and comprehensive concept, which Shelder argues as being a *modest* concept. In part, its modesty has to do with its potential one-dimensionality. Some instances of accountability do not include aspects of *answerability*, while others do not include elements of *enforcement*. Fundamentally, political accountability is a modest endeavour in such a way that it accepts the reality of power and its relative opacity (Schelder, 1999, p. 18).

The different political cultures are relevant. In some countries, accountability is conceived from a purely administrative or economic approach. In contrast, in other countries, the core of accountability is essentially political and is associated with democratic representation and exercising political responsibility.

Types of accountability: vertical, horizontal, and diagonal

Traditionally, two levels of accountability have been distinguished, following a spatial metaphor: (a) a 'vertical' axis that includes external mechanisms used by non-state actors to hold policymakers accountable; (b) a 'horizontal' axis comprising internal institutional oversight, checks *and balances within the* state (Goetz & Jenkins, 2001, p. 366). However, the increasing role of civil society actors has given rise to new theorisations proposing new axes or complements to the above, such as a 'diagonal' axis, horizontal socially driven accountability, or direct vertical accountability.

Vertical accountability means that through reasonably free and regular elections, citizens can punish or reward those in power by voting for or against them or their preferred candidates in the next election (O'Donnell, 1998, p. 10). The guarantee of freedoms of opinion and association and access to reasonably varied sources of information, which make it possible to make demands on public authorities and eventually denounce their wrongdoing, are prerequisites of this form of accountability. The functioning of reasonable free media also included in the definition of polyarchy, contributes to this. In elections, social demands can be articulated without suffering from state coercion and media that at least regularly cover the most visible pressures and alleged wrongdoing by public authorities (O'Donnell, 1998, p. 11).

In the context of democratic societies, Manin, Przeworski, and Stokes distinguish between the *mandate approach* and the accountability *approach* to the role of citizens, politicians, and elections. In the 'mandate' approach, elections select good policy proposals or politicians with particular policy schemes. Parties or candidates make such submissions during campaigns and explain how these policies affect the welfare of citizens; the latter decide which of these proposals they want to be implemented, while politicians are responsible for their realisation and elected governments to administer them. Elections emulate a direct assembly, and the winning platform becomes the 'mandate' that the government pursues. In a second approach, called 'accountability', elections hold governments responsible for the outcome of their past actions. Because they anticipate voters' judgement, governments are induced to choose policies they believe will be positively evaluated by citizens at the time of the next election (Manin et al., 1999, p. 29).

Democracies are not all the same, and some democratic systems may foster representation better than others. Some institutional factors deserve attention, as highlighted by Manin, Przeworski, and Stokes:

> Voters should be able to clearly assign responsibility for the performance of government. Voters should be able to vote out of government, the parties responsible for poor performance, and the parties they select should be able to get into government. Politicians should have an incentive to want to be re-elected. The opposition should monitor government performance and report back to citizens. Indeed, any reasonable understanding of representation must include the opposition. The media have a particular role to play. Unless they have clear partisan interests, they are more credible than either the government or the opposition. Finally, perhaps most importantly, voters should have some institutional instruments, in different spheres, to reward and punish governments for the results they deliver. However, elections are inherently a blunt instrument of control: voters only have to make one decision regarding the whole package of government policies.
>
> (Manin et al., 1999, pp. 47–48)

Horizontal accountability, on the other hand, presupposes the existence of state agencies with legal authority that are factually willing and able to take action, ranging from routine oversight to legal sanctions or even, in some democracies, *impeachment* concerning acts or omissions of other state agents or agencies that may, in principle or presumptively, be qualified as wrongful (O'Donnell, 1998, p. 26). Examples of horizontal accountability mechanisms include institutions such as ombudsmen, independent electoral institutes, corruption watchdogs, legislative commissions of enquiry and administrative tribunals. These are all public institutions specifically designed to evaluate, monitor and direct the behaviour of government officials (World Bank, 2004, p. 9).

There are two fundamental directions in which *horizontal accountability* can be violated. Although, in some instances, these directions may overlap, they are different. The first occurs when one state agency unlawfully infringes on the authority of another; the second involves unlawful advantages that a public official obtains for himself or his associates. O'Donnell (1998, p. 34) called the first kind 'transgression' and the second 'corruption', although the latter encompasses certain conduct that does not precisely fit the term. The horizontal dimension refers largely to the effective functioning of *checks and balances* and due process in governmental decision-making. The vertical dimension focuses instead on elections and other mechanisms citizens use to control their government (Smulovitz & Peruzzotti, 2000, p. 148).

Regarding the problems that give rise to horizontal accountability, O'Donnell presents a picture of the different tensions involved.

Firstly, the sphere of democracy suffers from decisions that cancel freedoms of association or introduce fraud into elections. Another field, the liberal one, is infringed when state agents violate, or allow private actors to violate, freedoms and guarantees such as the inviolability of the home, the prohibition of domestic violence and torture, the right of every person to a fair trial, and the like. Most of these violations are perpetrated on the borderline between the state apparatus and the weaker and poorer segments of society by low-ranking officials not directly accountable to the electoral process (although when these episodes spread to become systematic features, they often involve the participation or coexistence of more highly placed officials). The third sphere affected is the republican domain. These are actions by officials who, be they elected or not, often occupy high positions in the state or regime. These actions imply serious disregard for the demands of the republican tradition; that is, they subordinate themselves to the law or give clear priority to public, not private, interests (O'Donnell, 1998, p. 27).

The participation of community groups, NGOs and citizens, in general, is one of the most important factors behind successful accountability arrangements (World Bank, 2004, p. 9). Firstly, a distinction will be made between *direct vertical accountability* to distinguish it from *electoral vertical accountability*, based on the formal periodic election of members of the three branches of government. The first is that civil society participation can reinforce accountability structures in three different ways: first, direct monitoring and lobbying by civil society actors; and popular votes on particular issues or policies, which can complement elections as additional elements of vertical accountability. This increases the frequency and clarity of accountability signals that citizens send to public officials and thus enhances their vertical accountability to the public. Examples of such participation range from surveys that monitor the effectiveness of public services to the media exposing bureaucratic irregularities to the organisation of plebiscites and referendums (World Bank, 2004, pp. 9–10).

Secondly, there is *socially driven horizontal responsibility* or *social accountability.* For example, in their analysis of the social response to two extrajudicial killings in Argentina, Catalina Smulovitz and Enrique Peruzzotti documented how the combination of mobilisation, legal action and media exposure can effectively ensure that the court system functions impartially, even when the perpetrators are well-connected or even part of the government apparatus itself. Another example of this type of civil society participation would be the human rights ombudsmen, a distinctly 'horizontal' institution whose actions are constantly improved and often driven by social demands (World Bank, 2004, p. 10). Smulovitz and Peruzzotti argue that the concept of *social accountability* addresses both types of arguments: first, it presents an alternative control mechanism that, if taken into account, would lead to a different diagnosis of the overall state of accountability in Latin American democracies. Secondly, social initiatives can address some structural problems plaguing elections as accountability mechanisms (Smulovitz & Peruzzotti, 2000, p. 151).

Arguing for *social accountability*, Smulovitz and Peruzzotti make several arguments: first, social mechanisms control by exposing and denouncing wrongdoing. Exposures bring issues to light in a way that citizens can relate to and so help put them on the public agenda. As a result, the number of problems for which public officials can be held accountable increases. Secondly, social mechanisms control because they can trigger the operation of horizontal mechanisms. The social mobilisation around particular demands, media coverage and investigations, and the initiation of proceedings in oversight or judicial agencies put corrupt politicians at risk of losing their reputation or even being taken to court. In democratic contexts, where the political life of elected officials depends on getting as many votes as possible, they can be expected to avoid committing certain acts if they fear high reputational costs. However, public officials will not continually assess these risks in the same way. In some cases, the efficiency of social mechanisms depends on how public officials weigh the risks of engaging in corruption against the benefits. In other cases, however, social mechanisms trigger horizontal ones that do not depend on a cost-benefit calculation (Smulovitz & Peruzzotti, 2000, p. 152).

Thirdly, there is the diagonal accountability proposed by Goetz and Jenkins. Examples of this form of participation include citizen advisory boards that perform public functions such as auditing government spending, procurement oversight or election monitoring (World Bank, 2004, p. 10). This engagement breaks down the division between vertical and horizontal accountability mechanisms, as it involves the participation of 'vertical' actors in 'horizontal' mechanisms. It is a 'hybrid form of accountability' (World Bank, 2004, p. 10).

There are five critical institutional features proposed by Goetz and Jenkins that could theoretically allow citizen-initiated versions of hybrid accountability to assume an even more promising institutional form:

1 Legitimisation of non-governmental observers in the monitoring of public sector institutions;
2 The continuous presence of these observers throughout the agency's work process;
3 Well-defined procedures for the conduct of meetings between citizens and public sector actors in meetings;

4 Structured access to the flow of official documentary information; and
5 The right of observers to issue dissenting reports directly to legislative bodies (Goetz & Jenkins, 2001, p. 369).

COVID-19 and accountability: the case of Spain

The global spread of COVID-19 is much more than a biological phenomenon, as Diab et al. explain, as it has rapidly taken on political, economic, social and geographical characteristics. This is evidenced by subsequent confinements, mobility limitations, stay-at-home orders, financial rescue packages, interstate tensions, the closing of state borders, digital surveillance, the concentration of diseases in cities and the politics of expertise. The COVID-19 pandemic highlights some key elements of state power and its reproduction in health and economic policy. This has many other consequences for financial "lock-in" that have resulted in a considerable slowdown in global economic activity and increased social instability, disproportionately impacting those less advantaged in various monetary respects (Diab et al., 2021, p. 3).

This situation has also posed a challenge to understand the proper role of accountability in policy. For Shimizu and Mossialos, it has become clear that preparedness for health emergencies is governed with little accountability and obscurity. Who determined which countermeasures and for what purposes remains unknown to this day. The decision-making process was controlled by politicians and bureaucrats who lacked expertise in infection control, and the views of specialists were occasionally ignored (Shimizu & Mossialos, 2021, p. 114). The COVID pandemic has been a global phenomenon highlighting the weaknesses and strengths of different political systems and associated accountability mechanisms. In his work *Pandemocracy. A philosophy of the coronavirus crisis*, Innerarity makes the following reflection: 'from the people's point of view, it is said that those most affected by the coronavirus crisis will be the most vulnerable, but from the ideological point of view, the most affected will be populism. There are three things that populist leaders detest and that this type of crisis revalorises: expert knowledge, institutions and the global community' (Innerarity, 2020, p. 49).

If there is one thing that public administration scholars can learn from COVID-19, it is the need to know objectively and without bias from crises and disasters. The inherent human vulnerability becomes more evident. Boin et al. argue that COVID-19 reminds us that we must learn effectively and quickly in a world characterised by various disruptions, such as a changing climate, unstable financial systems and persistent cyber threats andhow can this be achieved while preserving democratic principles, institutions, and practices (Boin et al., 2020, p. 344)?.

The answer comes from a proper approach to accountability, a central element of democratic governance. As Ojiagu et al. argue, accountability keeps people informed and exposes and questions the administration, carries an implicit connotation of virtue, a positive quality in government, organisations or management, leading to several aspects of accountability: fiscal honesty and avoidance of fraud, good governance, adherence to mission and demonstration of government effectiveness. The literature indicates that accountability implies that government, individuals and organisations are responsible for adhering to specific standards and commitments; they are accountable for their activities and will face repercussions if standards are not met (Ojiagu et al., 2020, p. 26).

To avoid a global economic collapse and likely depression, according to Diab et al., UN member states have taken drastic and substantial measures, such as direct cash transfers, short- and medium-term forgiven loans and deferred payments, and unemployment insurance. UN member states have inevitably weakened protections by sacrificing compliance, oversight and accountability for speed of reaction and quick effect, thus providing ample opportunity for corruption. The lack of adequate accountability and control systems in allocating and distributing economic stimulus packages increases the danger of corruption and fraud. The simultaneous emergence of all these changes transformed the management and understanding of global geopolitics (Diab et al., 2021, p. 3).

As Boin et al. point out, the difficulty of reassessment is to recalibrate the policy mix in light of the changing morphology of the crisis and to decide which measures to maintain, soften or eliminate. This introduces a new difficulty: motivating employees, people and communities to respect the new system. Two approaches can be highlighted as follows:

- The task of *accountability*: opening up the records and creating a national dialogue on what was known and what was not known, what was done and what was not done: when, why and by whom regarding COVID-19.
- The challenge of *learning*: to reconstruct, question and reflect on one's own and other governments' actions to draw lessons to improve capacity for prevention, preparedness, response and resilience to future pandemics (or more generally, mega-crises) (Boin et al., 2020, p. 342).

Despite the difficulty, making early decisions on epidemic prevention is crucial. Wang provides an interesting analysis of ways to improve China's early reaction. Given that the strict sanctions regime may have contributed to the delay in Wuhan, it is considered that a system that tolerates specific errors of judgement may increase the likelihood of a faster response. Based on this line of reasoning, two types of errors of judgement are differentiated using the example of Wuhan during COVID-19. During the early stages of an infectious disease, when there are many unknowns and dangers, a decisionmaker may opt for early action that may be unwarranted and a false alarm. This is known as a Type I error or a false positive in decision-making. It is argued that such errors of choice should be allowed so that decisionmakers are not penalised by pre-emptive efforts that turn out to be overly aggressive, such as the decision to blockade the entire city and disrupt economic operations. During COVID-19 in China, many jurisdictions took proactive measures, especially Qinjiang (or Yichang – a city 100 miles west of Wuhan), which closed almost a week earlier than Wuhan and consequently had far fewer contagions *per capita*.

Conversely, decisions to under-report diseases or to postpone action should be severely penalised. These decisions are called 'Type II errors' or *false negatives*. During epidemics of communicable diseases, public authorities who delay action should be seriously punished (Wang et al., 2020, p. 3). These penalties or rewards for decision-makers are an element that is usually considered within the realm of accountability.

The unprecedented test of resilience posed by COVID-19, Cutter et al. argue, requires a shift away from fragmented solutions by individual hospitals and health systems in the design and delivery of healthcare. Integrating essential elements of *social accountability* frameworks is necessary for a successful adaptive response to the acute and post-acute demands of the COVID pandemic. This strategy highlights the accountability to population health required by the COVID pandemic and may lead to the emergence of a 'new normal' in healthcare delivery (Cutter et al., 2021, p. 4).

An oft-repeated conclusion is, following Leoni et al., that the COVID pandemic has uncovered and exacerbated substantial and systemic inequalities at multiple levels, including global and geographic disparities between developed and developing nations, socio-economic disparities within societies, and differences between individuals based on age, gender, education and ethnicity. The pandemic has not only produced a new lack of balance but also exacerbated existing inequalities and political problems. Unevenness is also embedded in national and international responses to COVID-19, as the provision and receipt of financial and monetary assistance and aid (including vaccine availability) are influenced by economic power and the politics of influence. There is an urgent need for scholars from all disciplines to contribute to debates and solutions on greater equality and the well-being of individuals in society in light of these issues (Leoni et al., 2021, p. 1314). It has been a frequent comment that the pandemic has affected persons unequally according to socio-economic criteria. This has a ring of truth that can be nuanced. On the one hand, the means to fight COVID-19, such as vaccines, are more available to rich countries; however, as it is a global epidemic and so contagious, it is in the common interest that no one is excluded from these treatments.

The following will briefly analyse the Spanish case of corruption and accountability in the situation caused by COVID-19. Firstly, it will reflect on Rose-Ackerman's approach in her article 'Corruption and COVID-19' (2021); secondly, it will examine various rulings of the Spanish Constitutional Court on the accountability – or lack thereof – in Parliament during the pandemic.

In an interesting analysis, Rose-Ackerman proposes three factors that favour corruption due to the pandemic:

Firstly, she argues that 'governments spend a great deal of money and make regulatory changes in a short period with little oversight, precisely when the very high speed of response means that oversight is especially necessary' (Rose-Ackerman, 2021, p. 39).

Among the specialised literature, there is a classic formula for approaching the concept of corruption proposed by Klitgaard. It is as follows:

CORRUPTION = MONOPOLY + DISCRETIONALITY − ACCOUNTABILITY[2]

This is explained, the author clarifies, in the sense that 'one will tend to find corruption when someone has a monopoly of power over a good or service, has the discretion to decide whether or not someone receives it and how much they get, and in doing so is not accountable' (Klitgaard, 1997, pp. 499–500).

Therefore, in this COVID pandemic, decisions must have been taken quickly, in situations of virtual monopoly and great discretion, over many resources and with hardly any accountability. The expected consequence is the appearance of cases of corruption or political clientelism.

Secondly, Rose-Ackerman states that 'in the case of COVID-19, the need for rapid response is not the only risk factor; multiple sources of uncertainty complicate the politics of response. The virus was and is poorly understood. When the pandemic began, there were no vaccines to limit the risk of infection or tested antivirals to give to the sick. There was significant uncertainty about the best testing strategies, treatments and safety protocols to balance safety with the continuity of economic and social life' (Rose-Ackerman, 2021, p. 39).

The underlying reflection is that severe uncertainty fosters corruption in a variety of ways that 'go beyond bribery and fraud. Individuals and companies seeking their own profit can take advantage of market disruptions and regulatory loopholes at the expense of the public good' (Rose-Ackerman, 2021, pp. 39–40).

In 2022, Spain achieved a Corruption Perceptions Index (CPI) score of 60 out of 100, representing a one-point decline compared to the year before. The CPI is maintained by the non-profit organisation Transparency International. This ranks it 14th/27th among European Union member states and 35th/180th overall. Two consecutive years of decline, despite the lack of statistical significance associated with a one-point decrease, are an unmistakable indication of peril and highlight the presence of enduring challenges that prevent the operation of democratic institutions and heighten the susceptibility to corruption in Spain (International Transparency Spain, 2002). The European Commission's December 2022 publication of a new Special Eurobarometer on Corruption is of particular interest; it reveals that 89% of Spanish individuals hold the belief that corruption is a prevalent issue, whilst the European average is at 64% (Eurobaremeter, 2022, p. 1).

According to Hernández and Moreno, the pandemic in Spain resulted in a sequence of adverse repercussions for the country's public transparency policy. These included, but were not limited to, the halt in procedure processing, which impeded the exercise of the right to access information, the withholding of information regarding emergency contract awards, the composition and reports of expert committees advising the government, and the distribution of information (Hernández Rodríguez & Moreno Martínez, 2021, p. 137).

As a result of the COVID-19-induced pandemic, the government issued an official declaration of state of emergency. The executive opted to suspend 'the deadlines for processing procedures of public sector entities' following the third additional provision of Royal Decree 463/2020, issued on 14 March 2020, which declared a state of emergency for managing the health crisis situation. This suspension would remain in effect until the Royal Decree or its extensions were repealed. The procedures to obtain information that was previously available were halted. However, it was specified in the fourth point of that section that inquiries concerning 'situations closely linked' to the coronavirus would trigger further access processes. It would be responded to adhering to the specified timelines. On 17 March 2020, however, Decree 465/2020 amended the regulation to permit the government to use discretion in determining whether or not to provide access to this particular request.

Confronted with this situation, which was accompanied by perplexing official statistics regarding the pandemic, non-public press conferences featuring predetermined inquiries, and postponements in disseminating emergency contracts on the Transparency Portal of the General Administration of the State. Additionally, ONG campaigns advocated for comprehensive documentation of all decision-making processes during the pandemic. This was done to ensure that information could be traced and readily accessible to the public and to bolster the transparency of public contracting executed during emergencies. Additionally, a gateway was needed to provide the most precise consolidation of information at the national, regional and local levels (Villoria & Jimenez, 2021, pp. 126–127).

The legal debate focused specifically on the third additional provision of Royal Decree 463/2020, 14 March, declaring a state of emergency to manage the health crisis caused by COVID-19, a provision that, according to Guichot Reina (2021, pp. 13–14), implies the general suspension of administrative procedures except, textually, those 'that refer to situations closely linked to the facts justifying the state of alarm', and for the author it can be understood that this exception may include the exercise of the right of access to information on the pandemic.

The fact that emergency contracts were not published until more than a month after the declaration of the state of alarm was also widely criticised (Hernández Rodríguez & Moreno Martínez, 2021, p. 137). Emergency procurement processes, which may feature exclusive sourcing, faster payment schedules, early payment requirements and general haste to obtain supplies, can reduce supplier due diligence and examination. Campos Acuña points out that these processes may be considerably more susceptible to acts of bad faith. Consequently, transparency should not be disregarded in rare circumstances or processes (Campos Acuña, 2022, pp. 119–120).

Over an extended period, this form of transparency laxity, Pineda and Pardo conclude, may not only foster corrupt practices but also impede market competition, neglect implementation of social criteria in contracting and ultimately erode the credibility of public administrations – all of which can disrupt the regular democratic operations of nations (Pineda Nebot & Pardo Beneyto, 2020, p. 339).

To promote openness in emergency public procurement, several civil society groups with expertise in this field have collaborated with Open Contracting Partnership to formulate the following recommendations, which Pineda and Pardo expose:

1 The use of emergency contracting should be justified, registered and made public;
2 Emergency contracting is the exception, not the rule and should be judged case-by-case;
3 Data on emergency contracting should be centralised in national e-procurement portals;

4 Full publication to maintain confidence;
5 Open data on emergency procurement;
6 E-procurement portals should be updated in the shortest possible time;
7 Transparency to avoid price speculation;
8 Open data to reinforce due diligence with suppliers and prevent fraud;
9 Make public penalties for fraudulent activities and bidding cartels;
10 Cooperation with civil society, investigative journalists and whistle-blowers.

Subsequently, the supervisory authorities must examine public procurement data to determine, if not retrospectively, whether there have been any deficiencies in the purchases executed, intending to detect potentially fraudulent activities, anti-competitive pricing, or other irregularities (Pineda Nebot & Pardo Beneyto, 2020, p. 339)

In addition to advancing the essential democratic regeneration, Gimeno Feliu affirms that the new public contract regulation must facilitate the redesign of public procurement as a public leadership strategy based on efficiency, openness and good administration. Furthermore, the health emergency should not justify 'opening the door to opacity'. The imperative for 'efficiency' in public decision-making precludes the compromise of integrity or openness. Transparency, political participation and the legitimacy of the separation of powers are a few of the fundamental principles currently under strain due to the pandemic and the need for immediate responses. In such circumstances, the culture and demands for prevention become even more critical. The unique circumstances need an increased emphasis on openness and accountability, not out of duty but because of the conviction that such principles underpin the proper use of authority and demand greater and better transparency. The current extraordinary circumstances necessitate a political administration that is profoundly unaligned with the notion of a power struggle, which rationalises an unwarranted strain stemming from the friend–enemy dichotomy. Opposition is not, nor should it ever be, the essence of political art; instead, it should be guided by a disposition towards broad accords that serve the collective good. Corrosion in politics poses a threat of veering into activities that deviate significantly from the principles of good governance – a fundamental right of every citizen, to be sure – and that we, as a community, cannot allow, and it must be condemned. Therefore, it is imperative to devise a brake mechanism to prevent a 'speed of inertia' towards zones of impunity and immunity, which is morally unjustifiable from every conceivable standpoint, even during critical situations (and even less from the idea of the democratic principle) (Gimeno Feliu, 2020, p. 32).

Thirdly, Rose-Ackerman argues that 'the health sector differs from the ordinary competitive market even in normal times, and market imperfections emerge in correlated insurance markets. Some libertarians argue that society can depend on the private sector for immediate response. Competitive markets, according to this view, will rush to develop the necessary tests, vaccines and anti-viral drugs and government interventions to increase the accessibility of these goods will only serve to suppress the profit incentives of producers. Individuals, at the same time, will take precautions to protect themselves without the need for government action' (Rose-Ackerman, 2021, p. 40).

Rose-Ackerman concludes that 'in short, unlike many natural disasters, the underlying structure of the health sector is riddled with inefficiencies that the pandemic has exacerbated. Of course, there may be price gouging and corruptly procured contracts in natural disaster and human conflict care, but having health at the centre of disaster recovery creates special problems' (Rose-Ackerman, 2021, p. 40).

The right to health has its own idiosyncrasies as a social right, and in extreme situations such as a pandemic, it can pose a particular problem. For example, conflicts of fundamental rights with infection prevention measures such as confinement, mandatory use of masks or vaccination conditions have been somewhat controversial.

On the other hand, in the case of COVID-19 treatment and accountability in Spain, the controversy over the declaration of a state of alarm should be highlighted. On the regulation of conditions of alert and exception, section 116 of the Spanish Constitution 1978 states:

> The Government must decree a state of alarm in the Council of Ministers for a maximum of fifteen days, reporting to the Congress of Deputies, which must meet immediately and without whose authorisation this period may not be extended. The decree must state the territorial scope to which the effects of the declaration extend. The Government must decree a state of emergency in the Council of Ministers, following authorisation from the Congress of Deputies. The authorisation and proclamation of the state of emergency must expressly state its effects, the territorial scope to which it extends and its duration, which may not exceed thirty days, though may be extended for an equal period, subject to the same requirements.

Organic Law 4/1981 of 1 June 1981 on states of alarm, exception and siege, in its section governing the state of emergency, provides:

> Section 4 – The Government may, under section 116(2) of the Constitution, decree a state of alarm, in all or part of the national territory, when any of the following serious alterations to normality occur.
>
> a Disasters, calamities or public misfortunes, such as earthquakes, floods, urban and forest fires or major accidents;
> b Health crises, such as epidemics and serious pollution situations;
> c Stoppage of public services essential to the community, when sections 28(2) and 37(2) of the Constitution are not guaranteed, or when any of the other circumstances or situations contained in this section are satisfied;
> d Situations of shortages of basic necessities (section 4, Organic Law 1981 of 1 June 1981).

This same statute establishes the circumstances of the state of emergency:

> When the free exercise of citizens' rights and liberties, the normal functioning of democratic institutions, the normal functioning of public services essential to the community, or any other aspect of public policy is so seriously

> altered that the exercise of ordinary powers is insufficient to re-establish and maintain it, the Government, under section 116(3) of the Constitution, may seek authorisation from the Congress of Deputies to decree a state of emergency.
>
> (section 13, Organic Law 1981 of 1 June 1981)

During the COVID pandemic, the Spanish government opted to decree a state of alarm without Parliament's intervention, which is required when declaring a state of emergency. One argument favouring the government's strategy is that 'health crises, such as epidemics and serious contamination situations', are expressly included among the assumptions of the state of alarm. A counterargument is that this pandemic and the subsequent confinements and reduced work have seriously disrupted citizens' rights and freedoms. This means that this situation has affected the essential content of fundamental rights, with the consequence that it has to be the Parliament that authorises this new state. This option was developed by the Constitutional Court, which considers the declaration of a state of emergency to be more justified in this case. It substantiated its rationale by stating:

> In view of all these circumstances, this court must limit itself to finding that the extraordinary restrictions on freedom of movement within the national territory imposed by section 7 (paragraphs 1, 3 and 5) of Royal Decree 463/2020, though aimed at protecting constitutionally relevant values and interests, and comply with the measures recommended by the World Health Organization in its document 'COVID-19 Strategy Update' (14 April 2020), exceed the scope of the state of alarm recognised by the World Health Organization, and comply with the measures recommended by the World Health Organization in its document 'COVID-19 Strategy Update' (14 April 2020), exceed the scope of the state of alarm recognised by the Constitution and the Organic Law referred to in section 116(1) of the Constitution (*LOAES* in Spanish).
>
> (Constitutional Court Ruling no. 148/2021 of 14 July, Finding of Law 11)[3]

Another element linked to accountability and the pandemic in the Spanish case is the suspension of parliamentary activity during the state of alarm. This was also the subject of a ruling by the Constitutional Court, in which the Court held that the declaration of the state of alarm, as would be the case for either of the other two conditions, must not under any circumstance interrupt the functioning of any of the constitutional powers of the state and, in particular, the Congress of Deputies. Consequently, the decision of the Bureau temporarily halted the processing of the appellants' parliamentary initiatives, thereby infringing their right to political participation. Specifically, the judgement states:

> Therefore, the decision to temporarily interrupt parliamentary activity, suspending calculation of the deadlines for registered initiatives contravenes the constitutional mandate addressed to the Congress of Deputies for the exercise

> of its own functions, particularly that of control of the Government, regardless of the duration of that interruption, since it is essential to this function that the functioning of the Chamber should not see its activity paralysed, even temporarily, not even and even more so in the case of a state of alarm applies. (…)
>
> The decision to suspend the processing of all parliamentary activity therefore affected the essential content of the appellants' *ius in officium* as Members of the House. As of the issuing of that resolution ordering the temporary suspension of the processing of the initiatives, the appellants found it impossible for any initiative they registered to be processed by Congress *sine die*, as long as the Bureau did not approve a new resolution deciding to lift the suspension.
>
> (Ruling 168/2021, 5 October 2021, Finding of Law 5)

If the state of alarm was decided by the government without parliamentary intervention, and parliamentary activities, especially in the Congress of Deputies, were suspended in parallel during this state of emergency, horizontal accountability and government political control can be considered weakened in this period. Nor was it an appropriate time to call elections and exercise vertical electoral accountability. It was, therefore, an ideal situation for hybrid forms of accountability from civil society and the media.

As Boin et al. recall, accountability is the defining characteristic of a democracy. Knowing that an elected politician must justify certain policy decisions imposes various constraints on the policy-making process. The literature reminds us that these circumstances impose accountability on politicians. The sacred norm is that responsible politicians must be well-informed, which may be the greatest burden. This norm has inspired a number of methods and conventions that have characterised democratic policy-making (Boin et al., 2020, p. 343).

With these decisions, the Constitutional Court has shown how accountability in the Spanish Parliament during the pandemic could have been improved. The fact that the parliamentary situation is not entirely favourable to the government should not make us lose sight of the need for accountability, even in exceptional situations, especially in the case of a state of alarm decreed by the government.

A relevant point of analysis is whether it has intensified *social accountability* mechanisms during the pandemic. According to the United Nations, Diab defines the NPM (lack of development of the abbreviation) as a voluntary, non-profit group of individuals established at the local, national or global level to solve problems for the public good. Task-oriented and composed of individuals with a common interest, NPMs carry out a range of humanitarian services and tasks, convey public concerns to governments and monitor the implementation of policies and programmes. They provide analysis and expertise, act as early warning systems, and help monitor and implement international agreements (Diab, 2021, p. 3). According to Diab, social control has shifted from the state (government) to societal professionals (who provide services) and individuals. Consequently, the social and informal nature of the environment can shape the accountability procedure (Diab, 2021, p. 7).

Conclusions

The notion of democracy is closely linked to the idea of accountability, where rulers are held accountable and responsible for their actions in government. This has various mechanisms and levels. Characteristically, the ideal elements of accountability are not always found in all cases, in all countries, and it is a concept under permanent construction. Nevertheless, the quality of democracy depends to a large extent on the effective exercise of accountability, with its elements and its different types, over its rulers.

The COVID pandemic has challenged various societies, especially democratic ones. Citizens have evaluated decision-making and accountability mechanisms on issues of major interest and where they were directly concerned. This is because, in many countries, movement rights have been restricted, and working patterns have been changed from a face-to-face model to an online one due to mandatory home confinement. There have been debates close to the classic question of when legal paternalism is justified (Ramiro Avilés, 2006) regarding whether the state can force people to wear masks or be vaccinated.

In Rose-Ackerman's analysis, this pandemic may have encouraged corruption due to several factors: 'First, the rapid unfolding of the pandemic and the correlative economic downturn have led to fierce competition for essential resources. Secondly, governments have rapidly mobilised public funds (both for health care and economic stability) on an unprecedented scale, creating opportunities for easy money of many kinds, including the overtly corrupt. Thirdly, politicians, civil servants and health professionals exercise substantial discretion in the allocation of resources. A loss of transparency and weakened oversight and enforcement have exacerbated problems of corruption and fraud, and public measures against these crimes have not kept pace with the unfolding crisis' (Rose-Ackerman, 2021, p. 41).

COVID-19 is a good place to gauge the quality of accountability because governments must report and justify their decisions. These must be advised by experts, although they have the final say as public decisionmakers. Rulers are rewarded or punished for their choices in one dimension of accountability. In another dimension, politicians must justify their decisions. In the case of COVID-19, a great deal of uncertainty and discretion in decision-making affected the vast majority of the population. As has been shown, accountability mechanisms are particularly relevant to avoid corruption. A remarkable element of the Spanish experience of accountability is that, although there is a political understanding, at the academic level, as opposed to a purely administrative approach, it is not popularly or journalistically rooted. The values of the culture of *accountability* remain hidden from the public at large, underlying the basis of democracy and indeed being the core on which the system of legitimacy is based. This makes it easier for a new ruler or political party to transgress these values, in whole or in part, more easily. In this sense, it has to be understood how accountability is a *modest* concept, which can sometimes manifest itself in some of its elements or types, and, at the same time, is the *touchstone* of democratic systems.

In Spain, in addition to these factors that would increase corruption, there has been a weakening of horizontal accountability during this pandemic, as the Constitutional Court has pointed out. On the one hand, the government has opted to declare a state of alarm, providing cover for house confinements. In the Constitutional Court's interpretation, this affects the actual content of fundamental rights, and it would have been preferable to announce a state of emergency with the intervention of Parliament for its approval. Secondly, during the state of alarm, parliamentary activity was suspended, thus limiting horizontal accountability and the right to political participation. Likewise, the Spanish Constitutional Court has not found this suspension justified.

States of alarm, exception and siege are part of the democratic *raison d'état*. The justification for this institution comes from the fact that, in exceptional situations, it is necessary to temporarily restrict certain rights to protect the proper functioning of the rule of law. These states have been previously regulated in an Organic Law, which establishes who, how, when and for how long rights can be suspended. It is a guarantee provided by law that, when warranted, certain rights may be limited temporarily, applying a previously established procedure.

The COVID pandemic has been a genuine opportunity to gauge the quality of the rule of law and the accountability system. The outlook is not so optimistic; there is still a need for those in power to be held *accountable* for their decisions, even in exceptional situations. Democracies will emerge stronger.

Notes

1 A previous and reduced Spanish version of this paper was published in *Aletheia, Anuario de derechos humanos y Filosofía del Derecho*, núm. 1, 2023, pp. 4—32.

2 Klitgaard explains the formula: 'illicit behaviour flourishes when agents have a monopoly of power over clients, when agents have great discretion, and when agents' accountability is weak' (Klitgaard, 1998, p. 75).

3 In declaring the state of alarm void, the Constitutional Court sought to avoid creating disproportionate consequences and limited the scope of its nullity: "It ultimately seems necessary to specify the scope of our declaration of unconstitutionality, modulating the effects of the declaration of nullity:

  1 Not only proceedings concluded by a judgment with the force of res judicata (as established in sections 161(1)(a) of the Constitution and 40(1) of the Constitutional Court Act [*Ley Orgánica del Tribunal Constitucional*]) or situations decided by final administrative actions (applying the criterion that we have been applying since Constitutional Court Ruling 45/1989, of 20 February, for reasons of legal certainty ex section 9(3) of the Constitution), but also other legal situations generated by the application of the annulled precepts, must be declared not to be subject to review as a consequence of the nullity declared here.

  This is because the partial unconstitutionality of Royal Decree 463/2020, of 14 March, does not derive from the material content of the measures adopted, the necessity, suitability, and proportionality of which we have accepted, rather from the legal instrument through which certain fundamental rights were suspended. Given the suspension has affected the general population, it is not justified to hear individual claims for review based exclusively on the unconstitutionality found when there are no other grounds for unconstitutionality. To understand it otherwise would conflict not only with the constitutional principle of legal certainty (section 9(3) of the Constitution) but also of equality (section 14 of the Constitution).

2 On the other hand, the review expressly provided for in section 40(1) in fine Constitutional Court Act is possible. That is to say: 'in the case of criminal or judicial review proceedings relating to a sanctioning procedure in which, as a consequence of the nullity of the rule applied, a reduction of the penalty or sanction or an exclusion, exemption or limitation of liability results'. This exception is imposed by section 25(1) of the Constitution, as criminal or administrative sanctions are prohibited for acts that at the time of their commission do not constitute a criminal or administrative offence, the maintenance of a criminal or administrative sanction resulting from a provision declared void would violate the right to criminal legality enshrined in the above constitutional precept.

3 Finally, as these are measures that citizens had a legal duty to tolerate, the unconstitutionality found in this judgment will not in itself be a basis for state liability (*responsabilidad patrimonial de la administración*), without prejudice to section 3(2) of Organic Law 4/1981, of 1 June, on states of alarm, emergency and siege" (Constitutional Court Ruling148/2021 of 14 July, Finding of Law 11).

Bibliography

Boin, A., Brock, K., Craft, J.,Halligan, J., Hart, P., Roy, J., Tellier, G.,Turnbull, L. (2020). Beyond COVID-19: Five commentaries on expert knowledge, executive action, and accountability in governance and public administration. *Canadian Public Administration, 63*(3), 339–368.

Bovens, M. (2010). Two concepts of accountability: Accountability as a virtue and as a mechanism. *West European Politics, 33*(5), 946–967.

Bustos Gispert, R. (2017). *Calidad democrática. Reflexiones constitucionales desde la teoría, la realidad y el deseo*. Marcial Pons.

Campos Acuña, C. (2022). Integridad y transparencia en la contratación pública como una herramienta de eficacia y eficiencia en la gestión pública pos-COVID. *Revista del CLAD Reforma y Democracia, 82*, 115–150.

Cutter, C., Nelson, C., & Abir, M. (2021). Accountability to population health in the COVID-19 pandemic: Designing health care delivery within a social responsibility framework. *Population Health Management, 24*(1), 3–5. https://doi.org/10.1089/pop.2020.0096

Diab, A. A. (2021). The accountability process during the time of COVID-19 pandemic and the emerging role of non-profit associations. *Academy of Strategic Management Journal, 20*(1), 1–9.

Diab, A. A., Metwally, A., & Mohamed, M. (2021). The failure of global leadership and accountability problems during the COVID-19 pandemic. *Academic of Strategic Management Journal, 20*(3), 1–8.

Eurobaremeter Special 523. (2022). Corruption, 24 March – 18 April 2022.

Gimeno Feliu, J. M. (2020). Integridad y transparencia en la contratación pública y su significado en tiempos de emergencia. *Anuario de Transparencia Local, 3*, 13–39.

Goetz, A. M., & Jenkins, R. (2001). Hybrid forms of accountability. *Public Management Review, 3*, 363–383.

Guichot Reina, E. (2021). La Ley de Transparencia sometida al test de la COVID-19. *Revista Española de derecho Administrativo, 212*, 11–54.

Hernández Rodríguez, E., & Moreno Martínez, C. (2021). La transparencia pública en el escenario post-covid: Hoja de ruta para una administración más abierta. *Revista Española de la Transparencia, 13*, 131–171. https://doi.org/10.51915/ret.170

Innerarity, D. (2020). *Pandemocracia. Una filosofía de la crisis del coronavirus*. Galaxia Gutemberg.

International Transparency Spain. (2002). Available at: https://transparencia.org.es/que-hacemos/investigacion/indices/indice-de-percepcion-de-la-corrupcion-2022/ (consulted 18-1-24).
Klitgaard, R. (1997). Cleaning up and invigorating the civil service: Summary. *Public Administration & Development*, *17*(5), 487–509.
Klitgaard, R. (1998). *Controlling corruption*. University of California Press.
Leoni, G. et al. (2021). Accounting, management and accountability in times of crisis: Lessons from the COVID-19 pandemic. *Accounting, Auditing & Accountability Journal*, *34*(6), 1305–1319.
Manin, B., Przeworski, A., & Stokes, S. (1999). Elections and representation. In A. Przeworski, S. C. Stokes, & B. Manin (Eds.), *Democracy, accountability and representation* (pp. 29–54). Cambridge University Press.
O'Donnell, G. (1998). *Accountability* horizontal. *Estudios Políticos*, *19*, 9–46.
Ojiagu, M. C., Nzewi, H. N., & Arachie, A. E. (2020). Accountability and transparency in nation building: A COVID-19 experience in Sub-Saharan Africa. *International Journal of Public Policy and Administration Research*, *7*(1), 23–33.
Pineda Nebot, C., & Pardo Beneyto, G. (2020). La contratación pública en tiempos de Pandemia del Covid-19 en España. *Revista da CGU*, *12*(22), 330–342. https://doi.org/10.36428/revistadacgu.v12i22.322
Ramiro Avilés, M. A. (2006). A vueltas con el paternalismo jurídico. *Derechos y Libertades*, *15*, 211–256.
Rose-Ackerman, S. (2021). Corrupción y COVID-19. *Eunomía. Revista en Cultura de la Legalidad*, *20*, 37–60.
Schelder, A. (1999). Conceptualizing accountability. In A. Schelder, L. Diamond, & M. Plattner (Eds.), *The self-restraining state. Power and accountability in new democracies* (pp. 13–28). Lynne Rienner Publishers.
Shimizu, K., & Mossialos, E. (2021). Accountability and transparency are vital in a pandemic response. *Journal of General and Family Medicine*. https://doi.org/10.1002/jgf2.401
Smulovitz, C., & Peruzzotti, E. (2000). Societal accountability in Latin America. *Journal of Democracy*, *11*(4), 147–154.
Villoria, M., & Jiménez, F. (2021). Rendición social de cuentas en España. El papel de las organizaciones de la sociedad civil en la promoción de buena gobernanza durante la pandemia derivada de la COVID-19. *Revista Española de Ciencia Política*, *57*, 111–137. https://doi.org/10.21308/recp.57.04
Wang, X., Xiao, H., Yan, B., & Xu, J. (2020). New development: Administrative accountability and early responses during public health crises—Lessons from covid-19 in China. *Public Money & Management*. https://doi.org/10.1080/09540962.2020.1819012
World Bank. (2004). *State-society synergy for accountability. Lessons from the World Bank*, World Bank Working Paper no. 30.

2 Enforcement of Equality Before the Law in Poland During the Coronavirus Pandemic

Roman Bäcker and Joanna Rak

Introduction

On 12 March 2020, the government declared the state of the epidemic in Poland. A day later, Prime Minister Mateusz Morawiecki informed about the ban on public gatherings of more than 50 people. On 24 March 2020, the government introduced severe constraints on freedom of movement. Citizens could leave their houses only in duly justified circumstances, such as going to work or buying food. The police began controlling pedestrians and drivers to verify whether their movement was justified. All economic and social restrictions resulted in an almost complete lockdown. However, the public administration has gradually lifted the restrictions since mid-April. The will for social survival and the ruling party's determination to secure the re-election of Andrzej Duda in the presidential elections appeared to be stronger than a fear of infection and readiness to respect civil rights. The presidential elections (the first round on 28 June and the second round on 12 July 2020), held in an atmosphere of no epidemiological threats, ended Poland's first pandemic wave.

The government claimed that the chief objective was to protect the safety of citizens. In the opinion of the main opposition political parties, namely the Civic Coalition (*Koalicja Obywatelska, KO*), the Polish Peoples' Party (*Polskie Stronnictwo Ludowe, PSL*), and the Left (*Lewica*), the authorities restricted the freedom of movement and assembly unconstitutionally (Musiał-Karg & Kapsa, 2021). Instead of introducing a state of emergency based on the 1997 Constitution, the government significantly limited civic freedom under ordinary law. If a state of emergency had been declared, the presidential elections would have had to be postponed (Drinóczi & Bień-Kacała, 2020). However, such a scenario disadvantaged President Andrzej Duda and the Law and Justice (*Prawo i Sprawiedliwość, PiS*) party supporting him. As a result, the administration limited liberties without declaring a state of emergency. Citizens who left their houses for purposes other than "to meet the necessary needs of everyday life" risked high fines and diverse repercussions, including court and detention proceedings. The public authorities did not classify exercising civil liberties, such as opposing democratic backsliding during protests, as a legitimate need (Orzechowski et al., 2021).

The clash between the ruling party, social groups, and political opposition uncovers opposing interests. On the one hand, the PiS strove for the highest possible

DOI: 10.4324/9781003482710-3

social conformism and aimed to stay in power. Exercising the latter without its own president would be much more difficult. On the other hand, the various opposition actors fought for the survival of elementary freedoms and civil rights, striving simultaneously to achieve electoral excellence (Guasti, 2020). These observations motivate the research problem of practising equality before the law in Poland during the pandemic.

Article 32 of the Constitution of the Republic of Poland (1997) establishes the principle of equality of citizens before the law. Everyone is equal before the law and has the right to be treated equally by public authorities. Moreover, no one may be discriminated against in political, social or economic life for any reason. As an expression of the pursuit of a fair and just legal system, this principle is at the core of the rule of law (Acemoglu & Wolitzky, 2021, p. 1429). Breaking this constitutional concept means transforming the structure of the rule of law into the prerogative state (Fraenkel, 2018).

This chapter aims to determine to what extent the Polish government respected equality before the law during the pandemic. It is a sensitive indicator of the changes in the trajectory of political structure. As such, it enables us to identify and account for the direction and pace of Poland's movements on a continuum between the rule of law and the prerogative state in 2020–2022.

The remainder of the chapter is divided into five parts. The first one offers a literature review on equality before law enforcement as an indicator of the rule of law. It also establishes a theoretical framework for the analysis, including theory-based coding and data interpretation. Then, the discussion goes on to methodological assumptions and a corpus of sources. This part presents the research design and rationale behind the adopted research procedures. The other two parts introduce research findings on the two dimensions of equality before law enforcement, that is respecting the freedoms of assembly and movement. The chapter finishes with a discussion and conclusions on the implications of the identified instances of protection and violation of equality before the law for the drift from the rule of law to the prerogative state.

Literature review and theoretical framework

The rule of law means that all citizens and institutions within the state structure are accountable to the same laws. This norm supports equality before the law and serves two main functions. While the first one is "to curb arbitrary and inequitable use of state power" (Bedner, 2010, p. 50), the second is "to protect citizens" property and lives from infringements or assaults by fellow citizens' (Bedner, 2010, p. 51). The prerogative state is the antinomy of the rule of law (cf. Schotel, 2021). It emerges when rulers restrict the freedom and rights of those they consider a threat to their authority regardless of the actual power of the latter to spark this potential threat (cf. Hendley, 2022). Accordingly, in the prerogative state, the state power is used arbitrarily, inequitably, and to secure the interest of rulers.

Researchers evaluate equality before law enforcement as one of the essential features of protest policing models since police officers play the role of law enforcement agents (Earl & Soule, 2006, p. 147). Jennifer Earl, Sarah A. Soule, and John D. McCarthy point to the threat approach as the most supported explanatory model in the scholarly literature. It assumes that the larger the threat to rulers, the greater and more severe the expected repression (Earl et al., 2003, p. 583). This means that authorities who cannot maintain their ruling positions according to the rule of law use the escalated force model of protest policing. They thereby breach the rule of law to eliminate the threat, which underlies the transition into the prerogative state.

At the same time, equality before the law is one of many, and therefore often marginalised, determinants of the style of protest control in current studies on contentious politics. della Porta and Reiter (1998, p. 4) differentiate between escalated force and negotiated management by applying the following criteria: the degree of force used by police, the number of prohibited behaviours, the number of repressed groups, police respect for the law, the timing of law enforcement, the degree of communication with demonstrators, the degree of "adaptability" understood as the capacity to adjust to emerging situations, the degree of formalisation of the rules of the game, and the degree of "preparation". Nevertheless, out of the factors included in the model, only the criterion of the number of repressed groups directly refers to equality before the law. While diffused repression is characteristic of escalated force, selective repression indicates negotiated management. Although della Porta and Reiter treat it merely as a quantitative indicator and thus aptly address mass arrest, its nature is qualitative as well.

The sheer number of repressed groups misses the other dimensions of protest policing selectiveness, which are qualitative, including partiality (when police repress some protesters and support or ignore others) and partisan actions (when police actions perform political interests of the ruling and act as their loyal supporters) (Suh & Tarrow, 2021). Recent studies draw attention to police partisanship and the political function of public order policing as one of its most under-theorised aspects (Smith, 2021). They emphasise that policing researchers must engage with the police's dependence on the government, the political context of their activity, and the resulting bias "to develop a comprehensive understanding of protest policing in the current era" (Gilmore et al., 2019, p. 48).

Clark McPhail, David Schweingruber, and John D. McCarthy developed the della Porta and Reiter's model of escalated force and negotiated management by reducing the number and changing some criteria for their distinction. Their modified model of protest policing draws upon the willingness of law enforcement to protect the right to assembly (also called the extent of police concern with the First Amendment rights of protesters), the extent of police tolerance for community disruption, the nature of the communication between the law enforcement officers and assembly participants, the extent and manner of arrests as a method of managing assembly participants, and the extent and manner of using force instead of or in conjunction with arrests to control assembly participants (McPhail et al., 1998, p. 51). Here, only the first dimension concerns equality before the law directly. Nevertheless, since the very willingness may remain beyond the scope of empirical observation, it should be treated as the protection of the political right to peaceful assembly by police. According to McPhail, Schweingruber, and McCarthy, in the escalated force model, police officers consider selected public gatherings illegitimate and act to repress them. In the negotiated management model, they acknowledge the universality of the right to peaceful assembly and tolerate protests regardless of their political aims. At the same time, law enforcement officers aim to protect human rights, life, and property (McPhail et al., 1998, p. 51). While escalated force is peculiar to the prerogative state, negotiated management is characteristic of the rule of law.

Another dimension of equality before the law is protecting freedom of movement. The rule of law assumes that the restriction applies to all citizens regardless of their characteristics. In turn, when members of the ruling elite do not have to obey the limitations, the prerogative state emerges. In the prerogative form, movement restrictions aim to increase social conformism and subordination, while in the rule of law, they protect public health and human lives. Adherence to procedures is another important indicator of the type of political structure. If the police act in accordance with their powers and the procedures provided for by law, the rule of law applies. In the prerogative state, the police operate outside the scope of the methods and thus expand their powers.

To sum up, this two-dimensional approach to equality before the law may be useful for understanding the dynamics of balancing between the rule of law and the prerogative state or the transition from the former to the latter. During the pandemic, the Polish police were engaged by the government to control compliance with the ban on movement, organising, and participating in public gatherings. The characteristic of the rule of law is that all citizens are treated equally in enforcing these bans. At the same time, the prerogative state divides Poles into those affected by the prohibition and those excluded from its observance. The following parts of the chapter uncover the essential features of this engagement.

Research methods and data

The study addresses the following research question: to what extent did the Polish government respect equality before the law during the pandemic? Here, the authors emphasise that the ruling elite used police officers to enforce the law, and the latter were agents defining the attribute of equality before law enforcement. To gather data sufficient and necessary to tackle the research question, we carried out an intertextual qualitative document analysis of police statements and news released during the pandemic, from the declaration of the pandemic in Poland up until the lifting of the state of the epidemic from 12 March 2020 to 16 May 2022 (Rozporządzenie, 2022). We obtained validation, convergence, corroboration, and representativeness for law enforcement characteristics with data triangulation. Our corpus of sources includes the official governmental website, entries from the Polish Police official website, the Capital City Police (the Warsaw Police Headquarters), tweets of these two entities, and news distributed by the most opinion-forming Polish media (Onet.pl, TVN24, RMF FM, and *Rzeczpospolita*).

The governmental website was a major source of notifying Poles about restrictions. In turn, the police informed about the rules of enforcing the regulations and created their own image of relationships between police officers and citizens. As the watchdogs, the media provided independent views on the ruling administration, the police, and citizens' involvement in law enforcement during the pandemic.

The authors manually searched entries on the governmental website to determine binding restrictions. At the same time, we searched entries on the police's official websites and X (formerly Twitter) accounts to gather those containing at least one of (a) and (b1) or (b2) search phrase in one news or tweet: (a) we *and/or* law enforcement *and/or* police *and/or* police officers *and/or* officers; (b1) disorder *and/or* assembly *and/or* gathering *and/or* protest *and/or* demonstration *and/or* manifestation *and/or* rally *and/or* strike *and/or* riot *and/or* social unrest *and/or* participants of these contentious collective gatherings; (b2) movement *and/or* move *and/or* moving *and/or* travel *and/or* travelling *and/or* location.

We included our source corpus Onet.pl, TVN24, RMF FM, and *Rzeczpospolita* by drawing upon the Institute of Media Monitoring (IMM)'s reports on "The most opinion-forming media in Poland". While those titles had more than 3,000 citations during the pandemic, others gained about 2,000 or fewer citations (Rak, 2021). By applying the same search rules, we explored the media archives manually.

Additionally, we triangulated those sources with datasets of the Global Database of Events, Language, and the Tone Project database (GDELT Project), namely, the GDELT Event Exporter and the GDELT Event Database. It contains records from numerous news outlets worldwide, published in 65 languages (e.g. *BBC Monitoring*, *New York Times*). We thereby combined state and commercial media narratives to avoid bias in interpreting law enforcement agencies' behaviour. When in doubt concerning data interpretation, we used the dataset for fact-checking instead of reviewing the whole dataset. By inquiring the GDELT EVENT Exporter, we built the former with the following set of criteria: date = 12/03/2020; end date = 16/05/2022 (the official caesuras of the pandemic in Poland); Actor1 Country: Poland (location of event: Poland); Event Code: 14 (the type of event: protest); Event Country: Poland (type and state affiliation of the initiator of the action: Poland); weighting: NUMEVENTS (an aggregation of the CAMEOevent codes into four categories ranging from Verbal Cooperation to Material Cooperation, Verbal Conflict, and Material Conflict) (Rak, 2021).

After collecting data on law enforcement characteristics, the authors went on to skim, examine, and interpret information. We employed content and thematic analysis techniques to facilitate these stages. First, we separated text excerpts directly referencing police respect for and protection of the freedoms of movement and assembly. Second, we organised these excerpts into two categories: the protection of freedom of assembly (a selective or stated top priority for all) and the protection of freedom of movement (a selective or stated top priority for all). These stages of content analysis were followed by thematic analysis. The latter commenced with multiple readings and reviewing the text passages in the two categories. It aimed to discover themes (patterns of meanings) relative to equality before the law regarding the freedoms of movement and assembly enforcement across the dataset (Clarke & Braun, 2017). Then, we grouped text passages into instances of securing or breaking those selected civil rights. The coding rested on the groups of search terms from the theoretical framework. Evaluator triangulation and the constant comparative approach to data facilitated analysis and contributed to the validity. While individual instances were mutually listed together in text passages, codes were used to arrange ideas and isolate clustering concepts. When the corpus of sources contained contradictory evidence, we resorted to the generated GDELT dataset to delve into the cases further. It allowed us to define the possible values of the aspects of equality before law enforcement. Such data triangulation provided a convergence of evidence.

Equality before the law and freedom of assembly

On 13 March 2020, with the declaration of an epidemiological emergency, the government introduced a ban on gatherings with more than 50 people. On 24 March 2020, concerning the statement of the epidemic, the Council of Ministers ordered a total restriction on assemblies. These regulations were relaxed in May 2020. In October 2020, with the rise of the second wave of the epidemic, a ban on public gatherings of more than ten individuals was introduced, further reduced to five people from 23 October 2020. From June 2021, organising public meetings with no more than 150 participants became possible.

In Poland, civil rights and freedoms may only be restricted by acts of Parliament. Article 57 of the Constitution of the Republic of Poland of 1997 explicitly states that a legal provision (a statute) may only limit the freedom of peaceful assembly. Meanwhile, all restrictions, including a total ban on assemblies from 24 March 2020, were introduced by the Regulation of the Council of Ministers. Nevertheless, the government tried to force citizens to abide by the ban on public gatherings by controlling the activity of the police.

During the first wave of the pandemic, few protests were caused primarily by economic factors. On 24 April 2020, the Czech Republic and German border area inhabitants protested against closing their borders. This decision deprived them of the possibility of working abroad. In June and July, employees of LOT Polish Airlines, travel agencies, and coach companies joined protests. In each case, the police protected protest sites but avoided dispersing the crowd and checking their identity cards.

On 14 April 2020, the All-Poland Women's Strike (*Ogólnopolski Strajk Kobiet, OSK*) held a protest against attempts to tighten the abortion law. People in the streets, cars, and balconies kept homemade posters. They adhered to all sanitary restrictions. Nevertheless, the police checked the IDs of 24 protesters, fined 4 people, and brought 6 cases to court. They also sent applications to the Chief Sanitary Inspectorate (*Sanepid*) to fine the protesters for non-compliance with sanitary regulations and accused them of blocking traffic (Malecki, 2020). Coronavirus sceptics held two very numerous protests of hundreds of individuals on 6 June and 10 July 2020 but did not encounter any reaction from the police. They were organised by the editorial office of "Gazeta Warszawska", supporting the ruling party.

On 26 March 2020, the Citizens of the Republic of Poland (*Obywatele RP, 2020*) activists put up a huge banner to thank healthcare workers for their work.

Although they respected the principle of spatial distance, the police accused them of breaking sanitary rules and brought indictments before the court. Those activists were noted for opposing democratic backsliding in Poland. After reading the evidence and considering the accusation's legal basis, the courts acquitted them.

The first street demonstration of the Entrepreneur Strike (*Strajk Przedsiębiorców*) led by Paweł Tanajno took place on 9 May 2020. The police detained 62 individuals. During the second demonstration on 17 May 2020, law enforcement officers violently clashed with the participants and arrested 380 activists, including Senator Jacek Bury from the opposition Civic Coalition, despite his immunity (Mierzyńska, 2020; Police clash, 2020; Warsaw police, 2020). The police treated the protest as illegal, as officials did not register it. Thus, the police disregarded the decision of the Court of Appeal in Warsaw (*Sąd Apelacyjny w Warszawie*), which stated that the refusal to register does not constitute a decision prohibiting the demonstration. During the third demonstration on 23 May 2020, law enforcement officers detained Tanajno, a registered candidate for the presidency of the Republic of Poland and a counter-candidate of the incumbent Andrzej Duda, the president supported by the ruling party. It was the first time a candidate for president was arrested in post-communist Poland (Presidential candidate, 2020).

Other protests were far less numerous. On 3 May, activists from the Committee for the Defence of Democracy (*Komitet Obrony Demokracji, KOD*) walked in several cities with banners "Constitution" (*Konstytucja*). The police detained some of them, checked their IDs, and accused protesters of breaking sanitary regulations in a few cases. However, the organisers declared they adhered to the sanitary regime (Konstytucyjne, 2020). On 12 May 2020, KOD organised events to ridicule the farce of the presidential election that was to take place two days earlier. Again, law enforcement officers checked the identity cards of the protesters (Obywatelskie protesty, 2020). A one-person protest in May 2020 in Toruń ended with the prosecution sending an indictment of unlawful use of public property, that is the accused was leaning against a streetlamp. Nonetheless, the court acquitted him.

On 22 and 23 May 2020, over 200 protesters gathered in front of the state radio headquarters. Radio managers nominated by the ruling party cancelled a weekly hit list, as Kazik's song entitled "Your Pain is Better than Mine", criticising Jarosław Kaczyński, took the No. 1 spot. The police did not intervene.

On 8 June 2020, law enforcement officers arrested an activist from the Citizens of the Republic of Poland, the association also famous for opposing democratic backsliding. Her fault was putting up posters accusing the Minister of Health Łukasz Szumowski of corruption on sites belonging to AMS – the advertising company. Officers handcuffed the activist, took her to the police station, and searched her apartment. Moreover, they sent her personal data to the state media controlled by the ruling party. A demonstration in support of her, organised two days later, was dispersed by the police.

During the second wave of the pandemic, the All-Poland Women's Strike organised large demonstrations in over a hundred cities and towns after the ruling of the Constitutional Tribunal was announced, which strictly limited the right to abortion. In October 2020, law enforcement officers temporarily detained and checked the

IDs of a few individuals. Subsequently, the police began to protect churches, Law and Justice's parliamentary offices, and the places of residence of politicians from the ruling party, mainly Kaczyński's, not only during *escraches*. On 10 November 2020, Paweł Dobrodziej, the Commander of the Capital City of Police, issued an instruction in which he ordered more decisive action against the demonstrators. Since then, the law enforcement officers claimed that assemblies during the epidemic were illegal, blocked marches, used the police technique of "kettling" to separate protesters from the crowd, fined, checked the IDs of the protesters, and sent requests for punishment to the *Sanepid*. On 18 November 2020, police officers in plain clothes used telescopic batons against protesting women in Warsaw. During the eight weeks of the Women's Strike, the Warsaw law enforcement officers detained over 80 people (Rak & Bäcker, 2023, pp. 207–208).

In summary, the principle of equality before the law was violated. The police avoided repressing the participants of public gatherings which were not anti-governmental. Nevertheless, they used multiple repressions against the participants of anti-government protests. The mildest form was identity card checking. The other forms included transporting to police stations, temporal detention, directing motions for punishment to the *Sanepid*, and prosecutor's accusations to courts. However, the judges, due to the unconstitutionality of the ban on public assemblies, usually ultimately acquitted the participants of the assemblies.

Notably, the participants in protests organised by the presidential candidate Tanajno suffered from severe repression. His activities were treated as posing a threat to President Duda's position. In addition, the ruling elite might have perceived them as potentially engaging in political participation with those who had not previously participated in social life. Due to the programme and social structure of Tanajno's supporters, they would support the opposition candidate more than Duda in the second round of the presidential election. Thus, the level of repression was much higher than in other cases.

Equality before the law and freedom of movement

It is hardly possible to precisely determine to what extent the ruling administration failed to comply with the prohibitions on moving and staying in public places during the pandemic. This is due to many factors. The first is the whole system of privileges conferred by possessing a high official or political office. A company car at one's free disposal that is not subject to police control, together with a driver, is only one of many such privileges. It is also impossible to define the scope of remote work, even for individuals such as Kaczyński, the president of Law and Justice, who do not use the Internet. It is only possible to scrutinise the credible facts from the media regarding individual cases of violating the very variable prohibitions against moving and staying in public places.

The most famous are the numerous cases of breaking all restrictions by Kaczyński. Despite the ban on leaving the house, except for going to work and shopping, Kaczyński went to church every Sunday, and on 18 March 2020, he went to the Wawel Castle to the graves of his brother and sister-in-law. In the latter case, in addition to the bodyguards who were always with him, he was also accompanied by the MEP and former Prime Minister Beata Szydło (Koronawirus, 2020). Kaczyński was characterised by his disrespectful treatment of the obligation to wear masks and the lack of spatial distance during public meetings. It was he who decided that, despite the pandemic, ceremonies to commemorate the 2010 Smoleńsk aviation disaster would be held. The most famous example of this was the ceremony at the monument to the victims of the Smoleńsk catastrophe in the centre of Warsaw on 10 April 2020. Regardless of the gathered group of over 100 law enforcement officers, over 50 activists from the ruling party participated in these celebrations (Rządzącym wolno, 2020). In the following year (2021), the celebration of the Smoleńsk disaster anniversary attracted fewer people, and the majority complied with the obligation to wear masks and keep spatial distance.

Additionally, Kaczyński visited the Powązki Cemetery on 10 April 2020, that is at the time when its administrator, the Archdiocese of Warsaw, banned entry. This information was made public immediately after the incident. However, it gained publicity again after the government introduced a total ban on visiting cemeteries on the Day of the Dead, 1 November 2020. This information, especially on the day when the commonly observed custom of remembering the dead in cemeteries was forbidden,caused widespread outrage (Jurszo, 2020; Nie, 2020).

Also, on 10 April 2020, six Law and Justice politicians who neither wore masks nor respected the spatial distance appeared at the Wawel Castle. As the prosecutor's office discontinued the investigation, one of the NGOs under the watchdog (Centre for Monitoring Racist and Xenophobic Behaviour – *Ośrodek Monitorowania Zachowań Rasistowskich i Ksenofobicznych*) filed a complaint with the court. After a year, the court ruled that there was no violation of the law, as all prohibitions, including sanitary regulations, were unconstitutional. Limitations of civic rights may occur only through a legal act, not an ordinance of the Council of Ministers (Politycy, 2021).

In May 2020, right after the opening of cafes and restaurants, PM Morawiecki allowed himself to be photographed in a cafe in Gliwice. Contrary to the recommendations of the Ministry of Health, he sat at a table with people he did not live with, failed to keep spatial distance, and there was no Perspex cover between the individuals seated opposite each other. Morawiecki explained that these were recommendations, not bans (Premier komentuje, 2020).

On 3 October 2020, the then-candidate and then the Minister of Education and Science, Przemysław Czarnek, visited his severely ill grandmother in the hospital. After three days, it turned out that he had developed symptoms of COVID-19. At the same time, 90% of patients in the ward visited by Czarnek fell ill with the disease. The prosecutor's office refused to investigate this matter (Kandydat, 2020; Opozycja, 2020).

During his leave from official duties, Minister for Health Szumowski repeatedly visited the Institute of Cardiology in Anin despite the introduction of a total visit ban. This was also the case just before his isolation due to COVID-19 in September 2020. Szumowski confirmed that he had been in this hospital many times during his vacation ("GW", 2020).

To sum up, Kaczyński's behaviour shows that he completely ignored epidemiological threats at the beginning of the pandemic. It was only after many weeks that he hardly conformed to some of the restrictions imposed by the government created by his party. Despite the apparent evidence of non-compliance with the limitations they adopted, the ruling politicians did not feel obliged to bear any consequences. Their most important task was to look for some neat explanation so that the media would not continue dealing with it.

A tremendous volume of information on breaking the bans occurred during the first epidemic wave in the Spring of 2020. This is most likely due to the very high level of public concern about the consequences of the pandemic and, thus, the pursuit of the strictest possible compliance by all, without exception, of all restrictions. Their non-observance by the rulers was treated as a particular disregard not only for the rules they introduced but also a threat to public health and the lives of all citizens.

Conclusion

The police repressed the participants of those public gatherings, which were a sign of protest against the ruling party's policy or could have threatened its political position. Law enforcement officers used repression so as not to cause an even greater wave of protests and prevent civil disorder. Thus, the most brutal and mass forms of repression, such as dispersing the crowd or imprisoning almost all demonstration participants, were rarely used. Repressions of a completely unlawful nature were very seldom. The most glaring case was the Women's Strike participants beaten on 18 November 2020 by police officers in plain clothes mingled with the crowd. The actions of the police are definitely on the side of the prerogative state, although it is undoubtedly a moderate stage, not a radical one.

Similar conclusions can be drawn in the case of non-compliance by high-ranking politicians of the ruling party with government regulations concerning restrictions on movement in public places. The most frequently reported cases involved the first wave of the pandemic, although they undoubtedly occurred later. However, during the successive waves of the pandemic, they did not arouse much interest from journalists and the broadly understood public opinion. The manipulative and cynical attitude of members of the ruling elite towards public opinion is worth noting. Any justification was necessary because it was already known that their fate was ultimately decided by the president of Law and Justice, who himself did not comply with the regulations of his own government.

The ruling party significantly limited civic freedoms under ordinary law, although they could have declared a state of emergency by drawing upon the 1997 Constitution. The latter solution would allow it to impose legal restrictions, but at the same time, it would force the government to postpone the presidential election for at least three months. The logic of party interest and convenience won with the rule of law. Citizens were deprived of freedom of assembly and could not freely oppose the unconstitutional changes in electoral law. Furthermore, the ruling party attempted to tighten the abortion laws without public debate, although the issue was highly controversial. This way, they intended to avoid mass protests, which would have likely occurred under normal circumstances.

The enforcement of restrictions on the freedom of public assembly and movement in public places locates the Polish state on the continuum on the side of the prerogative state. However, this is a moderate stage mainly due to the judgements of the courts that adhere to the Polish Constitution and thus do not fulfil the will of the ruling elite. This applies to a lesser extent to the power of public opinion to influence the most prominent politicians of the ruling party.

The examination of Poland's case illustrates the method for assessing adherence to the principle of equality before the law. A higher degree of adherence places a political system closer to the ideal type of the rule of law, while a lower degree aligns it more with the perfect kind of prerogative state. This position on the continuum is influenced not only by the actions of the ruling elite but also by the resistance of independent state institutions and the extent of condemnation from public opinion. Notably, this principle applies even in exceptional situations like pandemics and wars.

Using the theoretical and methodological framework mentioned above to assess equality before the law is valuable. For instance, one could examine the situation in Ukraine following the Russian aggression that commenced on 24 February 2022 or in Israel after the Hamas attack on 7 October 2023. Investigating the extent to which a state aligns with the characteristics of a prerogative state or adheres to the rule of law yields valuable insights into the nature of its governance and the state of its legal system. This analysis serves as a critical tool for understanding the balance between state power and individual liberties. Governance quality is a prominent aspect of this evaluation. A higher alignment with the characteristics of a prerogative state may suggest a concentration of power in the hands of a few, potentially leading to authoritarian tendencies and a lack of checks and balances. Conversely, a firm adherence to the rule of law reflects a commitment to legal principles, accountability, and transparency, contributing to a more just and equitable governance structure. Simultaneously, the institutional strength of a state is a critical factor in this analysis. A system leaning towards a prerogative state may be characterised by weak or manipulated institutions, potentially susceptible to the abuse of power. In contrast, a commitment to the rule of law is often associated with strong, independent institutions that check governmental power, promoting stability and accountability.

Respect for individual rights is another crucial dimension. Characteristics of a prerogative state may imply a potential disregard for individual rights and freedoms, as decisions may be made without due process or consideration for legal protections. On the other hand, adherence to the rule of law indicates a commitment to protecting individual rights, ensuring fair treatment, and upholding the principles of justice. In a prerogative state, public dissent may be suppressed, and civil society may face restrictions, limiting the ability of citizens to voice concerns. In contrast, a society that upholds the rule of law typically allows for open discourse, encourages civic engagement, and values the participation of citizens in shaping governance.

Finally, the analysis based on the above tool provides insights into how a state handles extraordinary situations. In a prerogative state, the response to crises may involve concentrated decision-making, potentially at the expense of individual liberties. However, even in exceptional situations, a commitment to the rule of law ensures that responses are consistent with legal principles, maintaining a balance between security and individual rights. The analysis of whether a state embodies the characteristics of a prerogative state or upholds the rule of law offers a comprehensive framework for assessing the overall quality of a nation's governance and legal system.

Funding: This chapter results from the research project *Civil Disorder in Pandemic-ridden European Union*. It was financially supported by the National Science Centre, Poland [grant number 2021/43/B/HS5/00290].

Bibliography

Acemoglu, D., & Wolitzky, A. (2021). A theory of equality before the law. *The Economic Journal, 131*(636), 1429–1465. https://doi.org/10.1093/ej/ueaa116

Bedner, A. (2010). An elementary approach to the rule of law. *Hague Journal on the Rule of Law, 2*(1), 48–74.

Clarke, V., & Braun, V. (2017). Thematic analysis. *The Journal of Positive Psychology, 12*(3), 297–298. https://doi.org/10.1080/17439760.2016.1262613

Constitution of the Republic of Poland. (1997). *Konstytucja Rzeczypospolitej Polskiej. Tekst uchwalony w dniu 2 kwietnia 1997 r. przez Zgromadzenie Narodowe*. https://www.sejm.gov.pl/prawo/konst/polski/kon1.htm

della Porta, D., & Reiter, H. (1998). The policing of protest in Western democracies. In D. della Porta, & H. Reiter (Eds.), *Policing protest: The control of mass demonstrations in Western democracies* (pp. 1–32). University of Minnesota Press.

Drinóczi, T., & Bień-Kacała, A. (2020). COVID-19 in Hungary and Poland: Extraordinary situation and illiberal constitutionalism. *The Theory and Practice of Legislation, 8*(1–2), 171–192. https://doi.org/10.1080/20508840.2020.1782109

Earl, J., & Soule, S. A. (2006). Seeing blue: A police-centered explanation of protest policing. *Mobilisation: An International Quarterly, 11*(2), 145–164. https://doi.org/10.17813/maiq.11.2.u1wj8w41n301627u

Earl, J., Soule, S. A., & McCarthy, J. D. (2003). Protest under fire? Explaining the policing of protest. *American Sociological Review, 68*(4), 581–606. https://doi.org/10.2307/1519740

Fraenkel, E. (2018). *The dual state: A contribution to the theory of dictatorship*. Oxford University Press.

Gilmore, J., Jackson, W., & Monk, H. (2019). 'That is not facilitating peaceful protest. That is dismantling the protest': Anti-fracking protesters' experiences of dialogue policing and mass arrest. *Policing and Society, 29*(1), 36–51.

Guasti, P. (2020). The impact of the covid-19 pandemic in Central and Eastern Europe: The rise of autocracy and democratic resilience. *Democratic Theory, 7*(2), 47–60. https://doi.org/10.3167/dt.2020.070207

'GW'. (2020). *Szumowski odwiedził szpital mimo zakazu? Tak twierdzą pracownicy placówki.* https://www.wprost.pl/kraj/10372687/koronawirus-szumowski-odwiedzil-szpital-mimo-zakazu.htm

Hendley, K. (2022). Legal dualism as a framework for analysing the role of law under authoritarianism. *Annual Review of Law and Social Science* [online first view]. https://doi.org/10.1146/annurev-lawsocsci-050420-104012

Jurszo, R. (2020). *Gliński: Kazik dał się oszukać, Kaczyński nie jest równiejszy, cmentarz nie był zamknięty. Ale jak to?* https://oko.press/glinski-kazik-dal-sie-oszukac-kaczynski-nie-jest-rowniejszy-cmentarz-nie-byl-zamkniety-ale-jak-to/

Kandydat na ministra edukacji i nauki mimo zakazu odwiedził babcię w szpitalu. (2020). Jest zawiadomienie do prokuratury. https://glos.pl/kandydat-na-ministra-edukacji-i-nauki-mimo-zakazu-odwiedzil-babcie-w-szpitalu-jest-zawiadomienie-do-prokuratury

Konstytucyjne spacery. (2020). https://ruchkod.pl/konstytucyjne-spacery/

Koronawirus w Polsce. (2020). *Prezes PiS Jarosław Kaczyński pojechał na Wawel*. https://wiadomosci.wp.pl/koronawirus-w-polsce-prezes-pis-jaroslaw-kaczynski-pojechal-na-wawel-6490377933768321a

Malecki, M. (2020). Poland's coronavirus restrictions are unconstitutional, unlawful and risk years of legal chaos. https://notesfrompoland.com/2020/04/18/polands-coronavirus-restrictions-are-unconstitutional-unlawful-and-risk-years-of-legal-chaos/

McPhail, C., Schweingruber, D., & McCarthy, J. D. (1998). Policing protest in the United States: 1960–1995. In D. della Porta, & H. Reiter (Eds.), *Policing protest: The control of mass demonstrations in Western democracies* (pp. 49–69). University of Minnesota Press.

Mierzyńska, A., (2020). *Przedsiębiorcy, bezmaskowcy i antyszczepionkowcy nawołują do antyrządowej rewolucji. Zaskakujący miks*. https://oko.press/przedsiebiorcy-bezmaskowcy-i-antyszczepionkowcy-nawoluja-do-antyrzadowej-rewolucji-zaskakujacy-miks/

Musiał-Karg, M., & Kapsa, I. (2021). Debate: Voting challenges in a pandemic—Poland. *Public Money & Management*, *41*(1), 6–8. https://doi.org/10.1080/09540962.2020.1809791

Nie, J. (2020). *Kaczyński nie pojawił się na cmentarzu dzień przed Dniem Wszystkich Świętych*. https://demagog.org.pl/fake_news/nie-jaroslaw-kaczynski-nie-pojawil-sie-na-cmentarzu-dzien-przed-dniem-wszystkich-swietych/

Obywatele RP. (2020). *Obywatele RP zwracają się do klubów parlamentarnych w związku z działaniami Policji 8—10 czerwca*. Retrieved January 30, 2022 from https://obywatelerp.org/obywatele-rp-zwracaja-sie-do-klubow-parlamentarnych-w-zwiazku-z-dzialaniami-policji-8-10-czerwca/

Obywatelskie protesty i happening w dniu farsy wyborczej. (2020). Komitet Obrony Demokracji. Retrieved January 30, 2022 from https://ruchkod.pl/obywatelskie-protesty-i-happeningi-w-dniu-farsy-wyborczej/

Opozycja o odwiedzinach Czarnka w szpitalu: Jego ból jest lepszy niż twój. (2020, October 9). https://www.rp.pl/swiat/art8798061-opozycja-o-odwiedzinach-czarnka-w-szpitalu-jego-bol-jest-lepszy-niz-twoj

Orzechowski, M., Schochow, M., & Steger, F. (2021). Balancing public health and civil liberties in times of pandemic. *Journal of Public Health Policy*, *42*(1), 145–153. https://doi.org/10.1057/s41271-020-00261-y

Police clash with business owners protesting over coronavirus crisis in Poland. (2020). Notes from Poland. Retrieved January 30, 2022 from https://notesfrompoland.com/2020/05/08/police-clash-with-business-owners-protesting-over-coronavirus-crisis-in-poland/

Politycy PiS na Wawelu nie złamali prawa. (2021). *Sąd: zakazy związane z epidemią COVID-19 są niekonstytucyjne*. https://wiadomosci.gazeta.pl/wiadomosci/7,114884,26806679,politycy-pis-na-wawelu-nie-zlamali-prawa-sad-zakazy-zwiazane.html

Premier komentuje swoje zdjęcia z kawiarni. (2020). *Pewne odległości są zalecane, ale nie są nakazywane*". https://www.wprost.pl/kraj/10328227/premier-komentuje-swoje-zdjecia-z-kawiarni-pewne-odleglosci-sa-zalecane-ale-nie-sa-nakazywane.html

Presidential candidate detained by police during protest. (2020). https://polandin.com/48192856/presidential-candidate-detained-by-police-during-protest

Rak, J. (2021). Policing anti-government protests during the coronavirus crisis in Poland: Between escalated force and negotiated management. *Teorija in Praksa*, *58*(SI), 598–615. http://dx.doi.org/10.51936/tip.58.specialissue.598-615

Rak, J., & Bäcker, R. (2023). The role of cognitive and emotional factors in demobilisation: The pro-choice protest movement activity in Poland. *Sociologia*, *55*(2), 197–219. https://doi.org/10.31577/sociologia.2023.55.2.7

Rozporządzenie Ministra Zdrowia z dnia 12 maja 2022 r. w sprawie odwołania na obszarze Rzeczypospolitej Polskiej stanu epidemii. https://isap.sejm.gov.pl/isap.nsf/download.xsp/WDU20220001027/O/D20221027.pdf

Rządzącym wolno więcej? Bez masek, w grupie. (2020, April 10). *Zdjęcia liderów PiS z rocznicy katastrofy smoleńskiej wywołały oburzenie*. https://www.tokfm.pl/Tokfm/7,103087,25860818,bez-masek-rekawiczek-w-grupie-internauci-krytykuja-postawe.html

Schotel, B. (2021). Administrative law as a dual state. Authoritarian elements of administrative law. *Hague Journal on the Rule of Law*, *13*(1), 195–222. https://doi.org/10.1007/s40803-021-00156-4

Smith, W. (2021). The politics of protest policing: Neutrality, impartiality, and 'Taking the knee'. *The Harvard Review of Philosophy* [online first view]. https://doi.org/10.5840/harvardreview202172236

Suh, C. S., & Tarrow, S. G. (2021). Suppression by stealth: The partisan response to protest in state legislatures. *Politics & Society* [online first view]. https://doi.org/10.1177/00323292211039956

Warsaw police defend 380 arrests after protest against virus measures. (2020). Retrieved February 05, 2022 from https://www.dpa-international.com/topic/warsaw-police-defend-380-arrests-protest-virus-measures-urn:newsml:dpa.com:20090101:200517-99-91640

3 COVID-19 Entrepreneurs

Corruption and the Violation of the Rights of Health and Development in South Africa and Uganda

Marianne Séverin and Hannah Muzee

Introduction

While the COVID-19 pandemic caught many countries and governments unawares, some suffered more than others. In Africa, with a highly inefficient public service and dysfunctional welfare state, African governments had to act fast to prevent a high death toll. South Africa implemented a 23-day lockdown right after the first infection was reported, 18 days before Italy. The United States, having, had one of the world's most significant casualties, introduced COVID lockdowns in March 2020. Screening at ports of entry was instituted for those coming into the country, where travellers were required to present a negative PCR test that was not older than 72 hours and subsequently proof of vaccination. In addition, the government intensified the distribution of information to private and public healthcare workers and the public about the pandemic (Villiers et al., 2020). Furthermore, a National State of Disaster was declared on 15 March 2020 to not only enable the government of South Africa to slow down the infection rate but also ease the pressure on the healthcare system. Since the population was not economically active, several strategies were introduced to alleviate the suffering of the people, such as the R350 social relief of Distress Grant, the COVID-19 Temporary Employer/Employee Relief Scheme (TERS). It aimed to provide wage support to workers, and other relief schemes to small businesses, including the extension of validity of vehicle and driving licenses (South African Government, 2022).

Other stringent measures in South Africa included restrictions on travel from high-risk countries such as Italy, South Korea, Spain, Germany, the United States, the United Kingdom, and China imposed on 18 March 2020. Both land and seaports were also closed to passengers and non-essential personnel, and non-essential travel within and out of the country was prohibited. Mass gatherings and celebrations were restricted and inevitable small gatherings with stringent adherence to prevention and control protocols enforced and observed (Home Affairs, 2020). Similarly, in Uganda, when the first case was reported on 27 March 2020, the government imposed travel restrictions, closed the international airport and all boarders to passenger travel, and embarked on a mass hygiene campaign of hand-washing, social distancing, and mask-wearing. All educational institutions were shut down, and work from home was encouraged except for essential workers (The World Bank, 2021).

DOI: 10.4324/9781003482710-4

Like in South Africa, a lockdown was also instituted with grave economic implications for the country and the population. As cases increased, Uganda's healthcare system was stretched thin and in shortage of supplies such as oxygen and beds for the critically ill. While the private sector attempted to remedy the situation, their charges were quite exorbitant and unaffordable by the average Ugandan, and people resorted to self-medication with herbal or home remedies. The emphasis on biomedical sciences left other health sectors neglected, such as mental health, maternal and child health, and sexual and reproductive health, with severe implications for people's well-being (Seruwagi, 2021). The Uganda government had to solicit funds to cushion the poor and vulnerable masses, which included a US$300 million relief from the World Bank. Referred to as the Uganda COVID-19 Economic Crisis and Recovery Development Policy Financing, it was used to support immediate relief to individuals and businesses affected by the pandemic. The support included the provision of agricultural inputs to farmers, offering social protection in the form of cash to over 500,000 people, ensuring an interrupted supply of essential services like electricity, water, and sanitation through government subsidies, granting tax exemptions to supplies and equipment used in the fight against COVID-19, extending support to the private sector and businesses in distress (The World Bank, 2020).

However, some of these financial interventions in both South Africa and Uganda were marred by corruption scandals. Many public officials took advantage of their offices and utilised the COVID-19 relief funds for their own private gain (COVID-19 entrepreneurs), consequently violating the citizens' right to development (RTD) and health. In this case, bribery obstructed the realisation of these rights by facilitating the diversion of funds for health relief and other social services. In many instances, corruption by government officials affected its ability to provide healthcare equipment and procure and distribute medication to the population, thus violating the right to health (Mgbemere, no date). In Africa, corruption tendencies by politicians and leaders not only undermine the rule of law, given that it essentially goes unabated, but also place the vulnerable and poor in worse conditions. More than ever, we see African politics as less of service but an avenue for self-aggrandisement by public officials (Dlamini, 2020; Wafawarova, 2013). The COVID-19 pandemic revealed the complicities of the public sector in South Africa and Uganda and exposed what we termed as *COVID-19 entrepreneurs*. This chapter, therefore, examined how bribery undermined the fight against COVID-19 in the two countries concerning the violation of the right to health and development by those sworn to protect it. We present evidence of COVID-19-related corruption and argue that it revealed the international nature of bribery with its manifestation on the continent unabated by international monetary bodies. The chapter begins with discussing the rights to health and development in South Africa and Uganda, the state of corruption, violations of rights to health/development in those countries, and a conclusive way forward.

The rights to development and health in South Africa and Uganda

Recognised by the United Nations Declaration of the Right to Development (UNDRTD) (United Nations, 1986), the RTD comprises civil and political rights as well as socio-economic rights. The RTD as a "solidarity right" is a "necessary link to the duties or responsibilities that exist mutually between individuals and their families, communities, and societies" (Gutto, 2006, p. 111). According to the Declaration's Article 1, the RTD is "an inalienable human right by virtue of which every human person and all peoples are entitled to participate in, contribute to, and enjoy economic, social, cultural and political development, in which all human rights and fundamental freedoms can be fully realised" (United Nations, 1986). Adopted by 171 countries, the Vienna Declaration and Programme of Action has reinforced the fact that since 1993 "all human rights derive from the dignity and worth inherent in the human person, and the human person is the central subject of human rights and fundamental freedoms, and consequently should be the principal beneficiary and should participate actively in the realisation of these rights and freedoms" (United Nations, 1993).

In a particular context with a strong geographical and cultural dimension, the RTD, as a universal human right, takes on a different aspect. In the African frame of reference, the RTD is emphasised in Article 22 of the African Charter (AC) on Human and Peoples' Rights, adopted in 1981, long before the UNDRTD. Considering its implementation, the RTD "entails addressing numerous [African] issues, including the sanctity of the rule of law, African cultures, development assistance, corruption, the gender question, and the migration crisis" (Kamga, 2020, p. 6). Consequently, through the African prism, the RTD must be read as follows: the RTD holders being the African peoples and the duty bearers the African States: "(1). All peoples shall have the right to their economic, social, and cultural development with due regard to their freedom and identity and in the equal enjoyment of the common heritage of mankind. (2). States shall have the duty, individually or collectively to ensure the exercise of the right to development (Article 22)" (African Commission on Human and People's Rights, 1981).

Indeed, while all peoples shall enjoy the provision of AC's Article 22, African States under Article 1 must "assume the obligation to adopt legislative or other measures to give effect to the rights protected under that treaty. States are (…) required to enact laws that support the recreation of an environment in which people can develop their full potential and lead productive, creative life in accordance with their needs and interests" (Okafor, 2013, p. 381). While most African countries signed and ratified the AC (African Union, 2017), as per the RTD through its Article 22, they are far removed from the reality regarding the respect of the RTD and its implementation. The brake on this RTD is the combination of weak states and institutions, poor governance, lack of democracy, vulnerable socio-economic contexts, and bribery. South Africa and Uganda (our geographical case studies) must be included in this description, especially regarding corruption in the context of the COVID-19 pandemic, which is our case of analysis.

If defining the RTD as a universal human right and in an African context has been the first step of this analysis, it is also vital to identify and discuss who are the duty bearers of the RTD and their role in implementing human rights and how they violate it.

The duty bearers of the RTD

The definition of duty bearers has some latitude based on the preamble of the Universal Declaration of Human Rights – UDHR (1948). The UDHR states "every individual and every organ of society (…) shall strive by teaching and education to promote respect for these rights and freedoms and by progressive measures, national and international, to secure their universal and effective recognition and observance, both among the peoples of Members States" (United Nations, 1948). Indeed, Serges D. Kamga translates this statement as "this provision calls upon every entity in the society or 'organ of society' to ensure that human rights are observed" (Kamga, 2018).

The Declaration of UNDRTD is much more explicit in its Article 2(3) regarding the state as a duty bearer having an obligation to implement the RTD: "states have the right and the duty to formulate appropriate national development policies that aim at the constant improvement of the well-being of the entire population and of all individuals, on the basis of their active, free and meaningful participation in development and in the fair distribution of the benefits resulting therefrom" (United Nations, 1986). The Declaration's Article 6(3) also states that "states should take steps to eliminate obstacles to development resulting from failure to observe civil and political rights, as well as economic social and cultural rights".

While the UNDHR leaves a broad margin of what the duty bearers are, the UNDRTD exclusively mentions the states as duty bearers. The private sectors must also be considered, even though they were initially not referred to. The reason has been "a doctrinal idea that this sector of the society did not need to take responsibility in human rights issues on the grounds [when usually] governments are the violators of human rights and not private companies" (Kamga, 2018). With the launch of the United Nations Global Compact (2000), the idea of private companies being outside the human rights corpus went against the grain. As a result, all private sectors are invited to meet human rights values derived from the Guiding Principles on Business and Human Rights (United Nations, 2011).

South Africa and Uganda being bound to the RTD and the AC, both states and their private sectors are without dispute the duty bearers of the RTD and so shall respect, implement, and protect both country holders' RTD (People of South Africa and Uganda are more specifically the most vulnerable). This observation underpins our analysis of South Africa and Uganda during the COVID-19 pandemic, which saw the birth of COVID-19 corrupt entrepreneurs who violated the RTD (and, as we will see, the Right to Health) – in being involved in corruption.

Right to development: the case of South Africa and Uganda in practice in the pandemic context

Signatories of the AC, such as South Africa and Uganda, are bound by the RTD. They translated it into their own constitutions. While Uganda signed and ratified the AC in 1986, it was only in 1995 that the RTD was enshrined in its Constitution (1995) through the National Objectives and Directive Principles of State Policy. In the South African case, it took the end of apartheid and the election of a new regime to see the signature and ratification of the AC by the country in 1996; as a result, the RTD was consecrated in its new 1996 Constitution through its Chapter 2, Bill of Rights. In the COVID-19 pandemic context, the RTD was put to the test to face the emergency. As principal duty bearers, South African and Ugandan governments had no choice but to decide on key measures to implement the RTD to face disastrous health and socio-economic consequences affecting their respective populations. Regarding socio-economic protections, South Africa created a Solidarity Fund "to put in place measures to mitigate the economic impact both of this disease and South African economic response to it" (South African Government, 2020).

The South African government also increased social grants. It introduced an extraordinary COVID-19 social relief of distress grant, expanded food rollout, and finally put a moratorium on evictions and temporary housing facilities for homeless people. For its part, the government of Uganda adopted a development policy (budget support) comprised of two pillars. The state strengthened the crisis response and protection of the most vulnerable. It reduced the poverty impact of the crisis by supporting the most unprotected through cash transfers and temporary relief). The second pillar is the fast-track economic recovery and debt sustainability (temporary relief to distress through tax payment postponement and loan restructuring, for example).

How did South Africa and Uganda implement the right to health in the context of the COVID-19 pandemic? Before answering this question, the right to health must be defined through the human rights vision and analysed in how it is enshrined in the South African and Ugandan Constitutions.

Right to health in South Africa and Uganda

While health is defined by the World Health Organisation (WHO) as a state of complete physical, mental, and social well-being, the right to health, part of the RTD, is an inclusive one that includes "a wide range of factors that can help us lead a healthy life" (United Nations, 2008). These factors are linked to the UDHR of 1948, which states in its Article 25 that "everyone has the right to a standard of living adequate for the health and well-being of himself and of his family, including food, clothing, housing and medical care and necessary social services, and the right to security in the event of unemployment, sickness, disability, widowhood, old age or other lack of livelihood in circumstances beyond his control" (United Nations, 1948). The International Covenant on Economic, Social and Cultural Rights (ICESR) of 1966 meanwhile claims that all governments are mandated to "(c) the prevention, treatment and control of epidemic, endemic, occupational and other diseases; (d) the creation of conditions which would assure to all medical service and medical attention in the event of sicknesses". In the African context, the right to health is mentioned in Article 16 of the African Charter on Human and Peoples' Rights: "1. Every individual shall have the right to enjoy the best attainable state of physical and mental health. 2. States parties to the present Charter shall take the necessary measures to protect the health of their people and to ensure that they receive medical attention when they are sick" (African Commission on Human and People's Rights, 1981, p. 5).

As state parties of these treaties and conventions, Uganda and South Africa have enshrined the right to health in their own constitutions. In accordance with Uganda's Constitution of 1995 with Amendments through 2017, "all Ugandans enjoy rights and opportunities and access to (…) health services, clean and safe water, work, decent shelter, adequate clothing, food security and pension and retirement benefits" (Article 14(b) – General social and economic objectives) (Constitution of the Republic of Uganda, 1995, p. 8). Article 20 – Medical services – of this Constitution continues by claiming "the State shall take all practical measures to ensure the provision of basic medical services to the population" (Constitution of Uganda, 1995, p. 9). In its Chapter 2 – Bill of Rights-, Article 27 – Health care, food, water and social security, the South African Constitution states "(1) everyone has the right to have access to (a) health care services (…); (b) sufficient food and water; and (c) social security, including, if they are unable to support themselves and their dependents, appropriate social assistance. (2) The State must take reasonable legislative and other measures, within its available resources, to achieve the progressive realisation of these rights. (3) No one may be refused emergency medical treatment" (Constitution of the Republic of South Africa, 1996, p. 11).

The right to health faces COVID-19 in South Africa and Uganda

South Africa was the first to put itself on alert between the two countries. In January 2020, the Department of Health activated the device following the coronavirus alerts. As a result, a COVID-19 case was legally required to report any positive test that fell into the category of severe lung disease and was subject to the same sentinel surveillance as influenza during its season. This early activation of this warning system would have enabled health personnel to be prepared to deal with the extent of the spread of the virus. In addition, strong cooperation was strengthened between the private and public health systems, the national government, and the ministries of health in the nine provincial governments. Three thousand health actors [lepiej chyba workers] in private and public sectors were trained to face the pandemic. Finally, an "aggressive" policy of information on the virus was launched to educate the public and fight against misinformation on social networks. The most spectacular measure taken to face the acceleration of coronavirus contamination was the Declaration of the National Disaster (15 March 2020) by the Head of State, Cyril Ramaphosa, followed by the Department of Co-operative Governance and Traditional Affairs, under the Disaster Management Act (N° 57, 2002). This allows the government to suspend certain constitutional rights and implement emergency measures (Department of Co-operative Governance and Traditional Affairs, South Africa, 2020).

In March 2020, with the first case of COVID-19, the Ugandan government took initial measures that included restricting travel to and from high-risk countries, closure of places of mass groupings such as schools, universities, churches and other political, religious, and social gatherings, mandatory institutional quarantine for all incoming travellers, curfew, travel ban in and out of the country; only essential services were allowed to operate. This national response strategy included contract tracing across the country (District task forces), testing, risk communication, physical and social distancing measures, screening at all ports of entry, training health workers and repurposing hospitals, health centres and stadiums to manage COVID-19 cases.

Understanding corruption and violation of the right to development and health during the COVID-19 crisis in South Africa and Uganda

The presence of corrupt tendencies concerning the COVID-19 relief funds in both South Africa and Uganda signalled not only a violation of human rights but also inefficient governance systems. The COVID-19 pandemic measures, such as lockdowns, significantly strain the informal sector and consequently affected household earnings, especially for the poor urban dwellers that depend on a daily income. The relief funds, meant to cushion the population during the pandemic and after, when food prices increased and, in many instances, restrictions on public transportation heavily impacted the underprivileged, were, however, not used for their intended purpose and thus constituted a violation of human rights, for this case, the rights to development and health by citizens in South Africa and Uganda. Human rights are inherent conditions without which an individual would not be able to live as a complete human being and thus need to be protected from abuse by people in power (Mgbemere, no date).

The right to health precludes not only the access to medication and medical attention by health workers but also the duty of government to ensure that citizens live in healthy and sanitary sound conditions. Introduced in 1948, the UDHR, the right to health connotes "a standard of living adequate for the health and well-being of a *Household* including food, clothing, housing and medical care and necessary social services…." (United Nations, 1948). This right is also enshrined in the Constitution of South Africa, where the government pledges to protect the rights of the citizens concerning health by ensuring access to healthcare services, reproductive health, sufficient food and water, and any other assistance that would enable people to live decent lives (Hassim et al., 2007). However, the COVID-19 pandemic exposed loopholes in the governments' commitment to protecting this right.

In March 2020, Corruption Watch received over 4,780 reports of COVID-related corruption cases, making it the highest tally since 2021 (Africa Research Bulletin, 2021). This COVID-19 bribery exposed the health sector's vulnerability, leading to the Health Minister's resignation over COVID-19 funds fraud in which he was personally implicated. The Special Investigations Unit (SIU) found that he had benefitted from an R150 million tender awarded to Digital Vibes (Hunter, 2021). Other COVID-19-related corruption cases included a probe by the SIU into the Chief Financial Officer of the Department of Correction Services, where personal protective equipment (PPE) tenders worth R50 million were awarded to 23 companies linked to his family and friends, also revealing instances where some tenders were allegedly awarded to deceased people (Mokone, 2020). In similar cases, the

SIU froze properties and accounted for R42 million to a businessman Hamilton Ndlovu for defrauding the government, a total of R172 million awarded to eight of his companies and associates to provide PPE. The probe revealed that except for R15 million used to purchase PPE, the rest was not used to obtain PPE supplies (Mafolo, 2021). Aside from the health-related scandals, bribery was also seen in the food distribution programme. Public offices embezzled a fund for the stimulus package of R500 million to supplement 11.3 million citizens' monthly assistance for food and other social benefits. In some instances, the food distribution programme to feed over 4.5 million South Africans was marred by discrimination, resulting in 7.8 million South Africans being left out of a social relief grant. Thus, two ANC officials were suspended for their complicity, and the president's spokeswoman was investigated for over a US$7 million contract to supply PPE (Chutel, 2020).

In Uganda, similar incidents were registered. Uganda raised Ugshs4.36 trillion as COVID-19 relief funds through donations, grants, and loans. However, findings from the Auditor General's report, which focused on funds totalling Ugshs311 billion inclusive of Ugshs284 billion disbursed to government ministries, departments, agencies, and districts, revealed that Ugshs6.68 billion out of the Ugshs234 billion was not utilised by the close of the financial year and remitted to the consolidated fund contrary to the directive by the secretary to the treasurer to bank the funds. From cash donations totalling Ugshs17.24 billion, only Ugshs850 million was utilised by 56 entities, and the balance was banked in designated entities' bank accounts. However, 25 entities that undertook COVID-19-related procurement worth Ugshs143.84 billion did not follow the procurement rules and regulations. Procurement of supplies was done without signed contracts, was marred with late delivery of goods, and in some instances, payment was received before goods were delivered. Another Ugshs1.31 billion disbursed to 17 entities was unaccounted for during the audit. In comparison, 94 out of 135 entities that received donations in kind did not undertake valuation according to the Treasury instruction. Items worth Ugshs55.8 billion handled by the Office of the Prime Minister had no sufficient evidence of acknowledgement to enable verification of receipt (Parliament of The Republic of Uganda, 2021).

As was in South Africa, public procurement and tenders were the centres of COVID-19-related corruption in Uganda. For instance, a contract signed by M/s Silver Bucks Pharmacy Ltd on 6 May 2020 to supply and install oxygen plants for hospitals in the central region – such as Mulago and Entebbe, at the cost of Ugshs6.4 million, with an invoice paid by June 2020 – had not supplied and installed the equipment by September 2020. Similar contracts were made by the Health Ministry to M/s Elsmeed EA Ltd worth Ugshs26 billion to procure and install emergency intensive care unit equipment in regional referral hospitals. Still, shipments were delayed to December 2020 for a contract signed in June 2020, with expected deliveries in August 2020. Apart from healthcare equipment, a contract for procurement of megaphones for disseminating information worth Ugshs2.9 billion signed on 11 May 2020 had not been fulfilled by 22 June 2020, and some districts had not received the megaphones by September 2020. A contract worth Ugshs1.3 billion was awarded to M/s Joint Medical Stores (JMS) to supply 1,000 beds and mattresses, 2,000 blankets and bedsheets for hospital and quarantine facilities; however there was a flaw in delivery of these items. Only 331 beds and mattresses could be verified, and when about 300 beds were moved from a quarantine centre to the national referral hospital, only 290 were acknowledged (VOX POPULI Investigations Unit, 2021). As punishment, the top four government officials in the Office of the Prime Minister were arrested and charged with abuse of office while running a programme providing food relief to vulnerable people during the pandemic. Evidence showed that while credible suppliers offered lower prices, the defendants rejected them for unqualified suppliers who took on higher prices and consequently cost the government losses of more than US$528,000 (Athumani, 2020). In another case, the Danish ambassador in Uganda and her deputy were recalled after a Zoom meeting recording revealed a plot to misappropriate funds meant to assist in the COVID-19 repatriations of Ugandan citizens (The Local dk, 2020).

Therefore, regarding the state of affairs with rights to health and development in South Africa and Uganda, grand corruption schemes investigated by the SIU in South Africa revealed that 70% of government funding for coronavirus by the end of August 2020 and 930 PPE across South Africa were plagued by allegations of bribery and irregularities (Mokone, 2020). In Uganda, too, high levels of corruption meant a violation of the right to health; Uganda citizens were not repatriated for fear of overwhelming the country's healthcare system, yet funds were set aside for that (Barugahare et al., 2020). Focus on the pandemic had other areas, such as sexual and reproductive health, neglected; the travel ban and curfews made it difficult for people to access hospitals or medical centres for professional attention. Concerning the violation of the RTD, the lockdown measures put a strain on the informal sector and household earnings, especially for the poor urban dwellers in both countries, and bribery led to increased food prices, making it hard for people to cope during the COVID-19 pandemic.

Discussion on corruption and a way forward

More often than not, when bribery is spoken about on the African continent, in cognisance of the countries' performance on the Corruption Perception Index, for instance where South Africa ranks 44 higher than Uganda, which ranks 27 on the Corruption Perception Index 2021 (Transparency International, 2022) – emphasis and blame are placed on the political leadership. This is mainly because, what is evident, of the grand and political corruption. In this chapter, we argue that the escalation of the phenomenon in Africa is both from within and without. Bribery in Africa cannot be discussed in a vacuum without acknowledging that the continent's largely inherited colonial systems of governance and administration. Tracing evolutionary events from the slave trade to the development of mercantilism, colonialism, and capitalism, these conditions increased dependence on finance and investment, eventually giving birth to a massive banking network and credit financing. The need for one to get leverage over the other right from the industrial era in Britain and onto the continent necessitated concessions in which money was involved. This became normalised and was instilled in colonial administrative structures passed on to the Africans in the 1950s at the attainment of flag independence and continued to be the norm in this neo-colonial era. Bribery in colonial structures was embedded in the related tax systems of the hut and poll tax. The taxes were only payable in monetary terms, and money was used to fund the colonial administration and generate cheap African labour. This tax was present in British protectorates and colonies such as Botswana, Kenya, Zimbabwe, and Uganda. Unfortunately, given the prevailing conditions, Africans were mainly unable to afford to pay the tax. The forceful and humiliating manner of collection provided a breeding ground for corrupt behaviour, especially among the so-called African leaders and chiefs who were employed as agents by the colonial governments. These chiefs exploited the inability of people to pay the tax, in which failure meant forced labour, consequently impoverishing populations left behind. Colonialists also used the money economy and bribery to control and subdue populations through divide and rule policy. Money created loyalties in different regions, such as the Ngonde in Malawi, Baganda in Uganda, Shona in Zimbabwe, and Igbo in Nigeria. These conditions eventually established a class society where loyalties were ultimately elevated to paramount status with privileged education and other economic opportunities, thus breeding social disparities as a fertile ground for corrupt behaviour to flourish (Mulinge & Lesetedi, 1998).

In the quest for independence, money was used to corrupt movements and gain collaborators in chiefs to help weaken African freedom fighters by infiltrating liberation organisations and betraying them to the colonial authorities; this was present in Kenya and the Congo. Besides, using chiefs as colonial agents gave them more power than was ordinarily vested in them, a similar phenomenon in public administration and political positions adopted by African elites after independence. Excessive power, authoritarianism, and lack of respect for the law became the order of the day. In addition, through the indirect rule that included the use of chiefs, colonial governments too managed to maintain a foothold in economic and political control of African countries even after independence; in situations where autonomy was achieved through a negotiated transition, colonists continued to manipulate government and economies through political elites who kept up to vent power in the person and not the institution, hence eliminating participatory democracy and increasing their ability to operate with impunity (Mulinge & Lesetedi, 1998).

It's no wonder that high-ranking officials carry out grand corruption on a large scale and transnationally involve the misuse of public funds, often laundered abroad. The abuse of significant funds is not only a violation of human rights but also perpetuates further such violations. Political elites utilise funds to increase their power and entrench their authoritarianism by limiting freedom of expression and access to justice, compromising judiciary independence (Transparency International, 2022). Thus, there is a need to prioritise grand bribery due to its adverse effects, such as the violation of human rights and the fact that grave incidents of grand corruption often go without sufficient or no punishment (United Nations, 2015).

Both countries (South Africa and Uganda) have "independent" institutions to fight against corruption. However, more must be done to ensure that corrupt tendencies are gravely dealt with and the tendency deterred from recurrence. South African lawyers call for the institution of an anti-corruption agency, accountable to parliament and not the president, to investigate and arrest corrupt suspects as a remedy for the laxity with which bribery is handled in the country. They argue that just like Singapore, Botswana, and Hong Kong, with independent anti-corruption agencies, those countries experienced a significant decline in bribery (Lekubu & Sibanda, 2020). Ugandan anti-corruption agencies suffer from presidential interference in their duties. Institutions such as the Inspector General of Government (IGG) are mandated to investigate bribery among public officers but, more often than not, get their activities curtailed. The President of Uganda, Yoweri Museveni, endorsed the Inspector General of Government's planned lifestyle audit meant as an accountability tool to detect and prevent bribery but later backtracked and publicly warned the IGG about the lifestyle audit, claiming that it might force corrupt individuals to hide stolen funds abroad, making it hard to track them. The president noted that Uganda was "…still lucky that our corruption people are corrupt here…" (Ngwomoya, 2021).

Political interference in the fight against bribery is endemic in Africa. Indeed, good governance practices, such as strict adherence to constitutionalism, separation of power, respect for the rule of law, an independent judiciary, transparency, and accountability in public administration, can go a long way in the fight against corruption. It's difficult not to underscore the importance of political will in the fight against bribery. African governments, let alone populations, are caught up in the politics of survival, which fuels corrupt tendencies (Nduku & Tenamwenye, 2014). The importance of a political will cannot be ignored to ensure implementation and reinforcement of laws against bribery. Thus, while colonial legacy and neo-colonial policies promoted by donor agencies that look the other way at atrocities facilitated through corrupt behaviour cannot be excused, political leadership and will on the continent towards the fight against bribery has been a major let-down. But it's crucial to underscore the fact the politics of survival is felt by the whole society as exacerbated by capitalistic tendencies that leave populations in continuous dependencies, impoverishment, inequality, and grave disparities and are the bedrock for corrupt tendencies.

Bibliography

Africa Research Bulletin. (2021). South Africa: Pandemic intensifies corruption, graft is hitting the covid-19 fightback. John Wiley & Sons Ltd.

African Commission on Human and People's Rights. (1981). *African charter on human and people's rights, African commission on human and people's rights*. Retrieved June 3, 2022, from https://www.achpr.org/fr_legalinstruments/detail?id=49

African Union. (2017). List *of countries which have signed, ratified/acceded to the African charter on human and people's rights*. African Union. Retrieved March 10, 2022, from https://au.int/sites/default/files/treaties/36390-sl-african_charter_on_human_and_peoples_rights_2.pdf

Athumani, H. (2020). Top Uganda officials arrested in COVID-19 purchasing scandal. *VOA*. Retrieved March 10, 2022, from https://www.voanews.com/a/science-health_coronavirus-outbreak_top-ugandan-officials-arrested-covid-19-purchasing-scandal/6187278.html

Barugahare, J. et al. (2020). Ethical and human rights considerations in public health in low and middle-income countries: An assessment using the case of Uganda's responses to COVID019 pandemic. *BMC Medical Ethics*, *21*(91). https://doi.org/10.1186/s12910-020-00523-0

Chutel, L. (2020). South Africa's big coronavirus aid effort tainted by corruption. *The New York Times*. Retrieved March 10, 2022, from https://www.nytimes.com/2020/08/19/world/africa/coronavirus-south-africa-aid-corruption.html

Department of Co-operative Governance and Traditional Affairs, South Africa. (2020). *Disaster Management Act, 2002(ACT No 57 of 2002)*. Retrieved June 3, 2022, from http://www.saflii.org/za/gaz/ZAGovGaz/2020/189.pdf

Dlamini, K. (2020). *Corruption is a crime against humanity, says Bekel-Thomas, corruption watch*. Retrieved June 8, 2022, from https://www.corruptionwatch.org.za/corruption-is-a-crime-against-humanity-says-bekel-thomas/

Gutto, S. (2006). The right to development: An implied right in South Africa's constitutional order. *Reflections on democracy and human rights: A decade of the South African constitution (Act 108 of 1996)*. South African Human Rights Commission. Retrieved March 10, 2022, from https://www.sahrc.org.za/home/21/files/Reports/Reflection%20of%20democracy%20and%20human%20rights_10%20year%20review_%20200.pdf

Hassim, A., Heywood, M., & Berger, J. (2007). A background to health law and human rights in South Africa. In *Health and democracy: A guide to human rights in post-apartheid South Africa*. Siber Ink.

Home Affairs. (2020). *Statement by President Cyril Ramaphosa on measures to combat covid-19 epidemic, Department of Home Affairs, Republic of South Africa*. Retrieved June 8, 2022, from http://www.dha.gov.za/index.php/statements-speeches/1332-statement-by-president-cyril-ramaphosa-on-measures-to-combat-covid-19-epidemic

Hunter, Q. (2021). Mkhize's resignation letter: "I am resigning to bring stability to health department"'. *news24*. Retrieved June 9, 2022, from https://www.news24.com/news24/southafrica/news/mkhizes-resignation-letter-i-am-resigning-to-bring-stability-to-health-department-20210805

Kamga, S. D. (2018). *The right to development in the African human rights system*. Taylor and Francis.

Kamga, S. D. (2020). *The right to development in Africa: Issues, constraints and prospects*. Pan African University Press.

Lekubu, B. K., & Sibanda, O. S. (2020). The thorny Legal question of whether grand corruption is a crime against humanity. *Daily Maverick*. Retrieved June 12, 2022, from https://www.dailymaverick.co.za/article/2020-08-27-the-thorny-legal-question-of-whether-grand-corruption-is-a-crime-against-humanity/

Mafolo, K. (2021). The bucks stop here: Businessman Hamilton Ndlovu to have properties and funds seized over PPE contracts. *Daily Maverick*. Retrieved March 10, 2022, from https://www.dailymaverick.co.za/article/2021-09-09-the-bucks-stop-here-businessman-hamilton-ndlovu-to-have-properties-and-funds-seized-over-ppe-contracts/

Mgbemere, P. E. (no date). *Submission of best practice that link anti-corruption measures with the realisation and protection of human rights*. Center for Grassroot Development and Crime Prevention. The effect of corruption on human right health—OHCHR. Retrieved June 8, 2022, from https://www.ohchr.org

Mokone, T. (2020). SA's astronomical Covid-19 corruption: Is a crime against humanity. *Sunday Times*. Retrieved June 9, 2022, from https://www.timeslive.co.za/sunday-times-daily/politics/2020-10-20-sas-astronomical-covid-19-corruption-is-a-crime-against-humanity/

Mulinge, M. M., & Lesetedi, G. N. (1998). Interrogating our past: Colonialism and corruption in Sub-Saharan Africa. *African Journal of Political Science*, *3*(2), 15–28.

Nduku, E., & Tenamwenye, J. (2014). *Corruption in Africa: A threat to justice and sustainable peace*. Focus 14. Globalehtics.net. Retrieved June 12, 2022, from https://repository.globethics.net/handle/20.500.12424/216698

Ngwomoya, A. (2021). Museveni to IGG: Go slow on lifestyle audit. *Monitor*. Retrieved June 12, 2022, from https://www.monitor.co.ug/uganda/news/national/museveni-to-igg-go-slow-on-lifestyle-audit-3647950

Okafor, O. C. (2013). A regional perspective: Article 22 of the African charter on human and people's rights. *Realising* the right to development: Essays in commemoration of 25 years of the United *Nations declaration* on the right to development. United Nations, 373–383.

Parliament of The Republic of Uganda. (2021). *Covid-19 funds mismanaged-auditor general, news*. Retrieved June 10, 2022, from https://www.parliament.go.ug/news/5019/covid-19-funds-mismanaged-auditor-general

Seruwagi, G. (2021). What Uganda has got wrong - and right in its struggle to contain COVID-19. *The Conversation*. Retrieved June 8, 2022, from https://theconversation.com/what-uganda-has-got-wrong-and-right-in-its-struggle-to-contain-covid-19-163826

South African Government. (1996). *Constitution of the Republic of South Africa.*

South African Government. (2020). *President Cyril Ramaphosa: Escalation of measures to combat coronavirus COVID-19 pandemic, newsroom*. Retrieved June 3, 2022, from https://www.gov.za/speeches/president-cyril-ramaphosa-escalation-measures-combat-coronavirus-covid-19-pandemic-23-mar

The Local dk. (2020). Uganda recalls Danish ambassador over Zoom plot to steal Covid funds. *The Local dk*. Retrieved March 10, 2022, from https://www.thelocal.dk/20200825/uganda-recalls-danish-ambassador-over-zoom-plot-to-steal-covid-funds/

The World Bank. (2020). *Uganda: World Bank provides $300 million to close COVID-19 financing gap and support economy recover, who we are*. Retrieved June 8, 2022, from https://www.worldbank.org/en/news/press-release/2020/06/29/uganda-world-bank-provides-300-million-to-close-covid-19-financing-gap-and-support-economy-recover

The World Bank. (2021). *Uganda COVID-19 crisis response and recovery budget support to mitigate COVID-19 pandemic, who we are*. Retrieved June 8, 2022, from https://www.worldbank.org/en/news/factsheet/2021/03/14/uganda-covid-19-crisis-response-and-recovery-budget-support-to-mitigate-covid-19-pandemic

Transparency International. (2022). *Corruption perception index 2021*. Transparency International, p. #22. Retrieved June 12, 2022, from https://images.transparencycdn.org/images/CPI2021_Report_EN-web.pdf

Uganda. (1995). *Uganda's constitution of 1995 with amendments through* 2005.

United Nations. (1948). *Universal declaration of human rights*. Retrieved June 9, 2022, from https://www.un.org/en/about-us/universal-declaration-of-human-rights

United Nations. (1986). *Declaration on the right to development, human rights instruments*. Retrieved June 3, 2022, from https://www.ohchr.org/en/instruments-mechanisms/instruments/declaration-right-development

United Nations. (1993). *Vienna declaration and programme of action, human rights instruments*. Retrieved January 20, 2022, from https://www.ohchr.org/en/instruments-mechanisms/instruments/vienna-declaration-and-programme-action

United Nations. (2008). *Fact sheet no. 31: The right to health, publications*. Retrieved June 3, 2022, from https://www.ohchr.org/en/publications/fact-sheets/fact-sheet-no-31-right-health#:~:text=The%20Fact%20Sheet%20explains%20what,international%20accountability%20and%20monitoring%20mechanisms

United Nations. (2011). *Guiding principles on business and human rights: Implementing the United Nations 'Protect, respect and Remedy'* framework. United Nations and United Nations Human Rights Office of the High Commissioner, p. #24. Retrieved June 3, 2022, from https://www.ohchr.org/sites/default/files/documents/publications/guidingprinciplesbusinesshr_en.pdf

United Nations. (2015). 'Statement submitted by the transparency international a non-governmental organisation not in consultative status with the economic and social council'. Conference of the state parties to the *United Nations convention* against corruption. United Nations. Retrieved March 30, 2022, from https://www.unodc.org/documents/treaties/UNCAC/COSP/session6/V1507500e.pdf

United Nations Global Compact. (2000). *The ten principles of the UN global compact, who we are*. Retrieved June 3, 2022, from https://www.unglobalcompact.org/what-is-gc/mission/principles

Villiers, C., Cerbone, W., & Zijl, V. (2020). The South African government's response to covid-19. *Journal of Public Budgeting, Accounting and Financial Management* [Preprint]. https://www.emerald.com/insight/content/doi/10.1108/JPBAFM-07-2020-0120/full/html#sec003

VOX POPULI Investigations Unit. (2021). *Inside opaque Covid-19 cash bonanza: Gov't report cites influence peddling, inflated costs, investigations*. Retrieved June 10, 2022, from https://voxpopuli.ug/inside-opaque-covid-19-cash-bonanza-govt-report-cites-influence-peddling-inflated-costs/

Wafawarova, R. (2013). Corruption: Crime against humanity. *The Herald*. Retrieved March 30, 2022, fromhttps://www.herald.co.zw/corruption-crime-against-humanity/

4 New World Order After the Pandemic

Can "New Political Thinking" Be Reinvented?[1]

A. Yu. Sungurov

Introduction

Scientific discussion on the nature and direction of changes in the new world order is essential to understand the development patterns of modern world politics (Baranovskij, 2019; Nikitin, 2018; Pantin & Lapkin, 2018). M.M. Lebedeva quite rightly notes, "In most studies of the world order, the analysis is carried out from the point of view of the power relations of states, and the analytical focus is primarily on the leading powers" (Lebedeva, 2019). At the same time, as early as the beginning of this Century, A.M. Slaughter stressed that today's states form "government networks" with the help of various complex interstate relations (Slaughter, 2004). In addition, non-governmental organisations of different types are beginning to play an increasing role in world politics (Stecko, 2012; Tormosheva, 2017).

The COVID-19 pandemic and its consequences have undoubtedly made and will continue to make significant changes in the new world order. So far, these possible consequences have been the subject of several journalistic publications, some of which have been prepared based on expert opinions (Dunaevskij, 2020; Kuznecov, 2020), as well as expressed forecasts of scientists (Alekseeva-Karnevali, 2020). This chapter's author is in full solidarity with one of these opinions, which can be summarised as follows: "In the global world, we need a new 'conference' to develop new rules of the game because the impact of the pandemic is comparable to the world war. And at this conference, it is necessary to develop tools and institutions of global cooperation, which can be quickly adopted and implemented, taking into account the maximisation of the common good, rather than striving to hurt the neighbour" (Kuznecov, 2020).

If we adopt this view, in the case of the previous World War, the result of the "conference", or rather their series, was the creation of the United Nations (UN), the Charter of which solidifies respect for universal human rights. Therefore, in this chapter, some attention will be paid to the necessary (and highly desirable) reforms of the UN to make this organisation correspond to the realities of today's world. However, as a radiobiologist in my initial academic career (Sungurov, 1988), I want to start this discussion with the effects of another disaster, that of Chernobyl, including its impact on the political life of my homeland, which took the form of "New Political Thinking" as the foreign policy course of the USSR in the last years

DOI: 10.4324/9781003482710-5

of its existence. Special attention will be paid to the "new political thinking" itself, as well as to its predecessors and approaches close to it, hoping to contribute to the development of "new" (as of 2020) thinking in the renewed world order.

Comparing the COVID-19 pandemic with the Chernobyl disaster that occurred in the USSR in April 1986 (Babosov, 1992; Chernobyl disaster, 1998), let us leave the man-caused nature of the Chernobyl disaster itself and the involvement of the personnel who turned off the protective systems in order to have time to conduct an experiment for the May Day (according to the detailed information on the development of the Chernobyl emergency situation that was obtained as a result of the conversation with respondent A., one of the founders of the Chernobyl reactor, June 2003) – out of the picture. This text is intended to compare the Chernobyl disaster with the COVID-19 pandemic by the criterion of informing residents of their own country and those of other countries about the occurrence of the event. It is known that after the explosion at the Chernobyl Nuclear Power Plant, there was a delay in informing both Soviet citizens and the world community about the disaster in a situation where the wind was already spreading radioactive fallout to neighbouring countries. Moreover, academician V.A. Legasov – a member of the government commission from the USSR Academy of Sciences, who did a lot in the first days after the explosion at the nuclear power plant to eliminate the consequences of the disaster and also presented a detailed and truthful report on the accident in August 1986 at a conference of the IAEA in Vienna – faced severe obstruction both from party officials and from some colleagues, which led to his suicide in April 1988.

In the case of the outbreak of the COVID-19 pandemic, China is known to have withheld information on the number of cases in Wuhan, which led to the spread of the epidemic around the globe, via flights from China, which continued throughout January 2020 (Fukuyama, 2020; Illarionov, 2020).

It seems that in the USSR, the shock of the Chernobyl catastrophe that became a crucial milestone in the development of the perestroika process. It led to a understanding by M.S. Gorbachev and his associates in the leadership of the Communist Party and the USSR as a whole (which at that time were synonymous) that instead of secrecy and autocracy, openness and publicity was needed, along with the development of the unity of our world and "its interconnectedness, interdependence, and integrity" (Gorbachev, 1995, p. 293). The idea of the need for "new thinking in world politics", which soon became the defining line of the USSR's foreign policy during perestroika, was also a logical step forward (Gorbachev, 1987).

The concept of the new political thinking

"The concept of the new political thinking created during Perestroika implies that, while respecting autonomy and observing the principle of non-interference in each other's affairs, states and peoples recognise the common responsibility for the survival of mankind. The new thinking proposed a project to restructure the world in accordance with universal human values. The main of them are those related to human life, freedom and security for everyone" (Pandemic, 2020).

Unfortunately, at that time, this concept was not understood by the leaders of many countries and vanished from the global political scene after the end of M.S. Gorbachev's political career. However, today, discussing the state of the world system after (or, perhaps, in the midst of) the coronavirus pandemic, we can assume that the concept of new thinking could become the basis for a new vision of the world system, which could lead to new (by the end of the second decade of the 21st Century), more effective ways of global governance, global management, that is such management that would make it impossible – at the very least – to keep silence about such emergencies. The same assumption is made in the June 2020 Gorbachev Foundation report (Pandemic, 2020).

Let us now take a closer look at the very concept of "new thinking" and its predecessors and briefly discuss the possible reasons why it was already in the 90s on the far periphery of global public opinion.

The idea of the importance of universal human values, based on which it is possible to agree and prevent new wars, existed long before the mid-1980s. Indeed, the roots of the concept of new thinking can be seen in the works of Immanuel Kant, including his treatise "Towards Eternal Peace". The fundamental possibility for the representatives of different states to agree based on some common values underlies the liberal approach in the theory of international relations. These were the prerequisites for Woodrow Wilson's proposals on the principles of the League of Nations. It was also unacceptable for the Communist Party of the Soviet Union (CPSU) Secretary General to refer to such ideological predecessors. However, it is possible that at that time, M.S. Gorbachev was unaware of the roots of his proposed concept.

The Gorbachev Foundation's report "The Pandemic as a Challenge and New Thinking in the 21st Century", already published in 2020, presents, in the opinion of the authors of the report, more similar predecessors, such as the post-World War II movement for nuclear disarmament and the Pugwash Movement against the use of atomic energy for military purposes, which was initiated in 1955 with the manifesto authored by A. Einstein, B. Russell, and other prominent scientists (Lebedev, 2004; Ryzhov & Lebedev, 2003). This movement, created 65 years ago, is still active today, including in modern Russia, judging by the constantly updated information on the website (http://www.pugwash.ru), as well as by the conference proceedings of the Russian branch of the Pugwash Movement (Global, 2018). In principle, this is a real example of a stable and influential (to some extent) epistemic community (Haas, 2011; Mihajlova, 2018). It is true, however, that the activities of this movement in Russia traditionally take place under the auspices of the Presidium of the Russian Academy of Sciences and the Ministry of Foreign Affairs, and it is still not widely known in the Russian scientific community.

The already mentioned report of the Gorbachev Foundation (2020) notes another precursor of the "new thinking" as a conception: namely, the writings of the Club of Rome, the regular publication of which, starting from 1968, contributed to the formation of the concept of sustainable development (Medouz et al., 1991; 1994; 2007). The Club of Rome, which emerged as an association of scientists, politicians, and businesspersons capable of generating serious, scientifically grounded predictions for scientists, represents not only a stable epistemic community but also a fascinating example of Paul Sabatier's influential "Coalition for the Defence of Public Interest" (Sabatier, 1998), working in the format of a unique "Factory of Thought", and the coalitions not at the national but at the global level (Club of Rome, 1997; Pechchei, 1980; Pechchei, 2020). The establishment and development of the Club of Rome and the reports commissioned by the latter require a separate in-depth analysis. It should be noted here that the Club of Rome, which, like any other club, had a somewhat limited membership, was soon supported by UNESCO and a much more open scientific and educational association. Consequently, the World Futures Studies Federation (https://wfsf.org) was established, which involved academic forecasters, scientists of other specialities and civil activists concerned about the problems of the Club of Rome. One of the founders of this association was a Soviet sociologist and forecaster I.V. Bestuzhev-Lada (Bestuzhev-Lada, 1984; 1998).

Let us return, however, to the concept of new thinking put forward by M.S. Gorbachev and his associates during perestroika. Already a quarter of a century later, the article by M.F. Polynov presents the main five provisions of this concept:

1. Recognition of a diverse but interconnected, holistic world, and, accordingly, the proclamation of the impossibility of solving international problems by force;
2. Prevalence of universal interests over those of class and nation regarding relations between states when solving global problems;
3. "Deideologisation" of foreign policy and refusal to consider the principle of peaceful coexistence as a specific form of class struggle;
4. Recognition of the right of each nation to choose its own destiny and, as a consequence, the refusal of the policy of proletarian and socialist internationalism;
5. Regulation on the "pan-European house". Creation of a new security system on the European continent that would include a reduced role for NATO and the Warsaw Pact and an increased role for the OSCE" (Polynov, 2012a).

In the author's opinion, these five theses succinctly reflect the main trends of the concept under discussion. In the foreword to his book *Perestroika and New Thought for Our Country and the World* in 1987, M.S. Gorbachev himself formulated the main messages of the book: "For all the contradictions of the modern world, for all the diversity of social and political systems existing in it, for all the different choices made at different times by peoples, it represents a certain integrity. We are all passengers on the same ship, the Earth, and it cannot be allowed to wreck. There will be no second Noah's Ark… We do not like any aspect of American politics and lifestyle. But we recognise the rights of the people of the United States, like everyone else's, to live by their own rules and laws, by their own customs and tastes… Time is running out, and we cannot lose it. We have to act. The situation does not allow us to wait for the ideal moment: a constructive and extensive dialogue is necessary today" (Gorbachev, 1987, p. 5).

In both cases, we can distinguish two main messages. The first, the most important one during perestroika, is the renunciation of the traditional messianic tendencies of the CPSU leaders, the recognition, both for the United States and for other nations, of the right to live as they please (which is equivalent to the renunciation of proletarian or socialist internationalism, as well as to the renunciation of ideology in foreign policy, as M.F. Polynov rightly stressed). This part of the concept of new thinking was highly relevant then, but today, it is more of historical interest.

The second message is the vision of our world, the world system, as diverse yet interrelated and holistic, as well as the prevalence of human interests over those of class and nation, which M.S. Gorbachev himself expressed in the form of a strong metaphor "We are all passengers of one ship, the Earth, and we can not allow it to crash", which remains hugely relevant today.

Let us now focus on a few more predecessors of the new thinking of M.S. Gorbachev, which neither himself at the time nor the Gorbachev Foundation report mentioned. The closest work in terms of time is Anat's monograph, A. Gromyko and V. Lomeiko's "New Thinking in the Nuclear Age" (Gromyko & Lomejko, 1984), the title of which already uses the words "new thinking". Although this book by Soviet diplomats is mainly devoted to the possibility of nuclear disarmament and was published in the year when K.U. Chernenko was still the Secretary General of the CPSU Central Committee – it contains many obligatory ideological stamps. Nevertheless, its last chapter is called "From block thinking to planetary", and there are words in it that are very well consistent with the new thinking of M. Gromyko. Gorbachev: "The interrelationship and interdependence of the world, whose vulnerability is growing, require from all members of the international community a much broader and more active partnership. Thus, there is an objective need for new thinking corresponding to the realities of the nuclear age and the growing global problems. *New thinking is planetary thinking imbued with the consciousness of common responsibility for the fate of mankind*" (Gromyko & Lomejko, 1984, p. 280).

Suppose we proceed from the last phrase of the quoted passage, from the planetary view of processes happening on Earth. In that case, we will inevitably come up with the ideas of the great Russian and Soviet scientist V.I. Vernadsky, including his notion of the noosphere as a phase of biosphere development: "Humanity, taken as a whole, becomes a powerful geological force. And before him, before his thought and work, becomes the question of biosphere reconstruction in the interests of free-thinking mankind as a single whole. This new state of the biosphere, which we are approaching without noticing it, is the 'noosphere'" (Vernadskij, 1989, p. 148). In the modern understanding of the noosphere, "a new evolutionary state of the biosphere, in which reasonable human activity becomes a decisive factor in its development" (Vernadskij, 1989, p. 148) (Big, 2006, p. 1062).

The recognition of science and scientific thought as leaders in the transition of the biosphere into the noosphere determines the special attention that science must attract. The beginning of consideration of science as a natural phenomenon has already been laid in the works of V.I. Vernadsky himself (Vernadskij, 1991). The analysis of the development of scientific thought and the role of science in the evolution of the biosphere has led him to a provision on scientists' special responsibility for the noosphere genesis process. It is possible to tell that the whole life of Vernadsky was a realisation of the conclusions arising from this position;

he actively participated in the so-called "zemstvo" movement, was one of the founders of Constitutional Democrats party and the permanent member of its Central Committee, and in the Summer of 1917 was the comrade of the minister of education in the government led by Kerensky.

Previously considered cases of predecessors of new thinking in politics – the Pugwash Movement and the Club of Rome – are perfect examples of the responsibility of scientists for the fate of our planet, that is the development of Vernadsky's ideas. The issue is that these ideas and Vernadsky's life and work are still not widely known to the global scientific community. Officially recognised in the USSR as a scientist-geochemist, he was still banned as a philosopher of science and author of the noosphere concept, as all these views diverged from the dominant ideology of "proletarian internationalism". Only the idea of new thinking of M.S. Gorbachev showed his general influences.

Unfortunately, in modern Russia, we also see no prominent examples of creative development of the concept of noosphere, taking into account the realities of the 21st Century. At the beginning of that century, an exciting work appeared: an anthology of Vernadsky's literature over 100 years, which included contemporary critical responses and polemics with them (Vernadskij, 2000). In recent years, only a book by one of the followers of geochemist G.B. Naumov (Naumov, 2014) has appeared in Russia; further criticism of Vernadsky's ideas found its continuation in mixing them with some philosophical theories of K.E. Tsiolkovsky (Fesenkova, 2008; 2018).

An interesting attempt to develop the concept of the noosphere was made by scientists from the Vernadsky University of Tauride in Simferopol, who prepared a publication of the collective monograph Noosferology (Noosferology, 2008), in which the author of these lines have also participated (Sungurov, 2008). Unfortunately, this initiative did not develop further, probably because it originated in a different country.

Let's mention here another Russian and, after his emigration, an international figure of cultural figure named Nikolai Roerich; whose proposal to sign the World Cultural Pact, which implies the preservation of cultural property as a planetary goal, was supported by US President Franklin D. Roosevelt. As a result, the first international treaty on the protection of artistic and scientific institutions and historical monuments in history was signed in 1935. In 1954, the Hague Convention for the Protection of Cultural Property in the Event of Armed Conflict was adopted under the auspices of the United Nations based on the experience of the World Cultural Pact (Roerich Pact) (Barenbojm & Zaharov, 2010; Kapustin et al., 2014). This initiative and Nikolai Roerich's and his sons' activities can also be seen as precursors to Gorbachev's new thinking.

In this way, we can see that most of the theses of the new thinking have already been expressed before; however, except for the 14 theses of Woodrow Wilson, they have never been mentioned by the leader of a large state. As we remember, Woodrow Wilson was not supported by the elite of his own country: the United States had not joined the League of Nations. More than 60 years later, Mikhail Gorbachev, in his call for collective realisation that we are all in one boat and another planet is not available to us, has not been heard by the elites of other countries. As Russian analysts rightly write, the US leadership regarded these proposals as a propaganda tool, as Gorbachev's retreat in all directions; that is they still operated with the logic of the Cold War (Brutenc, 2005; Barsenkov, 2017; Polynov, 2012b). Then, after the dissolution of the Warsaw Pact, NATO was not altered much, while the USSR ceased to exist. The evolution of the Russia–NATO relationship requires a separate analysis; however, in any case, it was not affected by the participation of M.S. Gorbachev.

Let's now turn to modernity. Unfortunately, the general trend of recent years is that of going against global thinking with its priority on universal values. For example, in March 2016, in Seoul, Korea, under the auspices of the Asian Association for Political and International Studies and with the support of the Ebert Foundation, one of the consequences of this trend was called "New Authoritarianism in Asia", and it discussed the reasons for the situation in which all but two of the Asian countries showed distinct authoritarian trends.

This trend can be observed in Asia and other countries, which means that the phenomenon of sovereignty is still gaining influence. This term appeared for the first time in a news report about the meeting of Kennan Institute graduates, which was scheduled for May 2020 in Prague but was not held due to the pandemic. In this message, sovereignty was understood as a global trend to strengthen independence and was echoed in the United States, Hungary, Poland, Russia, and other countries.

The world community's reaction to the COVID-19 pandemic may be expressed in an additional strengthening of sovereignty, which has already manifested itself in border closures, termination of flights, etc. This would be the worst scenario, in the author's view, as it implies further concealment of information about new threats. However, there is another option: the growth of human solidarity and mutual assistance, the return to universal values, as well as the strengthening of trends of global governance "with a human face". In other words, described principles and approaches of "the new thinking" may be beneficial, as naturally brought into line with the reality of the end of the second decade of the 21st Century.

If, considering the possible forms of strengthening global governance, we will be guided by the principle of W. Ockham, that is "not to create entities beyond necessary", then we should first of all address the United Nations as the only global organisation created by mankind. It is imperative that its creation recognised the universality of human rights, the defence of which was higher than the sovereignty of individual states (Sungurov, 2000). Indeed, the "sacred" principle of sovereignty enabled Nazi Germany to formally and "legally" exterminate millions of its citizens first and then unleash World War II.

The global shock of the horrors of this war allowed the UN founding countries to recognise human rights above the principle of sovereignty. Since then, more than 70 years have passed, and the horrors of the past war have been partly forgotten. Again, in many countries, politicians have begun to talk about the priority of state sovereignty. Going back to the UN, we can remember that shortly after its creation, various proposals and projects emerged to turn it into a much stronger organisation, for example by electing the UN General Assembly by direct vote of the inhabitants of our planet, which would make it possible to make the Security Council also elected by the General Assembly on a popular principle. This proposal was not adopted then and was most certainly ahead of its time. Moreover, some of the UN founding countries initially viewed the UN simply as a new type of forum for negotiations at the global level. It is no coincidence that the USSR and some other countries abstained from adopting the Universal Declaration of Human Rights in 1948, and the text of the Declaration itself was challenging to access for ordinary citizens of the USSR. Once again, returning to the new thinking of M.S. Gorbachev, it is vital to emphasise that recognising the priority of universal human values, which by definition included universal human rights, made up the strength and significance of this concept. Practical cases were also important: the return of A.D. Sakharov from Gorbachev's exile, the release of political prisoners, a significant easing of censorship, and, on the other hand, the establishment of the Office for International Humanitarian Cooperation and Human Rights in the USSR's Ministry of Foreign Affairs as well as the creation of a human rights division in the CPSU Central Committee (Barsenkov, 2017).

Today, all of this is political history. However, it is also our experience that lessons can help us not to make new mistakes today when the need to develop genuine global governance is growing stronger and stronger. Let's explore the possible ways to do it within this chapter's scope, which is focused on the United Nations reform.

The UN, established more than 75 years ago, has proven to be a successful instrument to prevent another World War, to take specific steps towards the recognition of the universality of human rights, as well as to update the sustainable development goals of the countries of our planet (70th anniversary of 2017). At the turn of the new millennium, the UN formulated well-defined plans in the Millennium Development Goals, a significant part of which has been achieved over the past 15 years (Goals, 2015). At the same time, there are more and more questions today about making operational decisions in critical situations in different regions of our planet. One of the issues causing constant disputes and discussions at the UN is the UN force intervention in case of mass human rights violations in specific countries, such as Rwanda and Kosovo, in the 1990s.

These circumstances, as well as the excessive bureaucratisation of UN structures and the complexity of making mandatory decisions, have already put the problem of reforming its activities on the agenda. One of the most pressing issues sis the reform of the UN Security Council, including the status of the five permanent members and their veto power over major decisions of the body. Indeed, such veto power of only five states is a clear rudiment of the last century, formed over 70 years ago, when these countries represented the five victorious powers in World War II. It isn't easy to understand why these countries are still in such an exceptional position in 2020. As a result, the effectiveness of this organisation decreases in many respects, especially when the interests of the member countries of the Security Council clash.

The topic of UN reform is the subject of attention of many Russian researchers (this text will be focused only on Russian authors); five of them directly devoted to this topic can be cited (Grishaeva, 2007; Palamarenko, 2018; Yurchenko, 2017; Zlokazova, 2008; Zverev, 2013). However, when you read these and many other works and analyse specific UN Security Council reform proposals, you may experience *deja vu* – a feeling that you have already read it. Accordingly, as Grishaeva (2007) wrote "It is impossible to let the current status of Russia, as a permanent member of the Security Council, be damaged. Undue expansion of the Security Council and revision of the veto right will cause the destruction of the entire organisation" (Grishaeva, 2007, pp. 51–52). Five years later, P.G. Zverev voiced the need to preserve the privileges of a permanent seat on the Security Council at the centre of the Russian agenda: "As long as Russian diplomacy has managed to retain a permanent seat on the Security Council after the collapse of the Soviet Union, a key UN post that provides important privileges but also requires great responsibility, the country's leadership must make every effort to restore Russia's international standing" (Zverev, 2013, p. 54). Another five years later, in 2018, Palamarenko's PhD thesis focused on the problems of UN reform. In retaliation to these provisions, the author argues: "At the current stage of development of international relations in the interests of international peace, the most important task is to maintain the current composition of the UN Security Council … Russia's specific interest in the issue of possible reform of the UN Security Council is to preserve its privileged status and to prevent revision of the veto principle" (Palamarenko, 2018, pp. 15–16).

We can see almost repeated theses about preserving Russia's privileged status. R. Yu. Palamarenko's thesis test contains, as it is supposed to, the formulation of the theoretical foundations of his study, where he specifies the following: "The methodology of the scientific school of political realism is applied in the analysis of goals, interests and strategies of actors, which allowed to reveal the correlation of forces between the leading and secondary players in the promotion of certain reform initiatives" (Palamarenko, 2018, p. 13).

In other words, the reasons for the same conclusions about the ways of the UN Security Council reforms can be explained. The authors of these studies adhere to the school of political realism, which by its very nature does not assume the possibility of any universal values; for this school of thought, the concept of "new thinking" is, by definition, unacceptable. Indeed, if only national interests are paramount in international relations, then all international organisations, including the UN, are just platforms for negotiations and nothing more. The values of sustainable development and, more, the existence of some universal human rights are just rhetoric, a cover for the realisation of national interests.

Suppose the analysis of possible ways of UN reform is carried out based on one of the liberal approach options. In that case, it seems likely to suggest re-evaluating the possible direct election of the General Assembly members, for example based on certain quotas for countries with different populations. Then, the General Assembly itself could elect the Security Council, as G. Clark and L. Song suggested more than 60 years ago. The author believes this would be a natural step towards making the UN a body of proper global governance.

Suppose we do not work in this direction. In that case, other centres of decision-making at the global level will inevitably be created, and individual countries or groups will act as they did in Iraq or Kosovo. The proposed path is long and complicated, but it is necessary to follow it by welcoming appropriate initiatives from both the Russian and international community of experts.

However, even today, it is possible for other actors in world politics, including NGOs, business structures, as well as representatives of the expert community, to participate more actively in decision-making within the UN (Ivanova & Ivanov, 2012; Lebedeva & Harkevich, 2018; Moskalchuk, 2016). In this regard, it is worth remembering the position of academician Sakharov, who in 1971 proposed to establish, under the auspices of the UN, the International Advisory Committee of Experts on Legal, Social, Environmental and Disarmament Problems from reliable and impartial individuals with the right to receive reasonable responses to their requests and recommendations from all governments. The statute of the Board and the procedure governing its composition should ensure maximum independence from the national interests of individual states and groups of states (Saharov, 1990, p. 27). Such a committee has not yet been established, and joint efforts may also be needed here.

At the same time, expert knowledge in the UN is undoubtedly utilised nowadays; the problem is that the leaders nominate experts in all areas of their respective countries. Therefore, there is a high probability that the governments of countries with authoritarian (and perhaps other) regimes will appoint only those experts who are loyal to these governments, similar to the way expert councils at the level of regional governments are formed in Russia today (Sungurov, 2000; Sungurov et al., 2020). Other channels for including independent experts in the work of the UN and other international organisations, including through the epistemic communities mentioned above, are needed. The discussed changes in the UN structure and activities do not exclude different directions of going beyond the boundaries of the national state; for examples O.S. Volgin writes about the necessity of developing supranational democracy (Volgin, 2017).

Conclusions

Summing up, it should be emphasised that the approaches to international relations declared more than 30 years ago under the concept of new political thinking have not exhausted their heuristic power, especially if we take into account the whole range of ideas and concepts briefly discussed in this chapter, close in spirit to the concept of Gorbachev's "new thinking". The idea of unity and integrity of human civilisation, along with the existence of universal human values, may prove to be a fruitful approach for creating collective solutions for complex problems of the modern "post-Covid" world, including possible ways of reforming the UN for it to become a viable alternative to the trend of excessive sovereignty.

The text presented here was mainly prepared two years ago. But considering it from today's perspective, the end of December 2023, I see that it has not lost its relevance today. Indeed, the world is even more rigidly divided into rigidly opposing parts. This is happening both as a result of the start of a "Special military operation" in Ukraine in 2022, the intensification of military operations on the territory of Palesstine this year, and an attempt to cancel the cults of individual countries. Today, in this rigidly polarised world, with efforts to find a new way of thinking, the ideas of Academician Sakharov and Nikolai Roerich are even more relevant – in short, everything that this text is dedicated to.

Note

1 A version of this chapter has been previously published in Russian by *Publichnaya Politika* [*Public Policy*] 2020, 4 (2), 39–59. The author is grateful to the journal for permission to reuse the material.

Bibliography

Alekseeva-Karnevali, O. (2020). Inflection point: The world after a pandemic COVID-19. Rossijskij sovet po mezhdunarodnym delam. Retrieved August 8, 2020, from https://russiancouncil.ru/analytics-and-comments/columns/global-governance/tochkainfleksii-mir-posle-pandemii-covid-19/

Babosov, E. M. (1992). The pain of Chernobyl. *Sociologicheskie Issledovaniya*, *6*, 14–21.

Baranovskij, V. (2019). The new world order: Overcoming the old or its transformation? *Mirovaya ekonomika i mezhdunarodnye otnosheniya*, *63*(5), 7–23. https://doi.org/10.20542/0131-2227-2019-63-5-7-23

Barenbojm, P., & Zaharov, A. (2010). The Roerich Pact in the XXI century. Letnij sad.

Barsenkov, A. (2017). Gorbachev's new thinking. *Website "Living History"*, *5*. Retrieved August 8, 2020, from http://lhistory.ru/statyi/novoe-myshlenie-gorbacheva

Bestuzhev-Lada, I. V. (1984). *Search social forecasting. Promising problems of society*. Nauka.

Bestuzhev-Lada, I. V. (1998). *Prospects for Russia's transformation: Expert scenario-predictive monitoring*. Izd-vo MGU.

Brutenc, K. N. (2005). Unfulfilled. Partial notes on perestroika. Mezhdunarodnye otnosheniya.

Dunaevskij, I. (2020). Life after COVID. *Rossijskaya Gazeta. Federal'nyj Vypusk*, *92*(8146), 27. aprelya. Retrieved August 8, 2020, from https://rg.ru/2020/04/27/eksperty-iz-ssha-i-evropy-rasskazali-kak-izmenitsia-zhizn-posle-pandemii.html

Fesenkova, L. V. (2008). Noospheric thinking and the current ecological situation. *Vysshee Obrazovanie v Rossii*, *1*, 142–147.

Fesenkova, L. V. (2018). Utopianism in modern ideas about the world: The concept of the noosphere. *Kul'turnoe Nasledie Rossii*, *4*, 9–14.

Fukuyama, F. (2020). Pandemic and political order. Retrieved August 8, 2020.

Global and regional security issues and prospects for cooperation: collection of scientific articles. 2018. SPb.: Mediapapir.

Gorbachev Foundation report (2020), The Pandemic as a Challenge and New Thinking in the 21st Century, https://www.gorby.ru/userfiles/file/pandemic_and_new_thinking.pdfo

Gorbachev, M. S. (1987). *Perestroika and new thinking for our country and the whole world*. IPL.

Gorbachev, M. S. (1995). Life and reforms: v 2 kn. Kn. 1. Novosti.

Grishaeva, L. E. (2007). UN reform—A way out of the crisis. *Vestnik RUDN. Seriya: Mezhdunarodnye Otnosheniya*, *4*, 47–59.

Gromyko, A., & Lomejko, V. (1984). UN Reform—A way out of Crisis Thinking in the Nuclear Age, Mezhdunarodnye otnosheniya.

Haas, P. M. (2011). Epistemic communities. In *IPSA encyclopedia of political science* (pp. 787–791). SAGE.

Illarionov, A. (2020). How China fought the coronavirus in the Wuhan seafood market. Retrieved August 8, 2020, from https://echo.msk.ru/blog/aillar/2645973-echo/
Ivanova, E. N., & Ivanov, V. I. (2012). Interaction of international non-governmental organisations with the UN and intergovernmental organisations. *Vestnik RGGU. Seriya: Politologiya. Istoriya. Mezhdunarodnye Otnosheniya, 19*(99), 57–67.
Kapustin, A., Barenbojm, B., Zaharov, A., & Kravchenko, D. (2014). *The Roerich Pact as the basis of the new UN convention on the protection of cultural property*. LUM.
Kuznecov, E. (2020). Three diseases of civilisation that have been exacerbated by the coronavirus. Forbs. 14 aprelya. Retrieved August 8, 2020, from https://www.forbes.ru/biznes/398231-tri-bolezni-civilizacii-kotorye-obostril-koronavirus
Lebedev, M. A. (2004). Learning to think in a new way: About the origin Pugwash movement of scientists. *Mir i Soglasie, 1*(21). Retrieved August 8, 2020, from http://www.pugwash.ru/publications/manifest/409.html
Lebedeva, M. M. (2019). Contemporary megatrends of world politics. *Mirovaya ekonomika i mezhdunarodnye otnosheniya, 63*(9), 29–37. https://doi.org/10.20542/0131-2227-2019-63-9-29-37
Lebedeva, M. M., & Harkevich, M. V. (2018). The role of business in the transformation of the political organisation of the world. *Kontury global'nyh transformacij: politika, ekonomika, parvo, 1*(11), 34–51. Retrieved August 8, 2020, from https://doi.org/10.23932/2542-0240-2018-11-1-34-51
Medouz, D. H., Medouz, D. L., Randers, J., & Berens, V. III. (1991). Limits of growth. Izd-vo MGU.
Medouz, D. H., Medouz, D. L., & Randers, J. (1994). Beyond growth. Study guide. Progress, Panageya.
Medouz, D. H., Medouz, D. L., & Randers, J. (2007). *Limits of growth. Thirty years later*. Akademkniga.
Mihajlova, O. V. (2018) Epistemic communities in the process of promoting ideas on the public administration agenda. *Vestnik Tomskogo gosudarstvennogo universiteta. Seriya: Filosofiya. Sociologiya. Politologiya, 46*, 167–175. https://doi.org/10.17223/1998863H/46/19
Millennium Development Goals: 2015 Report. (2015). N'yu-Jork: Organizaciya Ob" edinennyh Nacij. Retrieved August 8, 2020, from https://www.un.org/ru/millenniumgoals/mdgreport2015.pdf
Moskalchuk, E. I. (2016). Russian non-governmental organisations as a subject of international consulting activity. Avtoref. diss. kand. soc. nauk: 22.00.05. SPb.
Naumov, G. B. (2014). *Three space syntheses. Vladimir Vernadsky: The history of life and thought*. URSS.
Nikitin, A. I. (2018). The contemporary world order: Its crisis and prospects. *Polis. Politicheskie issledovaniya, 6*, 32–46. https://doi.org/10.17976/pps/2018.06.03
Noospherology: science, education, practice. (2008). Simferopol': Predpriyatie «Feniks».
Palamarenko, R. Y. (2018). The UN in the XXI century: problems of reform. Diss. kand. polit. nauk: 23.00.04.
Pandemic as a Challenge and New Thinking in the XXI Century Report. (2020). Mezhdunarodnyj fond social'no-ekonomicheskih i politologicheskih issledovanij ("Gorbachev-fond"). Retrieved August 8, 2020, from https://www.gorby.ru/userfiles/file/doclad_gf_16_06_20.pdf
Pantin, V. I., & Lapkin, V. V. (2018). Transformations of political spaces in the conditions of transition to a polycentric world order. *Polis. Politicheskie issledovaniya, 6*, 47–66. https://doi.org/10.17976/jpps/2018.06.04
Pechchei, A. (1980). *Human qualities*. Progress.
Pechchei, A. (2020). *Architects of the world. Notes of the club of Rome*. Rodina.
Polynov, M. F. (2012a). M.S. Gorbachev and new political thinking: Origins, main ideas, results. *Novejshaya istoriya Rossii, 2*, 136–152.

Polynov, M. F. (2012b). New political thinking: Emergence and main ideas. *Obshchestvo. Sreda. Razvitie*, *1*(22), 84–89.

Ryzhov, Y. A., & Lebedev, M. A. (2003). Paguosh. *Mezhdunarodnaya zhizn'*, *8*, 52–59.

Sabatier, P. A. (1998). The advocacy coalition framework: Revisions and relevance for Europe. *Journal of European Public Policy*, *5*(1), 98–130.

Saharov, A. (1990). *Peace, progress, human rights: Articles and speeches*. Sovetskij Pisatel'.

Slaughter, A.-M. (2004). *A new world order*. Princeton University Press.

Stecko, E. V. (2012). Global governance and the role of non-governmental organisations in its formation. *Obshchestvo. Sreda. Razvitie*, *4*, 110–115.

Sungurov, A. Y. (1988). Radiobiology of the cell surface. VINITI.

Sungurov, A. Y. (2000). World order in the XXI century: State sovereignty and protection of human rights. Miroporyadok posle Balkanskogo krizisa. Novye real'nosti menyayushchegosya mira. Dobrosvet, 82–93.

Sungurov, A. Y. (2008). The concept of the noosphere and the formation of civil society. Noosferologiya: nauka, obrazovanie, praktika. Simferopol': Predpriyatie "Feniks", 360–380.

Sungurov, A. Y., Dubrovskij, D. V., Karyagin, M. E., & Tinyakov, D. K. (2020). Public advisory councils as a form of involvement of expert knowledge in the process of political and managerial decisions (on the example of St. Petersburg). *Voprosy gosudarstvennogo i municipal'nogo upravleniya*, *2*, 7–31.

The Black Past of Academician Legasov. (2017). *Komsomol'skaya Pravda*, 27381, 26 aprelya. Retrieved August 8, 2020, from https://www.mk.ru/social/2017/04/25/kak-ubivali-akademika-legasova-kotoryy-provel-sobstvennoe-rassledovaniechernobylskoy-katastrofy.html

The Chernobyl disaster. [1986] (1998). Katastrofy konca XX veka. M.: URSS, 1998.

The Great Russian Encyclopedic Dictionary. (2006). Bol'shaya rossijskaya enciklopediya.

The Roman Club. (1997). *History of creation, selected reports and speeches, official materials*. URSS.

Tormosheva, V. S. (2017). Actors of the modern political space in the context of transnationalization. Vestnik Tomskogo gosudarstvennogo universiteta. *Seriya: Filosofiya. Sociologiya. Politologiya*, *3*, 167–175.

Vernadskij, V. I. (1989). *Biosphere and noosphere*. Nauka.

Vernadskij, V. I. (1991). Scientific thought as a planetary phenomenon. Nauka.

Vernadskij, V. I. (2000). pro et contra. Anthology of literature about V.I. Vernadsky for a hundred years (1898–1998). SPb., RHGI.

Volgin, O. S. (2017). About supranational democracy. *Pravo i Upravlenie*, *1*(42), 37–44.

Yurchenko, M. (2017). UN–70: Problems of reform. *Mirovaya ekonomika i mezhdunarodnye otnosheniya*, *61*(5), 88–98.

Zlokazova, N. E. (2008). UN security council reform: Main scenarios and challenges. *Vestnik VGNA*, *2*, 1–13.

Zverev, P. G. (2013). On the need for reform of the United Nations and Russia's role in this process. *Moskovskoe Nauchnoe Obozrenie*, *5*(33), 41–44.

5 Models of Human Resource Management in Healthcare Systems During a Pandemic

The Example of Poland

Jędrzej Skrzypczak and Tomasz Maksymiuk

Introduction

The obligation to assist and act for the patient's benefit has always formed the foundation of the ethos of medicine and its practitioners. As epidemics, plagues, and pestilential air have always occurred, the knowledge and care of physicians in fighting them have been the principal element in the combat against illnesses since antiquity, especially in the case of mass diseases (Zieliński, 2020). Hence, probably the belief in the supernatural origin of medical knowledge, which, for example, was confirmed by the myth that the Roman god Aesculapius was to protect the centre and capital of the then world from the plague in 293 BCE. It is also no coincidence that the doctors were descended from the eminence of priests. However, allowing such secret knowledge was connected from the beginning with the obligation to assist (Nawrot, 2018).

Appropriate medical staff resources have always played an essential role in health systems and, thus, in state systems (Sztolcman, 1923; Kostrzewski, 1964; Pałka, 2018). Still, it proves to be otherwise fundamental in crisis situations such as epidemics.

Human resources as a strategic element of health systems

Just as there are all manner of terms for health systems (healthcare system, health protection system, health service system), which is a separate entity composed of many different elements related by various ties, pursuing the primary objective of addressing health needs of individuals, groups, and entire societies, so one can certainly find its numerous definitions, approaches, and models, both theoretical and practical Włodarczyk &Poździoch, 2001).What is relevant, however, is that in each of these approaches – human resources, that is medical staff – are a principal or even strategic element of such a structure. One can imagine the best organisational solutions for medical care, excellent medical infrastructure, and state-of-the-art diagnostic and therapeutic equipment, which, however, will not heal on their own. The human factor is one of the most critical in this case (Sadowska, 1997; Stahl, & Emanuel, 2017).

DOI: 10.4324/9781003482710-6

Medical professions as professions of public trust

Professions of public trust ought to be accompanied by a particular ethos. These professions directly impact the fate of individuals and society, serve to protect fundamental social values, and have a specific societal vocation(Różyńska & Łuków, 2013).

In some countries, such as this one, legal acts (in Poland, the Constitution) provide medical professions with a special official status, that is those of public trust (Garlicki & Zubik, 2016; Skrzydło, 2013; Tuleja, 2019; Boratyńska & Konieczniak, 2003).

Thus, as a representative of a vocation of public trust, a physician is subjected to specific requirements not only concerning the practice of the profession but also their personal attitude. Violating the doctor's dignity is not only improper behaviour of a physician in relations with patients, other doctors, medical staff and personnel members, or employees of institutions where they perform their activities.

The obligation to provide care results not only from deontological norms but also from legal regulations. Each physician, starting their professional career in Poland, submits a medical oath, which is a preamble to the Code of Medical Ethics (CME), in which they vow, among other things, to serve human life and health, counteract suffering, prevent disease, and help those affected by physical or mental illness without any differences (Hamankiewicz, 2020). It seems, therefore, that the imperative of fighting the epidemic by medical workers fits perfectly into such a vocation. However, a fundamental doubt arises, namely, whether such involvement of medics in the fight against the epidemic should only be recognised and analysed in terms of deontological obligations or in the form of appropriate legal norms being, in fact, work order or even forced labour (Jasudowicz 1993; Patulski, 2019). And if so, should it happen in any situation, even when the employing entity does not provide personal protective equipment, putting medical professionals in the face of a threat to their health or even life?

There is a relationship between the number and quality of medical staff and the health status of a given population. It should be noted that most European health systems suffer from severe medical staff shortages (Doctors per 1,000 people - Country rankings, 2020; Doctors (overall number), 2020; Medical doctors (per 10,000 population), 2020; OECD Data. Doctors, 2020; Fleck, 2023).

The situation in Poland in this area is particularly worrying. There is one of the lowest employment rates in Europe in particular groups of medical professions. Moreover, this one is characterised by an unfavourable age structure like other European countries. There are many reasons for this state of affairs. However, it is necessary to point out errors in health policy here, resulting chiefly from underfunding this sector but also from inadequate education system planning and improper human resources management. In the report from 2016, the Polish Supreme Audit Office alarmed that the education and vocational training system for medical students does not guarantee the provision of an adequate number of trained medical professionals to the health system, adapted to the changing health needs of the population (NIK, 2016). Poland had the lowest percentage of practising physicians per 1,000 inhabitants among EU countries – 2.4 in 2017 compared to the average of 3.6 in the EU. In addition, some unfavourable social trends are noted, such as the ageing of the population (which naturally causes an increase in demand for medical services), as well as emerging epidemiological, terrorist, or climatic threats. It should also be noted that the medical staff are drained by more developed countries, which tempts doctors to have much better social conditions, leading to professional emigration and weakening the health systems of less wealthy nations. And yet, each medical profession is so universal that the language barrier is usually not an issue here, which is characteristic of other occupations, such as law (Buchelt et al., 2020, pp. 78–83).

Principles for ensuring medical staffing during the COVID-19 pandemic in the world

The unprecedented magnitude of the COVID-19 pandemic has led most health systems to overburden or even to the brink of incapacity. This was the case during the first two waves of the pandemic in 2020 and the next in 2021, including in Italy, France, Spain, and Poland. Such a situation resulted not only from the scale and increase in infections and the shortage of specialist equipment and rooms (despite temporary hospitals being established in many locations worldwide) but mainly from the shortages of medical staff and personnel (Nurses, 2020). While many countries coped quite efficiently with the deficit in the material sphere of the fight against this phenomenon, there were more issues with ensuring the appropriate level of medical staff (Medical doctors, 2020). This was due to various factors. Indeed, the most serious were the numerous cases of infections, which sometimes even resulted in the death of medical staff and personnel despite the use of personal protective equipment (Amnesty International, 2020a). According to Amnesty International data, as of 13 July 2020, over 3,000 medical workers worldwide died from the first wave of infections. The number of deaths in this professional group after the second wave as of 3 September 2020 was already estimated at 7,000 (Amnesty International, 2020b). These data seem to be significantly underestimated because only in Poland – according to the official, not estimated, data of the Ministry of Health – 84,821 medical workers became infected with SARS-CoV-2, and 145 died from COVID-19. Details by the professional group are shown in Table 5.1 (Ważna, 2021)

Table 5.1 Number of infections, deaths, and people under mandatory quarantine by medical professional groups in Poland after the third wave of the pandemic. Status as of 3 September 2020

Medical occupation	*Infections*	*Deaths*	*Quarantine*
Dentist	1,884	10	8,511
Lab. diagnostician	1,555	0	6,670
Pharmacist	2,106	5	7,814
Medical Assistant	26	4	121
Physician	20,476	66	78,069
Nurse	50,990	51	158,073
Midwife	4,764	4	18,312
Paramedic	3,020	5	9,592

Source: Ważna, 2021.

The extraordinary circumstances and organisational actions taken to combat the pandemic have undoubtedly dramatically impacted the nature and scope of tasks performed by healthcare workers (Kopp, 2020; Zarefsky, 2020). According to research conducted in Poland between December 2020 and March 2021, respondents (i.e. medical workers) felt they were positively unprepared to work in conditions of a pandemic and general chaos. Naturally, as time passed and they gained experience, their opinions improved. Working under stress also significantly influenced mutual relations in medical teams. Over half of respondents declared no change in team interpersonal relationships, but almost 35% reported a deterioration, and only 1 in 10 registered improvement. The average self-rating of stress at work increased from 3.7 before the pandemic to 5.1 during it. Most interviewees were afraid of transmitting the infection to their relatives. Other concerns included the possibility of medical error, inability to assist the patient, lack of sufficient personal protective equipment, and contracting SARS-CoV-2. Interestingly, the study participants rated their own involvement in medical tasks slightly higher than their colleagues (average 4.9 and 4.4, respectively). Neverthless, the overall rating was high (Przyłęcki et al., 2023). Similar conclusions apply to the situation around the world. The report by the World Health Professions Alliance (WHPA) and the World Health Organisation (WHO), "What the COVID-19 pandemic has exposed: the findings of five global health workforce professions", shows the extent of the physical and psychological harm caused to health workers during the pandemic (MHA, 2020). At the same time, it was emphasised that the main reason for this state of affairs was the dysfunction of the healthcare systems in which they worked, especially the lack of appropriate guarantees to protect their situation. The lack or insufficient support and security of healthcare systems left many feeling unappreciated (Downey et al., 2023).

It is not surprising, therefore, that in many regions of the world, the attitude of medics – who, as is evident from the above data, often exposing themselves or their loved ones to the risk of disease or even death, frequently took heroic steps to ensure continuity of medical care for dying patients – was universally acknowledged in the public mind. In the first wave of the pandemic, such as in Belgium, people went out, in the evening, to balconies or through windows to reward its heroes in the fight against SARS-CoV-2 with applause (due to lockdown and the ban on leaving the place of residence).

Shortages in medical staffing and the resignation of personnel from work in such conditions sometimes stemmed from fear and lack of appropriate knowledge in this area. Extraordinary actions in the "frontline" conditions often result in burnout syndrome. Finally, in a number of countries, many years of neglect in healthcare investment had led to deficits or worrying trends in these occupational groups even before the pandemic (e.g. the average age over 60), and sudden waves of hospitalisation in such cases drastically exposed these deficiencies, bringing about the dramatic consequences to the quality of medical care.

For example, specific solutions have already been adopted in the United States during this pandemic. The Families First Coronavirus Response Act (FFCRA), which entered into force on 18 March 2020, allowed employees to be released from work for 12 weeks as part of the Family and Medical Leave Act extension, for example in the case of ordered quarantine. In addition, the FFCRA provides that an employer may exclude employees who are medical workers or emergency responders from protection under this law. Under these arrangements, doctors, nurses, and paramedics could lose their jobs if they did not turn up despite the risk, in line with the provisions of the comprehensive pandemic response package. The decision to maximise the number of healthcare workers treating patients by possibly excluding them from quarantine and sick leave may have been made as hospitals expected more waves of patients. In the United States, other solutions were also introduced, which could make it difficult for medics to take up work in light of local regulations. For example, it was possible to waive non-competition clauses, allowing the physician to continue the practice in the immediate vicinity of the employer. In the United States, on the other hand, it is noted that the pandemic is causing many doctors to retire early due to personal health issues. It is stressed that such a trend is particularly acute in primary medical care, which is already struggling with a shortage of physicians. It is recognised that many US medical entities put pressure on medical staff and personnel to keep working, even if they have symptoms of SARS-CoV-2 infection (US Hospitals, 2020).

In Canada, amid an exponential increase in the number of hospitalisations of patients with SARS-CoV-2, leading to fears of severely overloading the overall healthcare system, some provinces have started to turn to recently retired doctors and nurses to return to work. It must be admitted that such appeals received a comprehensive and positive response. The enthusiastic reaction from nearly 10,000 medics prompted Prime Minister Francois Legault to announce that he was "proud to be a Quebec citizen" (Morgan, 2020).

In Great Britain, under the pre-pandemic law, medical employers could cancel booked annual leaves. However, it was decided to introduce additional, temporary statutory provisions under which employees who could not exercise their entitlement to annual leave due to COVID-19 might transfer up to 20 days of accrued annual leave for two years. All NHS employers have used this option. In turn, the new situation's fatigue, weariness, and uncertainty have led hundreds of NHS physicians to avoid extra working hours in the fight against the coronavirus because they have lost death benefits. On the other hand, it was emphasised that no physician should feel forced to undertake duties they did not feel competent to perform. In addition, the UK government has published national guidelines on COVID-19 and pregnant female workers. It is said that, for example women of any kind should not be obliged to continue working unless a risk assessment supports this. At the pandemic's start, the General Medical Council (GMC) issued guidelines explaining how it intends to regulate the practice during the coronavirus outbreak. The guide covers doctors working outside their usual routine, protecting their health, and temporarily registering some physicians who may be asked to return to practice, such as those who have recently retired. Doctors in training may also have been asked to work flexibly, for example with alternative tasks outside their scope of competence or training. In the United Kingdom, 37.9% of respondents (medical workers) agreed that "health care workers should be able to refuse to work with infected patients" during an outbreak (MDU Journal 2020; Chalmers, 2020; COVID-19 Terms and Conditions: All Doctors, 2020; COVID-19. Physician Private Practice Guidance, 2020).

In some European countries, the situation has been so dramatic with the surge in cases and hospital admissions that, for example physicians from the Belgian city of Liège have been asked to continue their work, even if they have the coronavirus (Covid: Belgian Doctors with Coronavirus Asked to Keep Working, 2020).

Similarly, the surge in infection has forced most hospitals in Italy, especially in the northern regions, to rapidly transform their primary or secondary care facilities into dedicated "COVID structures". Almost all scheduled procedures have been postponed, and only emergency services have continued. This involved, for example the need for medics to work, even outside their specialisation, such as surgeons learned anew how to examine the respiratory system, and gynaecologists used non-invasive mechanical ventilation.

As reported at the time, under certain circumstances and for various unreasonable reasons, some patients refused treatment; similarly, there were instances when doctors refused to care for patients. In practice, most countries generally assume that a physician cannot be compelled to treat a patient, and the freedom to choose doctors is protected under international law. Healthcare workers may encounter conditions they consider unsafe during a pandemic or epidemic. In such a situation, refusal to work could be acceptable if the environment presents an unacceptable risk.

Regarding the COVID-19 outbreak, 28% of German medical workers said that "it would be 'professionally acceptable' for health care workers to leave their workplace", even if it were to protect themselves and their families (Ehrenstein et al., 2006).

Referring medical workers in Poland to fight the COVID-19 epidemic in the light of deontological codes

In the CME, already in the preamble, that is the Medical Oath, the duty to serve human life and health is included. Art. 2 of this document states that "the physician's calling is to protect human life and health, prevent disease, treat the ill and relieve suffering". On the other hand, cases of refusal to provide medical assistance and situations in which it cannot be done are dealt with in Art. 7 of the CME. According to this standard, in particularly justified cases, the doctor may not undertake or refrain from the patient's treatment, except in urgent cases. Not initiating or withdrawing from treatment, the physician should indicate another possibility of obtaining medical service for the patient. Art. 69 of the CME corresponds with this norm, in which a doctor may not refuse medical assistance in urgent cases if the patient cannot obtain it from institutions appointed to assist.

As can be seen, deontological norms fully harmonise with the directive contained in Art. 30 of the Act of 5 December 1996 on the professions of physician and dentist (Act of 5 December 1996), according to which doctors are obliged to provide medical assistance in any case when a delay in delivering it could result in a risk of loss of life, severe injury or serious health impairment.

A referral to work in combating an epidemic in the act of 2008 in Poland

In the current legal situation, the issue discussed here is regulated by Art. 47 of the Act of 5 December 2008 on preventing and combating infections and infectious diseases in humans. It should be noted here that the content of this provision underwent quite significant changes, especially during the 2020/21 pandemic, resulting – as it seems – from the poor quality of the legislature on the one hand and, on the other, from the urgent need to supplement the medical staff (Zimna, 2020; Waszak, 2020).

Currently, under Art. 47 paragraph 1 of the Act, the procedure of referral to work discussed here may be introduced to combat epidemics. If so, it is then necessary to quote the legal definition of this concept contained in Art. 47 of this normative act. Namely, under Art. 2 point 9, the term means "the occurrence in a given area of infections or cases of an infectious disease in a number clearly greater than in the previous period, or the occurrence of infections or infectious diseases that did not occur so far". According to the Minister of Health regulation of 27 February 2020, COVID-19 was included in the Act's provisions on infectious diseases analysed here. In turn, by the regulation of 7 March 2020, the disease was added to the list of illnesses requiring hospitalisation and those justifying quarantine or epidemiological surveillance (Zimna, 2020).

Pursuant to Art. 47 paragraph 1 of the just mentioned Act on infectious diseases, the subjective scope of the referral to work in combating epidemics may include employees of medical entities, individuals practising medical professions, and individuals with whom contracts for the provision of health services have been signed. The working time in which such a person is employed does not matter. Other individuals may also be directed to combat the epidemic if their referral is justified by the current needs of the entities managing the occurrence. As it follows from the above, referral in the mode discussed here may cover both individuals working based on an employment relationship (e.g. employment contract) and based on all types of civil law contracts (e.g. contracts for the provision of health services), as well as individuals working in the medical profession, based on the so-called self-employment, that is running their own business. However, importantly, the referral can be made to all other individuals, and therefore even unemployed, provided that such a decision is justified by the current needs of entities managing the epidemic. What is also essential in Article 47, section 2a was added that a person may be referred to work in combating an outbreak at their request submitted to the provincial governor. As it seems, it is also necessary for the analogous decision to be issued by the latter in such a case. An individual in a comparable situation will be able to use all the rights provided under this regulation. Under Art. 47 paragraph 1 of the discussed Act, other individuals may also be directed to combat the epidemic if their referral is justified by the current needs of the entities managing it. As seen above, the circle of individuals this obligation may cover is essentially unlimited. However, such a solution should be assessed as fully justified considering that the goal, that is the fight against the epidemic, serves to protect the health or life of patients (Waszak, 2020).

According to the amendment of 28 October 2020, section 1a was added to this provision, which obliges the self-governments of medical professions, that is medical chambers and chambers of nurses and midwives, to submit, at the request of the provincial governor or the Minister of Health, the list of individuals practising medical services that may be assigned to work in combating epidemics. Such a list should include the name, surname, place of residence, and licence number to practise the profession. Professional self-government bodies should fulfil this obligation within seven days from receipt of the application. This solution results from professional self-governments keeping a register of physicians, nurses, or midwives; therefore, they have up-to-date personal data. The Minister or the provincial governor does not have such data. However, it must be added here that even professional self-governments do not have the data that would provide a basis for avoiding taking up this type of work. And it seems that the collection of such data by these entities should not take place (Zimna, 2020).

The catalogues of cases and individuals excluded from this obligation and subsequent amendments to this provision aroused emotions and controversy. In the original wording of this provision, the roster of individuals excluded from this obligation lists individuals under 18 or over 60 years of age, pregnant women or individuals bringing up children up to 18 years of age, including single parents of children under 18; individuals diagnosed with partial or total incapacity for work; invalids and individuals with diagnosed chronic diseases; individuals referred to in Art. 2 of the Act of 31 July 1981 on the Remuneration of individuals Holding State Managerial Positions and Members of Parliament and Senators of the Republic of Poland. Such a list raised many serious doubts and reservations for many reasons. While it was possible to fully accept the age limits indicated here (adults who are over 60), as well as exempting pregnant women, individuals with an apparent incapacity for work, invalids, and individuals with diagnosed chronic diseases from this obligation, the privilege of absolving from this obligation individuals who are MPs or senators of the Republic of Poland and occupying leading state positions seems to be a completely unjustified privilege of the authorities, violating the principles of social and professional solidarity. On the other hand, in the case of individuals bringing up children, it seems that a legislative error was made here (Waszak, 2020).

On the one hand, individuals caring for children up to 18 were excluded from the possibility of referral in this mode, similar to single parents. Separating such a category as single parents, which is entirely correct, should involve particular treatment than when both parents are responsible for the child's care. However, after the outbreak of the SARS-CoV-2 epidemic, this regulation was amended under the provisions of 31 March 2020 to revise certain acts in the healthcare system related to the prevention, counteraction, and combating of COVID-19. Under this amendment, individuals under the age of 18 or over 60 years of age were still not referred to work that carries the risk of infection while fighting an epidemic, as well as pregnant women and single parents bringing up children to 18 years of age. On the other hand, individuals bringing up a child by both parents could use this privilege only until their offspring reached 14. The same applies to individuals bringing up a child with a certificate of disability or the need for special education. This catalogue also includes individuals diagnosed with a partial or total incapacity for work, as well as invalids and individuals with diagnosed chronic diseases. This privilege was still available to individuals holding state management positions, deputies, and senators of the Republic of Poland. Finally, in the subsequent amendment of 14 August 2020, the issue of excluding invalids and individuals with diagnosed chronic diseases from the possibility of referring to work in this mode was clarified. It was indicated here that it concerns only individuals with such a disability or chronic illness whose course may be affected by contracting an infectious disease causing an epidemic or a confirmed chronic affliction that impacts the course or contraction of an infectious disease. According to the Ministry of Health, following the recommendation of the Minister, "before sending a referral to work, the provincial governor should contact the person to whom the decision is issued to confirm whether it is possible to hand over the referral" (Przyłęcki et al., 2023).

The doctrine states, "In a situation where a person is protected under Art. 47 paragraph 3 of the Act on Infectious Diseases of 2008 on preventing and combating infections and infectious diseases in humans was assigned by the employer to work that is objectively assessed as carrying a risk of infection; this person should be able to refrain from work. In this case, it must not be the degree of probability of infection that will be decisive but the very fact of the occurrence of such a risk. Hence, before referral, the provincial governor should try to determine whether work with the risk of a hazard is planned through explanatory activities with the institution that reports the demand" (Bieniek & Górnicz-Mulcahy, 2020, pp. 36–44).

A referral to work in combating an epidemic occurs by way of an administrative decision, which may be issued by the provincial governor or the Minister of Health (Zimna, 2020). The first authority will be competent in the case of a referral to combat an epidemic in the Province where the person referred has their place of residence or is employed. The latter entity will have exclusive competence in the event of being assigned to work in another Province. Such a decision is open to challenge. The provincial governor's decision may be appealed against the Minister of Health.

On the other hand, if the Minister issues the decision, there is a possibility of applying for reconsideration of the case by the same authority, the so-called "right to remonstration". Such a request is treated accordingly as an appeal against a decision, with almost all the consequences of such procedures. However, it should be noted that in paragraph 6 of this provision, it is stated *expressis verbis* that the lodging of an appeal does not suspend the execution of the decision (Zimna, 2020).

When examining an appeal or a request for reconsideration of the case, the provincial governor or the Minister may apply to a provincial or national consultant, respectively, in the field of medicine related to the chronic disease or in the area of infectious diseases, to obtain a decision whether it is a type of chronic disease which may be affected by infection or contraction of contagious illness, or if the diagnosed chronic affliction has an impact on the course or contraction of an infectious disease (Zimna, 2020).

In the original wording of Art. 47 of the Act on infectious diseases of 2008, there were no special procedures for delivering such a decision. The so-called first wave of cases showed that the standard transmission of decisions, that is by registered mail with acknowledgement of receipt, is ineffective, if only because Post Offices did not function correctly during the lockdown period. In addition, some individuals were in quarantine, so they could not meet the obligation to collect such correspondence from the Post Office. Hence, the amendment to this provision, which entered into force on 1 April 2020, introduced unique solutions in this regard. According to the cited regulation, such correspondence may be delivered in any possible way, ensuring that the decision reaches the addressee, including orally, such as by a messenger (e.g. police or military officer) or by telephone. In cases like these, such decisions do not require justification. Decisions communicated in such a way, other than in writing, are then delivered in writing after the reasons for such service have ceased to exist (Waszak, 2020).

The decision to refer to work in combating an epidemic creates an obligation to perform for up to three months in a medical entity or another organisational unit indicated in the decision (Waszak, 2020, p. 100). The period of incapacity for work adequately confirmed by a doctor is not included in the referral period to work in combating an epidemic. Notably, the applicable law does not specify whether such a decision should define the activities, scope of duties, or the type of work to which the person is directed. Failure to comply with such a decision may result in a fine of PLN 5,000 to PLN 30,000, which may be charged by the competent provincial governor or the Minister of Health (Zimna, 2020).

But such a decision also results in the creation of a number of rights for such a person, including the right to unpaid leave from the current employer for a specified period, the establishment of an employment relationship with such an individual for the duration of a specific work, not exceeding the period indicated in the decision, and the right to basic salary in the amount not lower than 200% of the average basic pay for the given position. Moreover, such a person is entitled to reimbursement of the costs of travel, accommodation, and meals. For the duration of the duty, the current employment relationship may not be terminated with the individual assigned to work to combat the epidemic, or the employment contract may not be terminated unless there is a basis for concluding the employment contract without notice due to the employee's fault or in the event of a change or revocation decision. According to the Ministry of Health communication, insurance policies will be purchased for them due to the "need to protect persons assigned to work in combating epidemics" (Waszak, 2020).

Conclusions

Healthcare workers have been on the front lines of the fight against the COVID-19 pandemic and, as such, have been exposed to a variety of extreme risks. It was not only about the possibility of getting infected with the pathogen but also about dealing with such negative factors as long working hours, mental stress, fatigue, burnout, stigmatisation, and even, in drastic situations, physical and psychological violence. The lessons learned from the pandemic, mainly because it was painful in terms of its consequences, should be appropriately used in the future to improve the functioning of healthcare systems. This difficult period has shown that properly educated and motivated medical staff should be treated equally with the state's strategic resources. Although for centuries, the role of medical workers in emergencies and wars has usually been appreciated to a greater or lesser extent (albeit most often only during their occurrence), after the experience of this pandemic, the protection of this occupational group should be given a new impetus (Damery et al., 2010). A thorough reform of the professional status of medical staff and personnel is necessary. We believe that in terms of legal protection, medical professionals in similar states of emergency should be treated similarly to police or military officers. Moreover, just as the needs of patients in contact with the healthcare system are often framed in terms of human rights, the legal situation of medics should be treated according to the same model (Derse, 2005).

The organisation of medical care in the initial period of the pandemic, particularly hospital care for patients infected with SARS-CoV-2, was quite chaotic. This resulted in significant discomfort at work, including high levels of stress among medical workers (Dunne et al. 2020). Research shows that the most affected people were transferred from other places to work (often involuntarily, such as in Poland) in infectious diseases' wards. Not all medical workers were prepared to work with COVID-19 patients because they lacked experience in such settings, especially in intensive care units (ICU). Working under time pressure and in new, challenging conditions led chiefly to an increase in perceived stress and, consequently, to mental disorders as well as conflicts among staff and personnel (Przyłęcki et al., 2023). Identical conclusions apply to the situation of medical workers in many countries (Carbajal et al., 2020), such as in Italy (Felice et al., 2020), Great Britain (BMA Report, 2023), and the United States (ASPE, 2022; MHA, 2020). This situation resulted, naturally, from extraordinary circumstances. The priority then was to ensure the functioning of healthcare systems at all costs in the permanent shortage of medical staff and personnel. Therefore, the priorities must have been different then. This could create a feeling of discomfort (Gifford, 2020).

But let us add that the experiences of the pandemic period also bring positive solutions. For example, employing telemedicine, which was introduced on a large scale then, seems to need to be constantly developed. Not unexpectedly, online medical assistance will never replace a direct examination, but it may be the only possible substitute in emergencies (Pawlikowski, 2020).

Around the world, different approaches have been observed in individual states to provide strategic medical personnel resources in the fight against the pandemic. They operated there through persuasion, appeals and invoking ethical obligations. However, some countries, such as Poland, used tough legal instruments and state coercion. There is no doubt today that Polish solutions involving the introduction of forced labour of medical staff turned out to be highly ineffective and, at the same time, distinctly controversial from the point of view of human rights protection (Jasudowicz, 1993; Przyłęcki et al., 2023). Firstly, it created additional unnecessary stress, which was not conducive to work efficiency, and secondly, it caused the healthcare system in other sectors, such as oncology treatment, to practically collapse. It is not without reason that we are currently observing a marked increase in cancer cases in patients who, due to the pandemic and the inability to contact a doctor, sought medical assistance too late. These types of deaths, although not directly, should be added to the mortal toll of SARS-CoV-2.

Therefore, it is necessary to propose an appropriate mix of actions and strategies at the level of national, regional (e.g. in the European Union), and international legal regulations, which will guarantee proper protection of healthcare workers in the event of similar disasters in the future. It should be repeated once again that it is necessary to postulate that these issues, that is the rights of medical workers, should be raised to the rank of human rights. And this is both individual (on the side of medical workers) and collective (on the side of patients), and on several levels.

Firstly, ensuring adequate medical staff and personnel safety in all possible dimensions is imperative. It starts with fundamental issues such as providing all required preventive and protective measures to minimise workplace health and safety risks. This should be combined with appropriate occupational health and safety instruction and training (WHO, 2020). It is also necessary to provide suitable guarantees of personal safety, both physically and mentally. In addition to the exemplary attitudes of citizens supporting medics during this challenging period, unfortunately, cases of aggression against representatives of this professional group were reported, such as from anti-vaccine groups. Therefore, providing these individuals with easy and unlimited access to diverse help and support in the mental health field and legal assistance is indispensable. In addition, efforts should be made to create working conditions for medical staff free from all forms of physical and verbal violence, and follow-up measures and actions should be implemented, including support for victims (WHO, 2020).

Moreover, during the tragic period of the fight for human life described here, medics were repeatedly forced to take actions for which they were neither trained nor prepared (Giulio et al. 2020). This concerns both working in conditions of extreme fatigue and situations when providing medical care, doctors who did not have the required specialisations and professional training in this type of medical procedure were sent to "Covid wards". In some countries (e.g., Poland), dentists were even allowed to be appointed to fight the pandemic in such situations, equating their right to practice the profession with the professional licence of doctors. This is understandable because it was an obvious example of acting in a state of extreme necessity. However, such individuals should be provided with legal protection and freed (except in obvious cases) from being blamed for possible medical errors; therefore, a specific type of legal immunity should be established (WHO, 2020).

It is also necessary to provide the possibility of obtaining compensation, rehabilitation, and medical services for healthcare workers who have suffered any health damage in connection with the fight against the pandemic, and even such cases should be classified as occupational diseases resulting from working conditions (WHO, 2020).

In turn, from the patient's point of view, appropriate actions are needed to support and prepare healthcare systems in the event of similar disasters in the future. The best solution is to create appropriate strategic reserves for such an eventuality, not only in the material sphere but also – what we wanted to emphasise in this article – personal.

As the experience of not only this pandemic but also previous instances shows, a key element in the fight against such threats is medical staff, or at least paramedical personnel, that is recruited individuals with at least minimal medical training. Therefore, reforms in this area should start with medical education at the primary and continuing training stages. Here, emphasis should be placed on developing educational modules in emergency medicine and combating infectious diseases. However, as it turns out, in some critical cases, even such solutions may turn out to be insufficient. Therefore, it may be needed to recruit additional staff and personnel ready for such eventualities. Educating physicians and other lower-level medically qualified personnel is long and extremely expensive process, so most medical systems worldwide cannot afford to maintain too many physicians (NIK, 2016). It seems that a specific solution to this challenge is to create and develop human resources based on the contingent of military medical workers, which is present in virtually every country. Moreover, efforts should be made to obtain such resources from among people close to the healthcare system, although not normally active. For example, it is about adequately motivating retired medical workers to support the system in such extraordinary cases. It is also worth ensuring that medical students are prepared for such an event from the beginning of their education. Training in providing essential medical assistance to personnel who are part of the state's strategic resources, for example fire brigade officers, army, police, etc., and thus building a pool of paramedics also deserves consideration. This, of course, must involve appropriate financial outlays from the state for this type of activity. However, the price is – as the COVID-19 pandemic has shown – the life or health of thousands of citizens.

In summary, however, it should be said that when drafting any changes to the healthcare system, one should always be guided by the message resulting from the ancient Hippocratic paroemia, namely "Salus aegroti suprema lex esto". The good of the patient should guide us both when we design systems and consider doctors' professional status.

Bibliography

Act of 5 December 1996 on the professions of physician and dentist, *Journal of Laws of 2020.*, item 514.

Amnesty International. (2020a). Globalnie: pracownicy opieki zdrowotnej uciszani, narażeni i atakowani. https://www.amnesty.org/en/latest/news/2020/07/health-workers-rights-covid-report/

Amnesty International. (2020b). Global: Amnesty analysis reveals over 7,000 health workers have died from COVID-19. https://www.amnesty.org/en/latest/news/2020/09/amnesty-analysis-7000-health-workers-have-died-from-covid19/

ASPE. (2022). Impact of the COVID-19 pandemic on the hospital and outpatient clinician workforce. https://aspe.hhs.gov/sites/default/files/documents/9cc72124abd9ea25d58a22c7692dccb6/aspe-covid-workforce-report.pdf

Bieniek, B., & Górnicz-Mulcahy, A. (2020). Przesłanki odmowy podjęcia pracy przez osobę skierowaną do zwalczania COVID-19. *Praca i Zabezpieczenie Społeczne*, *5*, 36–44.

BMA Report. (2023). COVID-19: The impact of the pandemic on the medical profession COVID-19: The impact of the pandemic on the medical profession. https://www.bma.org.uk/advice-and-support/covid-19/what-the-bma-is-doing/covid-19-the-impact-of-the-pandemic-on-the-medical-profession

Boratyńska, M., & Konieczniak, P. (2003). Standardy wykonywania zawodu lekarza. In L. Kubicki (Ed.), *Prawo medyczne* (pp 41–84). Elsevier Urban & Partner.

Buchelt, B., Kowalska, & Bobko, I. (2020). Zarządzanie zasobami ludzkimi w systemie ochrony zdrowia w czasach pandemii, Kraków. https://politykipubliczne.pl/wp-content/uploads/2020/10/Zarzadzanie-zasobami-ludzkimi-w-systemie-ochrony-zdrowia-w-czasach-pandemii.pdf

Carbajal, A., Boluarte, A. S., Boluarte, A. R., & Merino-Soto, C. (2020). Working conditions and emotional impact on health care workers during COVID-19 pandemic. *Journal of Healthcare Quality Research*, *35*(6), 401–402. https://doi.org/10.1016/j.jhqr.2020.08.002

Chalmers, V. (2020). Hundreds of doctors are avoiding working extra hours in the NHS's coronavirus battle because they've lost death-in-service benefits amid pensions row and freelance contracts. https://www.dailymail.co.uk/news/article-8166889/Doctors-avoiding-work-coronavirus-patients-compensation-fears-die.html

Covid: Belgian Doctors with Coronavirus Asked to Keep Working. (2020). https://www.bbc.com/news/world-europe-54688846

COVID-19 Terms and Conditions: All Doctors. (2020). https://www.bma.org.uk/advice-and-support/covid-19/your-contract/covid-19-terms-and-conditions-all-doctors

COVID-19. Physician Private Practice Guidance. (2020). March, https://www.tuckerlaw.com/2020/03/20/covid-19-private-practice-guidance/

Damery, S., Draper, H., & Wilson, S. (2010). Healthcare workers' perceptions of the duty to work during an influenza pandemic. *Journal of Medical Ethics*, *36*.

Derse, A. R. (2005). What part of "no" don't you understand? Patient refusal of recommended treatment in the emergency department. *Mt Sinai Journal of Medicine*, *72*(4), 221–227.

Doctors (overall number) (2020). https://www.oecd-ilibrary.org/sites/b33ab4c1-en/index.html?itemId=/content/component/b33ab4c1-en

Doctors per 1,000 people - Country Rankings. (2020). https://www.theglobaleconomy.com/rankings/doctors_per_1000_people/

Damery, S., Draper, H., Wilson, S., Greenfield, S., Ives, J., Parry, J., Petts, J., & Sorell, T. (2010). Healthcare workers' perceptions of the duty to work during an influenza pandemic. *Journal of medical ethics, 36*(1), 12–18. https://doi.org/10.1136/jme.2009.032821

Ehrenstein, B. P., Hanses, F., & Salzberger, B. (2006). Influenza pandemic and professional duty: Family or patients first? A survey of hospital employees. *BMC Public Health*, *6*, 311.

Felice, C., Di Tanna, G. L., Zanus, G., & Grossi, U. (2020). Impact of COVID-19 outbreak on healthcare workers in Italy: Results from a national E-survey. *Journal of Community Health*, *45*, 675–683. https://link.springer.com/article/10.1007/s10900-020-00845-5

Fleck, A. (2023). The countries with the highest density of doctors. https://www.statista.com/chart/21168/doctors-per-1000-inhabitants-in-selected-countries/

Garlicki, L., & Zubik, M. (2016). Konstytucja Rzeczypospolitej Polskiej. Komentarz. Tom I, wyd. II, Wyd. Sejmowe.

Gifford, M. (2020). Doctors are retiring due to COVID-19: Why you might have a hard time finding a new one. https://www.healthline.com/health-news/doctors-are-retiring-due-to-covid-19-why-you-might-have-a-hard-time-finding-a-new-on

Giulio, M. et al. (2020). Being a doctor will never be the Same after COVID-19 pandemic. *The American Journal of Medicine*, *133*(6), 652. https://www.amjmed.com/article/S0002-9343(20)30216-3/fulltext

Hamankiewicz, H. (2016). Przyrzeczenie lekarskie jako Preambuła do Kodeksu etyki lekarskiej. *Medyczna Wokanda*, *8*, 23–32.

Jasudowicz, T. (1993). Zakaz niewolnictwa i poddaństwa oraz pracy przymusowej lub obowiązkowej w Europejskiej Konwencji Praw Człowieka, „Studia Prawa Publicznego" No 3.

Kopp, E. (2020). Nurses, doctors exposed to COVID-19 who miss work may lose their job under aid bill. Retrieved January 1, 2021, from https://www.rollcall.com/2020/03/18/nurses-doctors-exposed-to-covid-19-and-miss-work-may-lose-their-job-under-aid-bill

Kostrzewski, J. (1964). *Choroby zakaźne w Polsce i ich zwalczanie w latach 1919–1962*. PZWL.

MDU Journal. (2020). Protecting the NHS from the medico-legal consequences of coronavirus. https://mdujournal.themdu.com/issue-archive/summer-2020/protecting-the-nhs-from-the-medico-legal-consequences-of-coronavirus

Medical Doctors. (2020). Medical doctors (per 10 000 population). https://www.who.int/data/gho/data/indicators/indicator-details/GHO/medical-doctors-(per-10-000-population)

MHA. (2020). The mental health of healthcare workers in Covid -19. https://mhanational.org/mental-health-healthcare-workers-covid-19

Morgan, L. (2020). COVID-19: Thousands of doctors, nurses rally to government call to fight coronavirus. *The Canadian Press*. Retrieved March 17, 2020, from https://nationalpost.com/news/thousands-of-doctors-nurses-answer-call-to-help-with-covid-19-effort

Nawrot, O. (2018). Historia prawa medycznego (pomiędzy Jerozolimą, Atenami a Rzymem—etyka, prawo i sztuka leczenia). In M. Safjan, L. Bosek (Eds.), *System prawa medycznego. Instytucje prawa medycznego* (vol. I). C.H. Beck.

NIK. (2016). Kształcenie i przygotowanie zawodowe kadr medycznych. Informacja o wynikach kontroli Najwyższej Izby Kontroli, Nr ewid. 220/2015/P/15/060/KZD. https://www.nik.gov.pl/plik/id,10242,vp,12565.pdf

Nurses. (2020). Nurses, doctors exposed to COVID-19 who miss work may lose their job under aid bill. https://www.rollcall.com/2020/03/18/nurses-doctors-exposed-to-covid-19-and-miss-work-may-lose-their-job-under-aid-bill/

OECD Data. (2020). Doctors. https://data.oecd.org/healthres/doctors.htm

Pałka, K. (2018). Świadczenia zdrowotne związane z chorobami zakaźnymi, w tym obowiązkowe i zalecane szczepienia in Safjan, M, Bosek, L. System prawa medycznego. Szczególne świadczenia zdrowotne, tom II.

Patulski, A. (2019). Wolność pracy i zakaz pracy przymusowej in Baran Krzysztof W. (ed.). System Prawa Pracy. Vol. IX. Międzynarodowe publiczne prawo pracy. Standardy globalne, WKP.

Pawlikowski, J. (2020). Etyczny wymiar decyzji priorytetyzacyjnych i alokacyjnych dotyczących stosowania zaawansowanych technologii medycznych w kontekście pandemii COVID-19. https://www.mp.pl/etyka/terapia_chorob/231724,etyczny-wymiar-w-kontekscie-pandemii-covid-19

Przyłęcki, P., Wieczorkowska, M., Pawlak-Kałuzińska, A., Cedrowska-Adamus, W., & Gulczyńska, E. (2023). The COVID-19 pandemic impact on the Polish medical personnel work: A survey and in-depth interviews study. *Frontiers in Public Health*, *11*. https://doi.org/10.3389/fpubh.2023.1187312

Różyńska, J., & Łuków, P. (2013). Narodziny i natura bioetyki in Różyńska, J., Chańska, W. (ed.), Bioetyka.

Sadowska, J. (1997). Zwalczanie ostrych chorób zakaźnych w Polsce w dwudziestoleciu międzywojennym (1918–1939). *Przegląd Epidemiologiczny*, *51*(3), 321–328.

Skrzydło, W. (2013). Konstytucja Rzeczypospolitej Polskiej. Komentarz, vol. VII, LEX.

Stahl, R. Y., & Emanuel, E. J. (2017). Physicians, not conscripts—Conscientious objection in health care. *New England Journal of Medicine*, *376*(14), 1380.

Sztolcman, G. (1923). Rola państwowej służby zdrowia w walce z epidemiami.

Tuleja, P. (Ed.). (2019). *Konstytucja Rzeczypospolitej Polskiej*. WKP.

US Hospitals. (2020). US hospitals pressure healthcare staff to work even if they have Covid symptoms. https://www.theguardian.com/us-news/2020/aug/13/us-nurses-doctors-covid-19-symptoms-working

Waszak, M. (2020). Skierowanie do pracy przy zwalczaniu epidemii. *Blaski i cienie* regulacji. *Medyczna Wokanda*, *14*.

Ważna, M. (2020). Ilu pracowników ochrony zdrowia zmarło z powodu COVID-19? https://www.medonet.pl/koronawirus/koronawirus-w-polsce,ilu-pracownikow-ochrony-zdrowia-zmarlo-z-powodu-covid-19-,artykul,66853781.html

Ważna, M. (2021). Ilu pracowników ochrony zdrowia zmarło z powodu COVID-19? https://www.medonet.pl/koronawirus/koronawirus-w-polsce,ilu-pracownikow-ochrony-zdrowia-zmarlo-z-powodu-covid-19-, article, 66853781.html

WHO. (2020). Coronavirus disease (COVID-19) outbreak: Rights, roles and responsibilities of health workers, including key considerations for occupational safety and health. https://www.whofreebasics.org/sections/advice-healthcare-workers/coronavirus-disease-covid-19-outbreak-rights-roles-and-responsibilities-health-workers-including-key-considerations-occupational-safety-and-health/

Włodarczyk, C., & Poździoch, S. (2001). Systemy zdrowotne. Zarys problematyki, Kraków.

Zarefsky, M. (2020). Amid COVID-19 upheaval, know your rights as an employed physician. https://www.ama-assn.org/practice-management/sustainability/amid-covid-19-upheaval-know-your-rights-employed-physician

Zieliński, A. (2020). Słowniczek terminów epidemiologicznych. http://www.przeglepidemiol.pzh.gov.pl/slowniczek-terminow-epidemiologicznych

Zimna, T. (2020). Skierowanie do pracy przy zwalczaniu epidemii, LEX/el.

6 Smart Quarantine vs Strict Lockdown

Restrictions on Political Rights in Anti-Pandemic Strategies in the Czech Republic

Maciej Skrzypek

Introduction

This chapter aims to trace the evolution of the state authorities' attitude to restrict fundamental political rights in the Czech Republic during the coronavirus pandemic from 11 March 2020 to the end of March 2021. At that time, the Czech authorities changed the anti-pandemic strategy, which impacted certain rights and freedoms. During "a second wave", the ruling elites decided to replace *smart quarantine* with a strict lockdown through an extra-constitutional state of emergency since February 2021. These changes aimed to extend the government's scope of power and allowed ignoring parliamentary opposition. The shift in strategy led to an intensification of the implementation of quasi-militant democracy instruments, which decreased the political nation's independence. Therefore, the author will address the motivations and results of anti-pandemic policy changes that impact the discussed sovereignty. That reflection is crucial for debate on implementing anti-democratic measures as part of the policy to deal with the subsequent widespread epidemics and other crises. In this chapter, the author refers to interdisciplinary studies on the effectiveness of pandemic strategies in the country, which, together with analysing the restriction of political rights, will provide answers to the legitimacy of changing the proposed action in the second half of 2020. The periodisation of the first year of the coronavirus crisis is presented in the diagram below.

This work differentiates between *smart quarantine* (March–September 2020) and strict lockdown (October 2020–March 2021). The first is based on the close cooperation of state authorities with epidemiologists and experts, thus adopting new technologies to deal with the coronavirus crisis. It was valid during the first state of emergency (March–May 2020). With that approach, modern states adopted digital innovations beyond restrictions on certain rights and freedoms, confirming that public officials trusted and recognised experts. In turn, strict lockdown is based on implementing a state of emergency, with a broad catalogue of restrictions on certain rights and freedoms. It was viable during the second state of emergency (October 2020–mid-February 2021) and an unconstitutional state of emergency (mid-February–March 2021). The governance style is characterised by concentrating power around the Prime Minister's cabinet and ignoring experts' opinions.

DOI: 10.4324/9781003482710-7

Based on that, the main reason for reducing the political nation's sovereignty was replacing *smart quarantine* with a more autocratic approach.

Literature review and theoretical grounding

This chapter is located in a part of renewed studies on militant democracy, resulting from the renaissance of holistic political theories, like institutionalism, and the growing threat from religiously motivated terrorism, especially Islamic fundamentalism. Karl Loewenstein conducted the first in-depth study on militant democracy. In 1937, in the face of the fascist threat to the Weimar Republic and other European democracies, Loewenstein suggested using legal instruments to protect democratic regimes (Lowenstein, 1937). Nowadays, a catalogue of militant democracy measures is expanded by scholarship, focusing primarily on the essential features of the imposition of anti-democratic means. The authors present single-case studies (Bogaards, 2020; Osiewicz & Skrzypek, 2020; Rak, 2020a; Rak, 2020b; Tyulkina, 2015) or propose comparative analyses (Bourne & Casal Bértoa, 2017; Skrzypek, 2020; Skrzypek, 2022; Steuer, 2019). It is worth quoting the approaches presented by Joanna Rak and Roman Bäcker (also present in this book). They assumed that the essential features of militant democracy rested on the self-defence ability of democracy to prevent it from being destroyed by anti-democratic forces (Bäcker & Rak, 2019).

Moreover, they proposed the antinomic ideal types of neo-militant and quasi-militant democracies. This distinction allows researchers to define the consequences of precisely adopting militant democracy measures. According to Rak and Bäcker, the essential features of neo-militant democracy are based on the self-defence ability of democracy from being destroyed by anti-democratic forces (Rak & Bäcker, 2022, pp. 3–7). In turn, quasi-militant democracy covers attempts to expand the ruling elite's scope and power competencies while reducing a nation's political sovereignty (Bäcker, 2020). This approach differentiates between the real intentions of democracy enemies and defenders of democracy; the author used this to determine which measures may be classified as quasi-militant democracy. Max Steuer's conclusions about militant democracy in the Czech Republic confirmed the applicability of this distinction in exploring modern political structures. He pointed out that anti-minority rhetoric and the normalisation of some forms of hate speech in the public discourse were crucial factors of the ANO party's success (Steuer, 2019, p. 201), an example of quasi-militant democracy. However, the author will analytically expand on the problem of using anti-democratic measures, which reduced the political nation's sovereignty. To sum up, quasi-militant democracy means reducing the political nation's independence. In turn, neo-militant democracy instruments do not diminish that sovereignty. In both analysed anti-pandemic approaches, only quasi-militant democracy means materialised. However, from September 2020 to May 2021, these instruments became a core of dealing with the pandemic in the Czech Republic.

The current academic works and NGO reports pointed out that the main factors threatening democratic institutions included widespread corruption and nepotism in the state administration, media dependence on businesspersons and politicians, increased anti-immigrant sentiment, lack of representation of the Roma minority at the level of central authorities, and the growing popularity of populist rhetoric (Kopeček, 2015; Kopeček, 2016; Kopeček, 2018). A similar opinion was expressed by Czech political scientists that considered ineffective technocratic governance, corruption, clientelism, and economic stagnation as conducive to de-democratisation (Dvořáková, 2012; Fiala, 2010; Kubát, 2013; Klima, 2015; Pehe, 2010; Švihlíková, 2015). Seán Hanley and Milada Anna Vachudova called changes within the Czech political structure an illiberal turn (Hanley & Vachudova, 2018). Their studies drew on the empirical analysis of the government's decision. In contrast, the author will analyse this phenomenon in the context of militant democracy and expand the time framework after the coronavirus crisis outbreak. Moreover, last month's scholarships published several articles about the consequences of the political and social structure of authorities' response to the COVID-19 pandemic in Europe (Buštíková & Baboš, 2020; Guasti, 2020a; Guasti, 2020b). The illiberal turn as a challenge for liberal democracy in the pandemic era was noted by Petra Guasti, who pointed out that it was an opportunity for the populists in the government to consolidate power. The coronavirus crisis gave populist leaders the ability to bypass checks and balances. Emergency measures strengthen the executive power, weaken parliamentary oversight, and suspend certain rights and liberties (Guasti, 2020a).

The first months of the pandemic in Czechia were discussed in detail, but this chapter refers to some articles where authors focus on the efficiency of the anti-pandemic policy. Several commentators, including in the international media, have called Czechs' experiences proof of "success". However, some Czech scholars formulated critical remarks on the anti-pandemic strategy. David Špaček argued "that at the beginning of the pandemic, the country was not sufficiently prepared for COVID-19 on planning, organisational or financial levels" (Špaček, 2020, p. 267). Despite that critical conclusion, he pointed out that "Czech politicians and public administration on all levels and also the society learnt clear and important lessons in a month, a relatively short time frame" and recommended continuing the *smart quarantine* approach (Špaček, 2020, p. 268). Therefore, he pointed out that the timing of public policy responses is a critical factor in dealing with the pandemic, which other scholars confirmed (Chubarova et al., 2020, p. 69). The fast and comprehensive anti-pandemic measures realised by the Czech and Slovak governments and the citizens' compliance with these measures were the recipe for success in Spring 2020.

However, before early Autumn, both countries functioned in relaxed regimes, introduced in early Summer when COVID-19 almost disappeared. In October 2020, the Czech Republic was one of the leading countries worldwide in the relative spread of COVID-19 infections (Nemec et al., 2020, p. 13). Other remarks concerned local governments. Their leaders' responses to the pandemic crisis depended on decentralisation, financial condition, administrative capacity, regulatory framework, and path dependency. Michal Plaček, David Špaček, and František Ochrana pointed out two different strategies. Firstly, municipal activism increases citizens' confidence in local governments and creates optimistic expectations among its citizens, thanks to stabilising the local economy and maintaining social cohesion. In turn, municipal passivism seeks primarily to continue fiscal discipline to maintain essential functions in the longer term. However, it led to lower confidence in the public sector. Their main conclusion is that lack of effective coordination between the central government and municipal actions, the complicated and bureaucratic administrative setting did not allow local authorities to make decisions to devise the optimal reaction strategy in a short response time (Plaček et al., 2020, p. 115). Luděk Berec's research team offered a complex view of the pandemic's beginning. They remarked that a local lockdown might reduce the number of cases more effectively than a state-wide one if the number of confirmed cases is not exceedingly high. However, personal protective measures, like face masks and increased hygiene, are more effective than reducing contact (Berec et al., 2020).

In sum, international experts formulated positive remarks about dealing with the pandemic during the Spring of 2020, while domestic researchers presented some critical and more detailed observations. The latter's calls to improve local authorities and continue *smart quarantine* to avoid strict national lockdowns were ignored. In this chapter, the author proves that the ruling elites ignored most of these opinions by changing anti-pandemic policy, significantly impacting the political nation's sovereignty.

Materials and methods

In this chapter, the circumstances of these decisions and their consequences for the functioning of the Czech democracy will be presented. Qualitative analysis of sources (legal acts, media content, and NGO reports) was used to examine official documents, politicians' statements, and legislation acts. Another method is process tracing to explore the phenomenon of dealing with pandemics and changes in anti-pandemic policy. The author's scientific approach included three steps: operarationalising of the research tool, collection and selection of sources, data analysis, and formulating conclusions. Firstly, based on the literature review, he referred to the theory of militant democracy and papers about the efficiency of anti-pandemic policy to prepare theses about the role of quasi-militant democracy means in dealing with the pandemic. Next, the author collected a national database of laws about limiting the nation's political sovereignty and media content about the coronavirus crisis in the Czech Republic. Finally, conclusions about the role of quasi-militant democracy measures in different pandemic strategies were formulated. In the research process, the author hypothesised that protecting fundamental political rights is conditioned by adopting a specific pandemic strategy. Different anti-pandemic approaches depend, among others, on the scale of cooperation between public officers and experts, the ruling elites' style of governance, and the level of the political nation's sovereignty. The case of Czechia provides evidence of a qualitative change in this regard due to the abandonment of *smart quarantine* in favour of a hard lockdown.

David Špaček classified anti-pandemic measures, forced in Spring 2020, into the following groups: (1) restrictions on citizens' rights, (2) restrictions on services (public and private), (3) restrictions on private services, (4) public administration obligations, and (5) economic measures (Špaček, 2020, p. 262). However, the author decided to refer to Joanna Rak and Roman Bäcker's proposition for analysing a political nation's sovereignty at the following pools: (1) the freedom of a political nation to make sovereign decisions, (2) the range of alternatives for selecting decision scenarios by a political nation, (3) the level of rationality of a political nation's deliberation before making decisions, and (4) institutions guaranteeing the sustainability of this sovereignty, generating situational compulsion precluding a political nation from straying off the path of sovereignty and democracy (Rak & Bäcker, 2022). Their proposition is more valid in analysing the level of protection of certain rights and freedoms. Based on them, the author examines which anti-pandemic measures influence the mentioned pools to verify which strategy reduced the political nation's sovereignty more. In his research, the author refers to data shared by Our World in Data and its COVID-19 Stringency Index. Those from the first year of the pandemic in Czechia allow him to divide this duration into two sub-periods, with a turning point in September 2020, when the state authorities re-adopted strict anti-pandemic policy. The main difference between these two sub-periods is a dominant approach to deal with the coronavirus crisis. After the success, in experts' opinions, of the first wave of the pandemic, thanks to mixing strict measures with technological achievements, in the Autumn of 2020, there was a change in the direction. It resulted from the Prime Minister's decisions in the Summer, which are discussed further in this chapter. However, these data did not include changes in political structure, like adopting an unconstitutional state of emergency, so the author decided to fulfil them by qualitative analysis of sources. Referring to other sources, like media content about the governing style and official reports about implemented measures, it is necessary to prove these changes.

Spring 2020 and smart quarantine

At the beginning of March 2020, in the face of a new pandemic challenge, Czechia adopted strict preventive measures after about a hundred cases of the infection were registered in the country. The Czech anti-pandemic policy complied with international practice in this regard, and on 12 March 2020, 11 days after the first three cases were confirmed, the country's parliament declared a state of emergency (Usnesení č. 194/2020 Sb). Before introducing it, all cultural and sports events of up to 100 people were cancelled; direct flights to China and South Korea were suspended. The next step was closing all types of schools. According to the Constitution (Constitutional Act No. 110/1998 Coll.), the Czech Republic's government is responsible for declaring a state of emergency by its resolution. On 1 April, the government asked the Chamber to extend the state of emergency by another 30 days. This was approved on 7 April, but only until 30 April. In May, the opposition did not accept prolonging the state of emergency. They argued that over-extending it was economically unsustainable, and they could not submit bills due to the procedure for voting on the plenary session agenda. Despite being legally enforced, a state of emergency should be classified as a quasi-militant democracy measure. The government decided to reduce political sovereignty to protect public health and order. The possibility of resisting these measures and undermining the legitimacy of a state of emergency was minimal, and the circumstances of spreading coronavirus suggested adopting fast responses. The possibility of resisting measures adopted during the state of emergency was minimal.

Moreover, the circumstances of the spreading coronavirus suggested giving a fast response, which legitimised governance by resolutions. One of the first decisions was to postpone supplementary polls to the Senate (Usnesení Vlády České Republiky ze dne 15. března 2020 č. 218). Finally, this election was held on 2–3 and 9–10 (second rounds) in October 2020 alongside the regional polls. The state authorities stopped holding elections in the sanitary regime to postpone them. This decision abused the core of the political nation's sovereignty, that is the right to vote and the right to be voted, and interfered with the constitutional procedure of election.

Stricter measures for certain rights and freedoms were applied since 16 March 2020, when the state authorities prohibited the free movement of people, except for travelling to work and necessary journeys to family or hospital, banned entry to the territory of the Czech Republic, and leaving the territory for Czechia citizens (Resolution of the Government of The Czech Republic no. 203 of 13 March 2020, no. 203). The right to hold public gatherings was banned, too. There is no doubt that these measures, as a response to the COVID-19 pandemic, reduced the level of the political nation's sovereignty to minimise social contact. Despite reasons for adopting rules to guarantee social distance, political contentions cannot be efficient without public manifestation of freedoms, which is a kind of direct participation in the public sphere, among others, to undermine government policy. At the same time, the Czech public administration developed tools to minimalise the consequences of the coronavirus crisis, primarily through close cooperation with the IT sector to detect new coronavirus cases. *Smart quarantine* fixes limits on certain rights and freedoms and closes collaboration with experts to implement digital innovation in public administration. One of the initiatives was covid19cz.cz, an official website to inform about detected infection outbreaks. Those efforts sought to prevent the lockdown's unwanted effects and deal quickly with the pandemic (Kouřil & Ferenčuhová, 2020). It was an opportunity to reduce the risk of the rapid growth of new infections without limiting certain rights and freedoms domestically.

Returning to changes within pools of the nation's political sovereignty, the character of the parliament's work will be discussed. In that place, it is worth pointing out that the opposition criticised the government for not acting earlier. At the end of January 2020, the former demanded a debate on the government's coronavirus measures, but the Chamber did not allow it. In March, the parliament had to reorganise its activities and reduce sessions, and as was mentioned before, Babiš's cabinet started governing by resolution. These decisions were essential to avoid legislative bodies and an opposition majority in the Senate by ruling elites in the decision-making process. It should be classified as a quasi-militant democracy means due to the reduced impact on democratic decisions by members of parliament, that is the representatives of the political nation. In the face of attempts to concentrate power by the government, the opposition unified and forced the government not to re-authorise the state of emergency in May 2020, when the number of new confirmed cases decreased. Earlier, a group of senators announced the intention to bring the travel ban to constitutional review, which resulted in the government abandoning these restrictions.

Moreover, members of the Senate started preparing a complaint to the Constitutional Court but ultimately stopped it. These examples show that the opposition's actions in emergency conditions put adequate pressure on Babiš's cabinet to limit the political nation's sovereignty violations. Crucial for maintaining a proper level of the political nation's sovereignty in a democratic society during the pandemic is the possibility of undermining forced restrictions. In April 2020, the Prague municipal court recognised four emergency measures, including limiting freedom of movement, travel ban, and compulsory closure of large shops, which are illegal. However, the Prime Minister did not recognise that judgement. This decision challenged the pandemic-driven measures of quasi-militant democracy. It confirmed that the independence of the judiciary during the "first wave" was not endangered by political pressures.

Limiting the nation's political sovereignty during the first wave of coronavirus in Czechia had consequences for freedom of the press. Dire conditions for independent media in Czechia resulted from the buying of leading entities by Babiš's company in 2013. The Prime Minister used partisan media in political competition by putting pressure on journalists and media workers. Some independent journalists quit their jobs and started to run new outlets. In the Spring of 2020, the state authorities blocked access to public information about hospital issues for some journalists (Guasti, 2020b, p. 54), which limited freedom of the press and access to information. At the same time, disinformation campaigns on social media were getting stronger and more frequent. As a result, a large part of the Czech society believed that the pandemic was a lie, vaccination was just a way to control people or kill them, and death toll statistics were fictional or at least to a large extent manipulated. In Spring 2020, 17% of Czechs thought COVID-19 was not worse than the flu; 46% of the population did not consider it a threat (the Czech Republic is losing…, 2020). However, the government ran no counter-disinformation except a single communication campaign debunking disinformation or promoting vaccination. It did not aim to address false messages (the Czech Republic is losing…, 2020). This scale of misinformation about coronavirus decreased the rationality of a political nation's deliberation before making decisions because corona sceptics and anti-vaccination movement significantly impacted public opinion, which the data above confirmed. To sum up, restrictions against the nation's political sovereignty, adopted during the first way of the pandemic, may be classified into the pools as given in Table 6.1.

Autumn 2020–winter 2021

After a few months of pandemic situation stabilisation, in September 2020, the number of cases highly increased. In the face of the incoming "second wave", the government adopted restrictions again, including declaring a state of emergency

Table 6.1 Limited pools of the political nation's sovereignty by anti-pandemic measures during Spring 2020

Anti-pandemic measures forced (Spring 2020)	Limited pools of the political nation's sovereignty
State of emergency	The freedom of a political nation to make sovereign decisions; the range of alternatives for selecting decision scenarios by a political nation; institutions guaranteeing the sustainability of this sovereignty
Postponed supplementary elections to the Senate	The freedom of a political nation to make sovereign decisions; institutions guaranteeing the sustainability of this sovereignty
Changes in the schedule of parliamentary work	The range of alternatives for selecting decision scenarios by a political nation; institutions guaranteeing the sustainability of this sovereignty
Blocking access to public information	The freedom of a political nation to make sovereign decisions; the level of rationality of a political nation's deliberation before making decisions
Prohibiting the free movement of people	The freedom of a political nation to make sovereign decisions

on 5 October and restoring most of the measures well-known from "the Spring wave". Moreover, mass vaccination in Czechia started at the end of December 2020. In dealing with the second, more dramatic phase of the coronavirus crisis, the government focused chiefly on prolonging the extraordinary state. At first glance, there may be invisible changes compared with Spring 2020, considering the COVID-19 Stringency Index. However, in the middle of the Summer of 2020, Andrej Babiš decided to introduce significant changes in anti-pandemic governance. At the Strategic Forum in Slovenia in August 2020, he said "My profession is businessman, crisis manager (…) we have results, best in COVID" (Bled Strategic Forum, 2020). The high self-esteem of governing a state's response to the COVID-19 pandemic fits Babiš's guiding principle and technocratic political thoughts to run the state as a business. However, the death rate and number of cases at the beginning of 2021 showed that Babiš carried the matter too far.[1] The essential feature of the changes in dealing with the pandemic was quitting close cooperation with epidemiologists and the IT sector to concentrate power into the Prime Minister's hands.

The end of September 2020 was a turning point in dealing with the coronavirus crisis. In the face of rapidly growing new cases, the Prime Minister fired Adam Vojtech, the Health Minister. That decision started a period of instability in anti-pandemic policy. During the first year of the pandemic, Czechia had four Head of Health Ministry officers, which led to chaotic governance and a lack of stable and long-term solutions (Janicek, 2021). The decision to remove Vojtech was a symbol of the shifting Czech anti-pandemic policy into a more authoritarian style, where the decision centre is located around the Prime Minister, who did not want to develop digital innovations and hearing epidemiologists in order to concentrate power, according to technocratic style promoted by him. It was the first time collective actions transformed into civil disorder, leading to clashing with police officers (Skrzypek, 2023, p. 31).

The main instrument of dealing with the second wave was prolonging the state of emergency and re-adopting most restrictions from Spring 2020. However, these practices in the constitutional framework stopped in February 2021 when the Senate refused a request to extend it on 18 February 2021. In justification, deputies referred to the fact that the pandemic was not improving and the economic consequences of the lockdown might have ravaged domestic entrepreneurs. In response, the Czech government applied a new law, which allowed the Minister of Health to impose lockdown measures and restrict freedom of movement without a state of emergency (Vlada, 2021). They claimed this law would effectively address the dramatic pandemic situation (Czech MPs refuse, 2021; Czech Republic COVID restrictions, 2021). The government replaced the constitutional state of emergency with "a new-unconstitutional state of emergency" (Usnesení č. 96/2021). In fact, the Minister of Health achieved the extraordinary power competencies to implement restrictions without parliament's agreement. In practice, it reduced the opposition's opportunities to discuss and challenge strict measures. Expansion of power competencies by the government and the violations of liberal democracy rules (a tripartite division of power, legislation initiative for deputies, possibilities to refuse act drafts by parliament) took place. That decision was the apogee of using quasi-militant democracy means during the pandemic, emphasising attempts to replace the rule of law with prerogative state rules. Since 1 March 2021, it has been forbidden to leave a place of residence without a good reason, such as travel to work or see a doctor (Resolution of the Government of The Czech Republic of 26 February 2021, no. 216). This form of state of emergency was prolonged until 11 May 2021. To sum up, in the second analysed period, anti-pandemic measures may be classified in Table 6.2.

Table 6.2 Anti-pandemic measures in the second analysed period

Anti-pandemic measures forced (Autumn 2020–Winter 2021)	Limited pool of the political nation's sovereignty
State of emergency/unconstitutional state of emergency	The freedom of a political nation to make sovereign decisions; the range of alternatives for selecting decision scenarios by a political nation; institutions guaranteeing the sustainability of this sovereignty
Changes in the schedule of parliamentary work	The range of alternatives for selecting decision scenarios by a political nation; institutions guaranteeing the sustainability of this sovereignty
Prohibiting the free movement of people (i.e. banning public gatherings)	The freedom of a political nation to make sovereign decisions

Conclusions

Summing up, the Czech response to the coronavirus crisis transformed from *smart quarantine* into strict lockdown. Despite adopting more rigorous measures, the pandemic had worsened since September 2020. That change allowed the ruling elites to attempt autocratisation of the political structure by reducing the nation's political sovereignty. Moreover, despite the similar character of restrictions, their implementation had different scopes and consequences. The policy of limitations, which started in September 2020, depended on the Prime Minister's willingness. He literally ignored the statements of the nation's political representatives.

In contrast, during the "first wave", anti-pandemic measures had parliament legitimisation and were fixed by digital tools. Moreover, in Spring 2020, the timing of policy reactions was swift, while "the second wave" was characterised by long-term stringency, which the pandemic situation may explain. Another difference between the analysed periods is social mood and attitude towards official policy. In the Spring of 2020, public opinion supported the adopted approach when restrictions and other measures worked adequately. In turn, during the "second wave", a dramatic situation and one of the worst results in Europe led to untrust in anti-pandemic policy and the government's decisions. At the beginning of 2021, mistrust of Babiš's policy forced the Prime Minister to apologise for those conditions and promise to rescue public health. However, that statement did not change anything in public governance. He continued ruling the state as a company, a typical approach for technocratic populists. Analysed transformation failed, showing experts' analysis as limited and chaotic (Nemec & Maly, et al., 2021, p. 288). Finally, the mentioned experts and parliamentary majority were ignored by the ruling elites who sought to expand their power. These attempts at autocratisation, in the name of dealing with the pandemic, can be summarized in Table 6.3.

Table 6.3 Limited pools of the nation's political sovereignty by anti-pandemic measures during the first year of the coronavirus crisis

Pools of the political nation's sovereignty	Spring 2020 (*smart quarantine*)	Autumn 2020/Winter 2021 (Strict lockdown)
The freedom of a political nation to make sovereign decisions	State of emergency; banning public gatherings	State of emergency/ unconstitutional state of emergency; banning public gatherings
The range of alternatives for selecting decision scenarios by a political nation	Postponing supplementary elections to the Senate; changes in the schedule of parliamentary work	Changes in the schedule of parliamentary work
The level of rationality of a political nation's deliberation before making decisions	Lack of complex campaign to combat misinformation and fake news about coronavirus	
Institutions guaranteeing the sustainability of this sovereignty,	State of emergency	State of emergency/ unconstitutional state of emergency;

Czechia's experience delivered evidence that changes in anti-pandemic policy affected the scope of protecting certain rights and freedoms and public trust in the adopted strategy. Moving from one grand design to another led to a decrease in the political nation's sovereignty, even if the latter was not more efficient. It means that in the face of the worsening pandemic situation and the introduction of subsequent limitations of fundamental rights and freedoms, the change of strategy led to transforming collective actions into civil disorder. The latter was crucial for destroying the stability of the political regime. Therefore, changes in anti-pandemic policy might affect public opinion support for that style of government. In Czechia's case, growing dissatisfaction led to more frequent calls to withdraw the government during mass demonstrations. Lost public support may be the potential cost of changing anti-pandemic policy towards more authoritarian, even if the pandemic worsens.

Funding of financial support

This work was supported by the National Science Centre, Poland [grant number 2021/43/B/HS5/00290].

Note

1 By March 2021, the Czech Republic recorded the second-highest confirmed death rate in the world, after San Marino. The dramatic situation in the country impacted social mood.

Bibliography

Bäcker, R. (2020). Kategoria narodu politycznego. In J. Wojnicki, J. Miecznikowska, & Łukasz Zamęcki (Eds.), *Polska i Europa w perspektywie politologicznej. Księga jubileuszowa dedykowana profesorowi Konstantemu Adamowi Wojtaszczykowi z okazji 45-lecia pracy akademickiej* (pp. 35–46). Oficyna Wydawnicza ASPRA-JR.

Bäcker, R., & Rak, J. (2019). Trajektoria trwania opancerzonych demokracji. *Studia nad Autorytaryzmem i Totalitaryzmem*, *41*(3), 63–82. http://dx.doi.org/10.19195/2300-7249.41.3.5

Berec, L., Smycka, J., Levinsky, R., Hromádková, E., Soltes, M., Slerka, J., & Vidnerová, P. (2020). The COVID-19 epidemic in the Czech Republic: Retrospective analysis of measures (not) implemented during the spring first wave.

Bled Strategic Forum. (2020). *BSF 2020—Opening and leader's panel: Europe after Brexit and Covid-19*. https://livestream.com/zivo/bsf2020/videos/210474867

Bogaards, M. (2020). Militant consociational democracy: The political exclusion of the extreme right in Belgium. In *Compromises in democracy* (pp. 175–200). Palgrave Macmillan.

Bourne, A. K., & Casal Bértoa, F. (2017). Mapping militant Democracy': Variation in party ban practices in European democracies (1945–2015). *EuConst*, *13*, 221.

Buštíková, L., & Baboš, P. (2020). Best in covid: Populists in the time of pandemic. *Politics and Governance*, *8*(4), 496–508. https://doi.org/10.17645/pag.v8i4.3424

Chubarova, T., Maly, I., & Nemec, J. (2020). Public policy responses to the spread of COVID-19 as a potential factor determining health results, a comparative study of the Czech Republic, the Russian federation, and the Slovak Republic. *Central European Journal of Public Policy*, *14*(2), 60–70. https://doi.org/10.2478/cejpp-2020-0008

Constitutional Act No. 110/1998 Coll. https://www.zakonyprolidi.cz/cs/1998-110

Czech MPs Refuse to Extend the State of Emergency Despite Government Pleas. (2021). https://www.euronews.com/2021/02/12/czech-parliament-refuses-to-extend-the-state-
Czech Republic COVID Restrictions: PM Babiš defies MPs to Extend State of Emergency. (2021). https://www.euronews.com/2021/02/15/czech-republic-covid-restrictions-pm-Babiš-defies-mps-to-extend-state-of-emergency
Czech Republic is Losing the Information War, Experts Warn. (2020). https://www.euractiv.com/section/digital/news/czech-republic-is-losing-the-information-war-experts-warn
Dvořáková, Z. (2012). (ed.). Řízení lidských zdrojů, C.H. Beck.
Fiala, P. (2010). *Politika, jaká nemá být.* Brno.
Guasti, P. (2020a). Populism in power and democracy: Democratic decay and resilience in the Czech Republic (2013–2020). *Politics and Governance*, *8*(4), 473–484.
Guasti, P. (2020b). The impact of the covid-19 pandemic in Central and Eastern Europe: The rise of autocracy and democratic resilience. *Democratic Theory*, *7*(2), 47–60. https://doi.org/10.3167/dt.2020.070207
Hanley, S., & Vachudova, M. (2018). Understanding the illiberal turn: Democratic backsliding in the Czech Republic. *East European Politics*, *34*(3), 276–296. https://doi.org/10.1080/21599165.2018.1493457
Janicek, K. (2021). *4th Czech health minister resigns since start of pandemic.* https://apnews.com/article/europe-pandemics-coronavirus-pandemic-health-government-and-politics-ac1a2f335b6676abb6bbe2ac0c530fc0
Klima, M. (2015). *Od totality k defektní demokracii: Privatizace a kolonizace politických stran netransparentním byznysem.* Praga.
Kopeček, L. (2015). *Czech Republic.* https://freedomhouse.org/country/czech-republic/nations-transit/2015
Kopeček, L. (2016). *Czech Republic.* https://freedomhouse.org/country/czech-republic/nations-transit/2016
Kopeček, L. (2018). *Czech Republic.* https://freedomhouse.org/country/czech-republic/nations-transit/2018
Kouřil, P., & Ferenčuhová, S. (2020). Smart quarantine and blanket quarantine, the Czech response to the COVID-19 pandemic. *Eurasian Geography and Economics*, *61*(4–5), 587–597. https://doi.org/10.1080/15387216.2020.1783338
Kubát, M. (2013). *Současná česká politika: Co s neefektivním režimem?* Praga.
Nemec, J., Drechsler, W., & Hajnal, G. (2020). Public policy during COVID-19, challenges for public administration and policy research in Central and Eastern Europe. *The NISPAcee Journal of Public Administration and Policy*, *XIII*(2), 11–20. https://doi.org/10.2478/nispa-2020-0011
Nemec, J., Maly, I., & Chubarova, T. (2021). Policy responses to the COVID-19 pandemic and potential outcomes in Central and Eastern Europe: Comparing the Czech Republic, the Russian Federation, and the Slovak Republic. *Journal of Comparative Policy Analysis: Research and Practice*, *23*(2), 282–290. https://doi.org/10.1080/13876988.2021.1878884
Osiewicz, P., & Skrzypek, M. (2020). Is Spain becoming a militant democracy? Empirical evidence from freedom house reports. *Aportes. Revista de Historia Contemporánea*, *35*(103), 7–33.
Pehe, J. (2010). *Demokracie bez demokratů: Úvahy o společnosti a polityce.* Praga.
Plaček, M., Špaček, D., & Ochrana, F. (2020). Public leadership and strategies of Czech municipalities during the COVID-19 pandemic–municipal activism vs municipal passivism. *International Journal of Public Leadership*, *17*(1), 108–117.
Rak, J. (2020a). Conceptualising the theoretical category of neo-militant democracy: The case of Hungary. *Polish Political Science Yearbook*, *49*(2), 61–70. https://doi.org/10.15804/ppsy2020204
Rak, J. (2020b). Quasi-militant democracy as a new form of sacred in Poland during the corona crisis. *Journal for the Study of Religions and Ideologies*, *19*(57), 111–128.

Rak, J., & Bäcker, R. (2022). *Neo-militant democracies in post-communist member states of the European union*. Routledge.

Resolution of the Government of The Czech Republic no. 203 of 13 March 2020, no. 203. https://www.mvcr.cz/mvcren/file/resolution-of-governemnt-of-the-czech-republic-of-march-13th-2020-no-203-on-the-adoption-of-a-crisis-measure-594585.aspx

Resolution of the Government of The Czech Republic of 26 February 2021, no. 216 on the adoption of crisis measures. https://www.mvcr.cz/mvcren/article/coronavirus-information-of-moi.aspx

Skrzypek, M. (2020). The banning of extremist political parties as a measures of neo-militant democracy: The experience of post-communist States. *HAPSc Policy Briefs Series*, *1*(2), 67–73.

Skrzypek, M. (2022). Between neo-militant and quasi-militant democracy: Restrictions on freedoms of speech and the press in Austria, Finland, and Sweden 2008–2019. *European Politics and Society*. https://doi.org/10.1080/23745118.2022.2063229

Skrzypek, M. (2023). From collective action to civil disorder: A comparative analysis of pandemic-ridden Czechia and Slovakia. *Studia Securitas*, *2*, 26–37.

Špaček, D. (2020). COVID-19 – National government approach in the Czech Republic. In P. Joyce, F. Maron, & P. S. Reddy (Eds.), *Good public governance in a global pandemic*. The International Institute of Administrative Sciences.

Steuer, M. (2019). Militant democracy on the rise: Consequences of legal restrictions on extreme speech in the Czech Republic, Slovakia and Hungary. *Review of Central and East European Law*, *44*(2), 162–201.

Švihlíková, I. (2015). *Jak jsme se stali kolonii*. Praga.

Tyulkina, S. (2015). Militant democracy: An alien concept for Australian constitutional law. *Adelaide Law Review*, *36*, 517–539.

Usnesení č. 194/2020 Sb. https://www.zakonyprolidi.cz/cs/2020-194

Usnesení č. 96/2021 Sb. https://www.zakonyprolidi.cz/cs/2021-96

Usnesení Vlády České Republiky ze dne 15. března 2020 č. 218. https://www.zakonyprolidi.cz/cs/2020-88

Vlada. (2021). The government declares state of emergency until 28 March, free movement and retail rules to be tightened from Monday, schools to close again. https://www.vlada.cz/en/media-centrum/aktualne/the-government-declares-state-of-emergency-until-28-march–free-movement-and-retail-rules-to-be-tightened-from-monday–schools-to-close-again-187038/

7 Is Obligatory Vaccination Against COVID-19 Acceptable from the Human Rights Perspective?

Tomasz Litwin

Introductory remarks

The COVID-19 pandemic caused the death of more than 6 million people worldwide (Covid-19 WHO, 2022). This disease is regarded as severe, possibly leading to death, and also very infectious. Even after being recognised as cured, many individuals infected by the SARS-CoV-2 virus suffer from long-term adverse effects. The pandemic forced governments to introduce *lockdowns* that limited rights and freedoms and worsened the economic situation of individuals and states.

Vaccination against COVID-19, easily accessible in Western countries, is universally recognised as the only method to limit the possibility of infection and the dangerous effects of the disease. However, less than 70% of the population in many countries is fully immunised. This could shortly result in an increasing number of infections and deaths caused by the pandemic and lead to another series of *lockdowns* worldwide. The main aim to diminish the above-mentioned possible effects of the following "wave" of the illness is to vaccinate the possibly most extensive number of people. Not immunised individuals cause threats not only for themselves, as they could be easily infected and heavily suffer from the disease, but they could also infect many others.

However, those who contest inoculation justify their approach by using arguments based on internationally recognised human rights:

- the obligatory vaccination is against the principle of inviolable dignity and personal freedom connected with the right to protect private life and freedom of thought and conscience;
- the vaccines are unsafe because they were not adequately checked during scientific research, so compulsory immunisation should be prohibited, forcing an individual to participate in medical experimentation.

This chapter is based on the hypothesis that although the above arguments of the opponents of vaccination against COVID-19 are serious, obligatory immunisation as the only effective measure encouraging more people to get inoculated, necessary to gain herd immunity would still be in accordance with human rights. The chapter is written from the perspective of legal science and uses judgements and literature as sources.

DOI: 10.4324/9781003482710-8

The possible obligatory vaccination against COVID-19 – detail analysis

The scientific sources confirm two basic facts about different experiences of COVID-19 by vaccinated and unvaccinated individuals. Those who have been inoculated are better protected from being infected with COVID-19. This fact also leads to the conclusion that there is a lesser chance that an immunised person will infect other individuals. Another critical point is that when vaccinated individuals get infected, they mostly have only light symptoms of the disease; sometimes, they may not even experience any symptoms. They generally need to rest at home for approximately two weeks and do not require hospital care (WHO Emergencies, 2022). Since the infected yet vaccinated individuals typically have light or no symptoms, a hypothesis could be presented that they would unleash fewer viruses into the environment. An infected person releases many viruses when sneezing and coughing (Borak, 2020, pp. 297–299). Therefore, it seems that vaccinated individuals, even when contracting COVID-19, will potentially infect fewer people than unvaccinated ones.

The generally light course of COVID-19 in inoculated people is crucial because severe cases of the disease require hospital treatment, often using respirators. The number of such devices is limited even in the Western states. Infections concerning a considerable number of unimmunised individuals will result in relatively many severe cases of the disease, requiring hospital treatment using respirators. Such circumstances could lead to the situation that because of the lack of such equipment, numerous unvaccinated patients will die because appropriate medical assistance will be impossible. Moreover, it seems conceivable that the health sector, even using extraordinary measures, will be unable to handle it in such a situation. This could also result in the total collapse of the health sector or in focusing only on the medical treatment of COVID-19 cases and neglecting patients with other severe diseases such as cancer or diseases requiring transplantation of organs who, because of that, would not receive appropriate medical treatment. In such a critical situation, the governments have no other solutions to limit the number of infections than introducing *lockdowns* with already known side effects: a global and country-level economic crisis also concerning families.

In most Western countries, voluntary vaccination started at the beginning of 2021. However, the results are not satisfactory. In many Western states, such as the United States and countries of Central-Eastern Europe, the immunisation rate in the population is below 70% (Covid-19 WHO, 2022), a value necessary for obtaining herd immunity at vaccine efficacy of at least 80% (Tetteh et al., 2020, p. 1). This lack of population immunity could result in the next wave of the pandemic with all its consequences.

It seems that only compulsory vaccination could encourage more people to get inoculated. Two types of sanctions could accompany it. The first one should be a fine imposed on nonimmunised individuals. The second one should limit the right to enter indoor public spaces or places of entertainment, such as libraries, museums, pubs, restaurants, cinemas, theatres, among others, only for vaccinated individuals. It should be mentioned that visiting such places is only leisure, not a necessity for life; hence, such sanction cannot be regarded as harassment. The required immunisation would not concern the individuals who should not be vaccinated because of health issues.

Compulsory immunisation is nowadays a part of healthcare policies in many countries. Generally, it concerns children with their parents or legal representatives being responsible for its accomplishment. Moreover, not undertaking the vaccination could result in a penalty sentence. Sometimes, the sanctions also concern not inoculated children; for example they cannot attend preschool education.

In some Western countries (France (French Government), 2022 and Denmark (Coronasmitte, 2022)), the state authorities were trying to force people not vaccinated against COVID-19 to immunise by introducing regulations that were not allowing such people to visit publicly accessible indoor spaces. Vaccinated individuals entering such areas showed their paper or digital certificate of inoculation. People who are not fully immunised could have temporary access to those locations only after presenting a valid negative test for COVID-19.

In the United States, unvaccinated individuals working for federal administration faced unpaid suspension, and then their employment relationship was terminated (Bloomberg, 2022).

In Indonesia, anyone who refused to get inoculated could face consequences such as denial of social assistance or government services, or they may be fined. The penalty was determined by regional health agencies or by local governments (Reuters, 2022).

Stringent steps against the COVID-19 pandemic were taken in Austria. A temporary *lockdown* was in force from 22 November until 13 December 2021. Moreover, proof of complete vaccination or recovery was necessary to enter public places after the *lockdown*. Valid negative COVID-19 tests (PCR and antigen) only no longer allowed to enter such areas (Austria Info, 2022). However, in 2022, there was a plan to send a special invitation for immunisation to not vaccinated individuals, and on those who would not be inoculated after 1 February 2022, a fine of €3,600 (around $4,000) will be imposed; a penalty of €1,500 will also be imposed on those who refuse to take the booster shot of COVID-19 vaccine (Bloomberg vaccine fine, 2022; Time, 2022).

In Singapore, free hospital treatment for COVID-19 did not privilege unvaccinated individuals. Individuals who required such treatment and were not immunised were forced to cover the costs (Fortune, 2022).

The arguments against obligatory vaccination

In the public debate, we can find many arguments against COVID-19 vaccination. However, only a few have authentic evidence, while most are irrational conspiracy theories.

The opponents of compulsory COVID-19 vaccination claim that:

1. They do not trust the government, so they will not get inoculated because governments organise COVID-19 vaccination;
2. Vaccines are dangerous to health;

3 COVID-19 does not exist or is not dangerous to health;
4 They have freedom of choice, and they choose not to be immunised;
5 Vaccination is a method of implanting some "micro-devices" (chips) to control people;
6 Pharmaceutical companies created the COVID-19 virus and vaccines;
7 "Natural methods" of protection against the disease are better than vaccines;
8 The vaccines against COVID-19 do not actually exist or do not work;
9 The vaccines have not been adequately tested; they were developed too quickly; an example is the swiftly developed swine-flu vaccine, which has had many adverse effects (e.g. narcolepsy);
10 No one is responsible for the vaccine's potential side/adverse effects (Wawrzuta et al., 2021, p. 5).

From the human rights perspective, argument no. 4 seems well grounded, as compulsory immunisation could be considered not in accordance with inviolable dignity and personal freedom connected with the right to protect private life and freedom of thought and conscience. Every person has the right to decide what to do with their body freely, and no one can be forced to treat their body in a way they do not want to. It is also only a private decision of every person how to treat their body. All these general considerations influence, naturally, individual choices on vaccination. Moreover, every person has the right to be against immunisation and publicly present their view. This right is also connected with living according to personal convictions. Therefore, being or not being inoculated is considered a personal issue that should be protected from public information.

Other arguments no. 2, 7, 9–11 could be developed regarding the immunisation against COVID-19 as a medical experiment in which only people who freely agree upon it could participate. The vaccination against COVID-19 should be regarded as a medical experiment for three reasons. Firstly, some adverse side effects of the procedure are not publicly known. Secondly, not all stages of medical research on COVID-19 vaccines are completed. Thirdly, not enough time has passed from starting the immunisation to consider it safe.

In a case before the US Supreme Court that was rejected for legal reasons, the applicants regarded compulsory vaccination against COVID-19 as offending their religious feelings. According to them, the vaccines developed by Johnson & Johnson required the use of abortion-related human cells. Moderna and Pfizer used abandoned fetal cell lines to come about with their vaccines. Such a connection between vaccines and the cells of aborted human fetuses violates the principles of their faith (John Does et al. v. Janet T. Mills, 2021).

Arguments supporting obligatory vaccination

Although the arguments presented above seem vital, compulsory vaccination against COVID-19 is still justified mainly through protecting public health.

From the human rights perspective, the author agrees that involvement in a medical experiment requires the consent of the person who participates in it

(Constantin, 2018, p. 143). However, he cannot entirely agree with the statement that vaccination for COVID-19 should be treated as such.

Only one profound adverse effect of COVID-19 vaccination was reported by medical sources: thrombosis. However, at present, patients at risk of thrombosis could be excluded from the immunisation based on the medical interview conducted before vaccination (Bilotta et al., 2021, pp. 1–13). According to circulating gossip or unofficial reports, some people suffered from various undesirable symptoms after inoculation – some of them could be true. Still, there is no proof that "undesirable symptoms" were caused by the COVID-19 vaccine – those symptoms could have had a coincidental character.

All stages of research on COVID-19 vaccines, including the most popular vaccine, BioNtech-Pfizer, are completed. The last phase of the clinical trial was finalised in January 2021 (Pfizer, 2022). The BioNtech-Pfizer vaccine was also officially accepted by the EU (EMA, 2022), Great Britain, and US special regulatory agencies controlling drugs and vaccines (Pfizer, 2022). Therefore, COVID-19 immunisation using the BioNtech-Pfizer vaccine cannot be regarded as participation in a medical experiment.

The vaccination cannot be treated as a violation of dignity. Generally, this procedure does not differ from other such activities. It is not painful; it does not leave any physical marks; it does not have any psychological impact on the inoculated person; it lasts less than a minute (from the moment of inserting the needle); it does not have any long-term effects on the body of the vaccinated person. It requires showing only the arm, so it does not infringe on intimacy. The final decision on immunisation remains with the particular individual, as the sanctions could only encourage one to get inoculated. Still, the person is not forced to use violence to do it. The primary purpose of vaccination is to protect the life and health of the inoculated person; another goal concerns safeguarding the life and health of other people. It cannot be regarded as some measure of imposing power on the individual by the state or a method of cruel treatment of the individual. As previously mentioned, the compulsory immunisation of children has been practised for many years in the Western states and has not raised doubts from the human rights perspective.[1]

The required COVID-19 vaccination does not oppose the freedom of conscience, as opponents of this procedure can still publicly criticise it. Moreover, being "forced" to vaccinate can be the basis of an appeal to the national or international courts. Compulsory immunisation could also be regarded as better protecting the privacy of conscience and views. If we know that someone is not inoculated, when there is a choice to be so or not, we could suppose that this person is against vaccination. However, more possible solutions exist for such cases when the procedure is obligatory and an individual is inoculated. A person could be a supporter of immunisation. Still, this person could also be against vaccination but decided to get inoculated to avoid the fine and to have the right to enter pubs, theatres, cinemas, etc.

The obligatory vaccination against COVID-19 could be regarded as an infringement of personal freedom connected with the right to protect private life. Generally, a person should have complete autonomy in deciding what to do with their body. The threat of a fine or limitation of the possibility of visiting broadly regarded public places of entertainment undermines this autonomy. However, it is justified by the reason of protection of public health.

Protecting public health is one accepted reason for limiting the individual's rights and freedoms. It focuses on safeguarding the health of many people or even the whole of society. This reason comes from the assumption that the individual, by using his/her rights and freedoms, cannot endanger the health and, consequently, the life of others (Jacobson v. Massachusetts, 1905, 30, and following).

As previously mentioned, COVID-19 should be regarded as a severe threat to the health and life of many individuals. Moreover, this disease is very infectious. The vaccination, which is now easily accessible on the social scale, protects not only vaccinated individuals but also others, as the inoculated ones are less vulnerable to infection; they are thus less likely to be the source of infection. Obligatory vaccination seems to be the only way to encourage more people to get immunised effectively. Vaccinating the largest possible number of individuals is also essential to protect people who cannot be inoculated. Therefore, compulsory vaccination against COVID-19 is justified by public health reasons (Vavricka et al. v Czech Republic, 2021, pp. 272–288 paras).

The opposition against COVID-19 vaccination cannot be explained by religious conviction. First of all, Moderna and Pfizer's vaccines were produced without using human cells (Health, 2022). Moreover, religious leaders are not against COVID-19 vaccination, and Pope Francis seems to regard it as a moral obligation (Ncroonline, 2022). Personal views, even based on religion, also cannot justify, in this case, the refusal of the vaccination, as it protects the life and health of the inoculated individuals and the health and life of others. The democratic state, which seems to be the only form of state that guarantees the appropriate level of protection of human rights and freedoms, is a state that is neutral concerning the worldview of its citizens. It cannot privilege (or discriminate) the citizens because of their religious convictions. These convictions cannot justify omitting the public obligations that concern all citizens. Therefore, if there seems to be a broad acceptance of the view that religious beliefs are not explaining, for example not paying taxes (Taylor, 2005, pp. 153–156) or not fastening the seatbelts, religious convictions also cannot justify the refusal of immunisation. The protection of the health and life of others by vaccination against COVID-19 does not require a lot of commitment from an individual. It is clearly more important than the preservation of religious feelings, doubtful in this case.

The compulsory COVID-19 vaccination also protects other rights and freedoms, especially those in danger because of *lockdowns*, which for the governments seem to be the only alternative to mass immunisation to protect the health and life of the citizens. Such infringements of rights concern the right to work and freedom of economic activity because some professional activities were prohibited or limited during the *lockdowns*. In Poland, for example hotels and fitness clubs were closed during the *lockdowns*, and the restaurants could serve only takeaway meals. One of the aspects of the right to work is the obligation of state authorities to protect individuals from unemployment. The state authorities should care for the existing and create new jobs (positive actions). They should also avoid the actions (negative actions) that support the growth of unemployment (Collins, 2015, pp. 23–24, 37). Therefore, the *lockdowns* should be regarded as situations that state authorities should avoid.

By the freedom of economic activity, the author means the right derived from one of the aspects of the right to work – "the right to free choice of employment or occupation". This right "consists at least of the freedom of each individual to pursue an occupation of his or her choice without unjustified restrictions". The term "occupation" in this context should be understood broadly and can be exercised in the form of employment or self-employment (Collins, 2015, p. 18, 21–22). The conception of this right could be developed as the prohibition of imposing an unjustified restriction on exercising the job chosen and gained by the individual. The *lockdown* when, for example a restaurant whose owner is not allowed to open is such a restriction, but it seems to be justified by protecting public health and the lives of others. However, the *lockdown* limiting the described right would not account for the case of mass immunisation leading to herd immunity.

Another right infringed on by the lockdowns concerns education when children and students are forced into online teaching. Such tuition is less effective and limits social interactions, harming children and even adult students. Therefore, online teaching does not ensure the appropriate quality of education, which is one of the aspects of the right to it (Beiter, 2006, p. 477, 627).

Final remarks

COVID-19 is a severe and very infectious disease causing millions of deaths worldwide and responsible for the global economic crisis, which endangered or sometimes ruined the lives of many people.

The easily accessible vaccination is the only effective medical way to protect an individual from this disease. Mass immunisation also seems to be the only effective way to create protection for society. Unfortunately, the voluntary inoculation system is ineffective in fighting the COVID-19 pandemic because insufficient people get vaccinated. Compulsory immunisation has become the only method of encouraging more individuals to do it.

However, the opponents of vaccination against COVID-19 presented diverse arguments against it. Many of them are irrational, and only two require consideration from the human rights perspective. The first one is that this vaccination is a sort of medical experiment, and the second one is that obligatory vaccination violates the human dignity connected with personal freedom and the right to protect private life. Both arguments are wrong. The most popular vaccine, BioNtech-Pfizer, was appropriately tested and checked, and it was allowed to be used by medical product control offices in the European Union, United States, and other Western countries. The protection of public health also justifies required immunisation, which is a broadly accepted reason accounting for the limitation of human rights and freedoms.

Therefore, vaccination against COVID-19 should have become obligatory in many countries to protect society's life and health. From the perspective of 2024, the COVID-19 pandemic already seems to be an increasingly distant memory. However, it should be remembered that this disease has not been eliminated, and the SARS-CoV-2 virus is still mutating into various forms. It cannot be excluded that some of its future variants may prove to be very dangerous. Moreover, the COVID-19 pandemic might not be the last one in the 21st century, and vaccines can again be the best way to combat its effects. Unfortunately, the anti-vaccine movement, which is becoming increasingly popular in Western societies, threatens to spread an irrational fear of vaccines. Consequently, the social effects of the next pandemic can be even worse than those of the last one. Moreover, dangerous diseases such as measles, which seemed to have been eliminated thanks to vaccines, are returning. All these considerations should also start the reflection on whether, apart from paying taxes, inoculation against different diseases should become a legal obligation for individuals in the democratic state.

Note

1 In the book that discusses in detail many sorts of violations of human dignity there is no comment concerning the obligatory vaccination, see: (Kaufmann et al., 2010, p. 1 and next).

Bibliography

Internet sites

Retrieved June 30, 2022, from https://covid19.who.int/

Retrieved June 30, 2022, from https://en.coronasmitte.dk/corona-passport

Retrieved June 30, 2022, from https://fortune.com/2021/11/09/singapore-covid-unvaccinated-free-health-care/

Retrieved June 30, 2022, from https://news.bloomberglaw.com/daily-labor-report/unvaccinated-federal-workers-to-face-unpaid-leave-termination

Retrieved June 30, 2022, from https://time.com/6123087/austria-covid-19-vaccine-mandate-protests/

Retrieved June 30, 2022, from https://www.austria.info/en/service-and-facts/coronavirus-information

Retrieved June 30, 2022, from https://www.bloomberg.com/news/articles/2021-11-22/vaccine-holdouts-face-4-000-fine-in-austria-s-virus-crackdown

Retrieved June 30, 2022, from https://www.ema.europa.eu/en/medicines/human/EPAR/comirnaty#authorisation-details-section

Retrieved June 30, 2022, from https://www.gouvernement.fr/info-coronavirus/pass-sanitaire

Retrieved June 30, 2022, from https://www.health.nd.gov/sites/www/files/documents/COVID%20Vaccine%20Page/COVID-19_Vaccine_Fetal_Cell_Handout.pdf

Retrieved June 30, 2022, from https://www.ncronline.org/news/vatican/pope-francis-suggests-people-have-moral-obligation-take-coronavirus-vaccine

Retrieved June 30, 2022, from https://www.pfizer.com/science/coronavirus/vaccine/about-our-landmark-trial

Retrieved June 30, 2022, from https://www.pfizer.com/science/coronavrus/vaccine/about-our-landmark-trial

Retrieved June 30, 2022, from https://www.reuters.com/article/health-coronavirus-indonesia-vaccines-idUSL4N2KO1ZD

Retrieved June 30, 2022, from https://www.who.int/emergencies/diseases/novel-coronavirus-2019/covid-19-vaccines/advice

Judgements

Jacobson v. Massachusetts, 197 US 11 (1905).
Vavřička and Others v. the Czech Republic Applications nos. 47621/13 and 5 others, Merits and Just Satisfaction, 8 April 2021.
US Supreme Court JOHN DOES 1–3, ET AL. v. JANET T. MILLS, GOVERNOR OF MAINE, ET AL. 595 U. S. (2021).

Literature

Beiter, K. D. (2006). *The protection of the right to education by international law. including a systematic analysis of article 13 of the international covenant on economic, social and cultural rights*. Brill.
Bilotta, C., Perrone, G., Adelfio, V., Spatola, G. F., Uzzo, M. L., Argo, A., & Zerbo, S. (2021). COVID-19 vaccine related thrombosis: A systematic review and exploratory analysis. *Frontiers in Immunology*, *12*, 1–13. https://doi.org/10.3389/fimmu.2021.729251
Borak, J. (2020). Editorial. Airborne transmission of COVID-19. *Occupational Medicine*, *70*, 297–299.
Collins, H. (2015). Is there a human right to work? In V. Mantouvalou (Ed.), *The right to work. Legal and philosophical perspectives* (pp. 17–38). Hart Publishing.
Constantin, A. (2018). Human subject research: International and regional human rights standards. *Health and Human Rights Journal*, *20*(2), 137–148.
Covid-19 WHO, (2022). Number of COVID-19 cases reported to WHO. https://covid19.who.int/ (Last accessed: 30 June 2022).
Kaufmann, P. et al. (Eds.). (2010). *Humiliation, degradation, dehumanisation. human dignity violated*. Springer.
Taylor, P. M. (2005). *Freedom of religion. UN and European human rights law and practice*. Cambridge University Press.
Tetteh, J., Nguyen, V. K., & Hernandez-Vargas, E. A. (2021). Network models to evaluate vaccine strategies towards herd immunity in COVID-19. *Journal of Theoretical Biology*, *531*, 1–14. https://doi.org/10.1016/j.jtbi.2021.110894
Wawrzuta, D., Jaworski, M., Gotlib, J., & Panczyk, M. (2021). What arguments against COVID-19 vaccines run on Facebook in Poland: Content analysis of comments. *Vaccines*, *9*(481), 1–12. https://doi.org/10.3390/vaccines9050481
WHO Emergencies, 2022, https://www.who.int/emergencies/diseases/novel-coronavirus-2019/covid-19-vaccines/advice (Last accessed: 30th June 2022).

8 Threats to Freedom of Expression in the Era of the COVID-19 Pandemic

Jędrzej Skrzypczak and Krzysztof Duda

Introduction

Freedom of expression and freedom of the media are among the elementary human rights underpinning the functioning of democratic societies and, at the same time, a necessary condition for the development of individuals.

The international system of guarantees for media freedom

A vital role in the international system of guarantees for media freedom is played by documents and regulations adopted in the second half of the 20th century, that is well before the digital revolution in the media sector began. This includes acts adopted by the United Nations, that is the Universal Declaration of Human Rights of 1948 (UN, 1948) and the International Covenant on Civil and Political Rights of 1966 (UN, 1966). International guarantees of freedom of expression at the regional level also play a significant role. On the European continent, the European Convention for the Protection of Human Rights and Fundamental Freedoms (CoE, 1950), adopted by the Council of Europe, plays a vital role in this respect. Thus, according to Article 10(1) of the European Convention: "Everyone has the right to freedom of expression. This right shall include freedom to hold opinions and to receive and impart information and ideas without interference by public authority and regardless of frontiers. This provision does not exclude the right of States to subject radio, television or cinematographic undertakings to a licensing procedure" (CoE, 1950). Paragraph 2 of this provision states that "The exercise of these freedoms entailing duties and responsibilities may be subject to such formal requirements, conditions, restrictions and sanctions as are prescribed by law and are necessary in a democratic society in the interests of state security, territorial integrity or public safety for the prevention of disorder or crime, for the protection of health and morals, for the protection of the reputation and rights of others, and for the prevention of the disclosure of confidential information or for guaranteeing the dignity and impartiality of the judiciary" (CoE, 1950).

In the case of the European Union, reference should be made to Article 11 of the Charter of Fundamental Rights of the European Union of 7 December 2000 (UE, 2000), which guarantees the very freedoms at issue here. According to this provision: "Everyone has the right to freedom of expression. This right shall include

DOI: 10.4324/9781003482710-9

freedom to hold opinions and to receive and impart information and ideas without interference by public authority and regardless of frontiers. The freedom of the media and its pluralism shall be respected" (UE, 2000). The Inter-American Convention on Human Rights (OAS, 1969, Article 13) plays a similar role in North and South America. Similar guarantees of freedom of expression and media are introduced on the African continent by Article 9 of the African Charter on Human and People's Rights (AU, 1979).

Most of these regulations, except the Charter of Fundamental Rights of the European Union, were adopted in the analogue media era long before the internet and social media emerged. However, there is no doubt today that the above-cited international guarantees of freedom of expression also apply in the digital age.

Particularly noteworthy is the jurisprudence of regional human rights courts, which creatively develop and interpret the above norms and adapt them to contemporary challenges in this area. The European Court of Human Rights has repeatedly pointed to several essential functions that the media fulfil in a democratic state, namely to perform a monitoring function and to play the role of a public watchdog, to transmit and thus make possible the reception of information and views of social interest and concerning public affairs; to make it possible to participate in the civic debate; to comment on events that are important for the society and of general concern (Voorhoof et al., 2016). It is emphasised that by providing the citizens with reliable information on the functioning of the political system as a whole and public life, the media gives voters a reliable basis for making choices between actors on the political scene. Secondly, it is stressed that the media plays a vital role in the democratic system by monitoring the three authorities, describing and denouncing law and ethics violations by the authorities' representatives. In this way, transparency of decisions taken, accountability, and public scrutiny of the resolutions of political decision-makers are ensured, and abuses of power and possible cases of corruption are exposed. Only then is the principle of control and oversight, essential in a democratic system, fully realised. Hence, the doctrine formulates the view that "To the role of the media as the chain dog of democracy, liberal creed attaches such great importance that it even grants them the status of a fourth power in the state. This authority is exercised on behalf of and in the interests of citizens and civil society/…/. In a narrower sense, the media as organs of the fourth power are supposed to control the legitimacy and ethics of the actions of state institutions and large corporations; in a broader sense, the media are also supposed […] to arouse interest in public affairs/…/" (Mrozowski, 2001, p. 200).

Noteworthy is the position of the Inter-American Court of Human Rights, which, in its ruling, Advisory Opinion OC-5/85 of 13 November 1985, para. 70 stressed:

> Freedom of expression is the cornerstone on which the very existence of a democratic society rests. It is essential to the formation of public opinion. … It constitutes, in short, the means by which the community, in exercising its options, is able to obtain sufficient information. Consequently, it can be said that a society that is not well informed is not a truly free society
>
> Hudson (2017).

However, it should also be noted that the norms mentioned above of international law allow the need to impose various types of legally prescribed states of emergency due to severe threats to citizens' life, health, and security in urgent situations. States may then take measures derogating from certain human rights obligations and commitments under instruments of international and regional law. Such provisions are conveyed *expressis verbis* in Article 4 of the International Covenant on Civil and Political Rights, Article 27 of the Inter-American Convention on Human Rights, and Article 15 of the European Convention on Human Rights. The exception in this respect is the African Charter on Human and Peoples' Rights, which does not contain such provisions (Barata, 2020).

Permitted restrictions on freedom of expression

Thus, freedom of expression is not an absolute value either. It may be subject to restrictions in specific situations. Article 19.3 of the International Covenant states that exercising rights entails special duties and responsibilities. It may, therefore, be subject to certain limitations, but only those provided for by law and necessary to protect national security, public order (*ordre public*), or public health. However, applying the so-called three-step test is always required in such cases. This means that any restriction on freedom of expression, to be lawful, must meet a three-part test, that is it must comply with the following three principles: the principle of legality, the principle of legitimacy, and the principle of necessity and proportionality. The first one means that the applicable law must clearly and explicitly lay down any restriction on freedom of expression. The principle of equity (legitimacy) requires that any limitation imposed must serve the overriding objectives listed expressly in the Covenant. Finally, the principle of necessity and proportionality indicates that any restriction on freedom of expression forced on a country must be strictly necessary, for a democratic society, to achieve its overriding objectives and be proportionate and appropriate to the aim pursued (Barata, 2020).

Similar clauses authorising states to apply certain restrictions on freedom of expression in cases of emergency have also been included in the regional conventions cited above, namely Article 13 of the Inter-American Convention, Article 10 of the European Convention, and Article 9.3 of the African Charter on Human Rights. In all cases, however, restrictions of this type must meet equivalent conditions to the three-tier test provided for in Article 19(3) of the Covenant (Barata, 2020).

Many countries took advantage of such opportunities to a greater or lesser extent during the COVID-19 pandemic and introduced restrictions on freedom of expression. Today, it can be said that in most of these cases, the health crisis was merely a pretext for applying oppressive regulations. Paradoxically, freedom of expression and unfettered access to public information proved to be powerful instruments in the fight against the pandemic and improved the population's health. On the one hand, reliable communications on coronavirus, presenting the number of infected and dead, showed the true extent of the tragedy, warning the public to the danger.

For example, the Polish website presented publications by experts associated with the Science Against the Pandemic initiative from 2020 to 2023.

Prominent representatives of the world of medical science prepared three comprehensive studies on COVID-19 disease, available prevention, treatment, and risks of post-COVID (Borkowski et al., 2021)

On the other hand, information based on up-to-date medical knowledge torpedoed mass emerging "conspiracy theories" about the causes and ways of spreading the pandemic and pseudo-scientific reports about "miraculous" ways to combat the pandemic (Błochowiak et al., 2022). Thirdly, by imparting reliable knowledge, they encouraged preventive vaccination (AP News, 2023; Cyberdefence, 2023; FactCheck.org, 2023; Google Fact Check Tools, 2023). Suffice it to say that, for example in Poland, when vaccines for SARS-CoV-2 began to be provided, information appeared *en masse* on social media that a chip was hidden in the preparations, which, once administered, would allow a person to be tracked. Such a plan resulted from an alleged global conspiracy by interest groups and world leaders. As a result, even among medical professionals, the vaccination refusal rate was surprisingly high (Zagórski, 2020). Yes, there may have been a few areas where, due to exceptional circumstances, such as the need to avoid panic among the public, it was necessary to impose certain restrictions in this respect. However, many examples can be identified where a public health crisis has been used to impose repressive restrictions on freedom of expression (UNHR, 2020). According to a report by the International Institute for Democracy and Electoral Assistance, freedom of expression severely declined during the pandemic. This document states that it was the most threatened human right during the public health crisis. No less importantly, the measures applied to restrict freedom of expression were often disproportionate to the intended purpose. As highlighted in the Global Monitor on the Impact of COVID-19 on Democracy and Human Rights prepared by International IDEA (IIGMC, 2020), in the case of 90 countries surveyed, that is 55% of the total number of cases analysed, legislation was enacted or measures taken to restrict freedom of expression. Such actions were justified by the need to combat disinformation. According to the report, 38 countries have introduced new laws criminalising disinformation about pandemics. The punishment for spreading it was imprisonment. In 18 countries, there are fines for this, nine of which are democracies such as Albania, Bulgaria, Mongolia, and the Philippines. In the latter country, such an act is punishable by a fine of up to US$20,000. A further 18 states used existing legislation in this regard but applied a more restrictive interpretation of the provisions than before the pandemic. In at least ten countries, the introduced legislation was permanent. This means they are also in force after the end of the pandemic. Remarkably, according to this report, the most restrictive ways of limiting freedom of expression were observed in the Asia-Pacific region (IIDEA, 2021).

It is worth recalling here that on 14 July 2020, just four months after the WHO announced the COVID-19 pandemic, the UN Human Rights Council adopted a resolution that obliged States to "refrain from using … public health laws to restrict the right to freedom of opinion and expression in a manner contrary to their obligations under international law, including by ensuring that all measures taken to address threats to public health are entirely consistent with international human rights obligations" (HRC, 2020).

A completely fundamental issue in the context of media freedom is ensuring the safety of journalists. It is about physical safety and the psychological and legal sphere. Hence, guarantees are also necessary to protect journalists from attack or intimidation (Horsley, 2020). Several worrying cases were also observed in this area during the COVID-19 pandemic. Moreover, it is worth recalling here that the safety of journalists, understood in this way, has been emphasised on many occasions in documents of international stature and at the either global or regional level. The following documents should be mentioned in this catalogue: the Resolution adopted by the Human Rights Council on 29 September 2016 (HRC, 2016), the UN Plan of Action on the Safety of Journalists and the Issue of Impunity (UN, 2012), Journalists' Safety Indicators (UNESCO, 2013), the Recommendation CM/Rec (2016)4 of the Committee of Ministers to member States on the protection of journalism and safety of journalists and other media actors, the Resolution of the General Assembly of the OAS on the right to freedom of thought and expression and safety of journalists and media workers (OAS, 2017), and 185 Resolution on the Safety of Journalists and Media Practitioners in Africa (OA, 2011).

During the COVID-19 pandemic, cases of physical attacks and intimidation of journalists, such as when they were forced under threat of punishment to use only official information sources or were arrested and questioned by law enforcement authorities on the broad basis of the existence of an emergency and exceptional situation, were reported worldwide (COVID-19 Pandemic, 2022). More often than not, the pretext for obstructing the work of journalists was the argument of the need to limit the danger of infection by avoiding contact with other people (Global, 2022).

Another area of media freedom that suffered severely from the restrictions imposed during the pandemic was the issue of access to information, chiefly public information. Nevertheless, this is one of the essential elements of media freedom and fair journalism (UNESCO, 2019). Without such access, the media cannot perform the control function described above in democratic systems. It is worth recalling here that the UN Sustainable Development Goals, adopted by the UN General Assembly and identified as Goal 16, are "to ensure public access to information and the protection of fundamental freedoms, under national legislation and international agreements".

Nonetheless, scandalous practices have repeatedly occurred during the crisis discussed here. One example is the case of Nicaragua, where the government banned independent national and international press editors from participating in Ministry of Health conferences during the pandemic (Roudik, 2020). On the other hand, it must be acknowledged that, during the pandemic period, 91% of the countries in the world set up separate websites with messages and information on COVID-19 (IIDEA, 2021). It is essential to note the many positive cases where state authorities published and regularly updated reliable and verified information on the spread of infection, the number of deaths, and up-to-date details on restrictions and vaccinations in force. In some countries (e.g., Italy, Sweden, and Taiwan), government agencies held periodic, almost daily press conferences to regularly update the public on critical events related to the spread of coronavirus. Social media was also used to communicate ongoing messages. In addition, online services and platforms were used to distribute vaccine messages, such as creating a national inoculation referral system and making medical appointments for vaccine administration (IIDEA, 2021).

As assessed, providing transparent access to reliable COVID-19 facts in these countries was crucial for preventing the spread of misinformation and coronavirus. At times, care was also taken to ensure that messages were accessible to linguistic minorities or to sign language-only speakers. Attempts were also undertaken to use different messaging forms, such as memes, cartoons, and other humorous digital campaigns, to make the message and communication about SARS-CoV-2 more attractive to the public. Different communication platforms and channels were also used. This was the case in Taiwan, for example. The same was true for some international organisations. Thus, the WHO launched a multilingual messaging service via WhatsApp to answer coronavirus questions (IIDEA, 2021).

However, it should be stressed that the mere launch of a website providing particulars on a pandemic cannot be considered identical to providing full access to public information. Naturally, it must be acknowledged that in many democratic countries, such websites have been characterised by objectivity and pluralism. However, there have been numerous cases, including in countries traditionally counted as democracies, where such websites only provided favourable material to the government and the ruling party and attempted to conceal or silence facts inconvenient to policy decision-makers. All this was motivated solely by a desire to make political capital. Thus, under the pretext of fighting the COVID-19 pandemic, these websites were part of propaganda strategies and governmental agitation (IIGMC, 2020).

Another example of the restriction of freedom of expression during the COVID-19 pandemic, which, in fact, also concerned access to information, was cases where people directly involved in the fight against the pandemic (e.g. medical workers) were banned from communicating their observations to journalists or where such activists disseminated their own opinions through private social media accounts (IIDEA, 2021).

For example one can point to the situation observed in the early days of the pandemic in the People's Republic of China when health workers and journalists from newsrooms related to civic media tried to inform the public about worrying developments in late 2019. However, they were attacked by various state authorities for reporting on the outbreak of a then-unknown disease. Over 5,000 criminal investigations were launched against individuals who published information about the then epidemic for "fabricating and deliberately spreading false and harmful information". In one case, civic media journalist Zhang Zhan travelled to Wuhan in February 2020 to report on the COVID-19 outbreak but mysteriously went missing in Wuhan in May 2020. It was later revealed that she had been detained by the police, charged with "starting quarrels and provoking trouble", and sentenced to four years in prison (Mawarire, 2020).

Examples were also noted from democratic countries such as Poland, where doctors and other medical staff in the early stages of the pandemic were instructed not to speak to journalists. Those who disregarded such instructions were threatened with inevitable repercussions, including loss of employment.

Nevertheless, another example of the restrictions imposed on citizens concerning the COVID-19 pandemic in the area of freedom of expression was the issue of access to the internet. As early as in the pre-pandemic period, the problem of such access was repeatedly raised and included among the components of freedom of expression and thus elevated to the status of human rights.

The United Nations Human Rights Council stated in its decision of 4 July 2018 that "the same rights that people enjoy offline must also be protected online, in particular freedom of expression, which applies regardless of borders and through any media of their choice" (HRC, 2018).

It can, therefore, be argued that freedom of expression includes the right to unrestricted access to the internet (IIDEA, 2021).

Firstly, it is vital to note the Declaration Establishing Guidelines for the Protection of Freedom of Expression on the Internet of 2011 (Declaration, 2011). This was a significant document in that it was signed by the Special Rapporteur on Freedom of Expression of the African Commission on Human and Peoples' Rights (ACHPR), the Special Rapporteur on Freedom of Expression of the Inter-American Commission on Human Rights of the Organisation of American States, and the Representative on Freedom of the Media of the Organisation for Security and Cooperation in Europe (OSCE).

This statement emphasised, on the one hand, the need to promote universal access to the internet and, on the other hand, recognised that cutting off access to it, or parts of it, to entire populations or specific groups is unacceptable, even in situations justified on grounds of public order or national security.

According to the European Court of Human Rights (ECHR, 2012), which examined the legislation of twenty Council of Europe member states (Austria, Azerbaijan, Belgium, the Czech Republic, Estonia, Finland, France, Germany, Ireland, Italy, Lithuania, the Netherlands, Poland, Portugal, Romania, Russia, Slovenia, Spain, Switzerland, and the United Kingdom), the ECHR stated at the time that the right to access the internet was protected by constitutional guarantees of freedom of expression and freedom to receive ideas and information. This right consisted of, on the one hand, the privilege of every person to participate in the information society and, on the other hand, the obligation imposed on states to guarantee internet access to their citizens. As highlighted by the European Court, the Council of Europe's standards on freedom of expression on the internet have been established in various resolutions, recommendations, and declarations, among which one should mention Recommendation CM/Rec(2007)16 of the Committee of Ministers to member States on measures to promote the public service value of the internet, Recommendation CM/Rec(2008)6 of the Committee of Ministers to member States on measures to promote the respect for freedom of expression and information about Internet filters (CoE, 2008), Recommendation CM/Rec(2012)3 of the Committee of Ministers to member States on the protection of human rights about search engines, as well as the Convention on Cybercrime (ETS No. 185). It is also worth mentioning other cases concluded before the ECHR on internet publications, namely KU v. Finland, Times Newspapers, Ltd v. the United Kingdom (Nos. 1 and 2), but in particular the case of Editorial Board of Pravoye Delo and Shtekel v. Ukraine, where the Court found:

> … the absence of a sufficient legal framework at the domestic level allowing journalists to use information obtained from the Internet without fear of incurring sanctions hinders seriously the exercise of the vital function of the press as a "public watchdog"…
>
> ECHR (2011)

In turn, the UN Special Rapporteur, in a June 2017 report (HRC, 2017), assessed that any disconnection from the internet should always be qualified as not meeting the standards of international protection of freedom of expression.

This issue has also been the subject of proceedings before international tribunals. It is worth recalling the case pending before the European Court of Human Rights, Ahmed Yildirim v. Turkey, on 18 December 2012 (ECHR, 2012). The Court stated that blocking an entire domain name to deal with a particular piece of allegedly illegal content always requires "a determination as to whether a less far-reaching measure could have been taken". The European Court unanimously held that the decision taken and upheld by the Turkish authorities to block access to Google Sites was a violation of Article 10 of the European Convention on Human Rights and Fundamental Freedoms, which guarantees the freedom to express, receive, and impart information and ideas "regardless of frontiers" (ECHR, 2012).

As emphasised by the European Court in this case:

> In the light of these documents and the practice of the States Parties referred to in the judgment's reasoning, the minimum criteria for Convention-compatible legislation on Internet blocking measures are: (1) a definition of the categories of persons and institutions liable to have their publications blocked, such as national or foreign owners of illegal content, websites or platforms, users of these sites or platforms and persons providing hyperlinks to illegal sites or platforms which have endorsed them; (2) a definition of the categories of blocking orders, such as blocking of entire websites, Internet Protocol (IP) addresses, ports, network protocols or types of use, like social networking; (3) a provision on the territorial ambit of the blocking order, which may have region-wide, nationwide, or even worldwide effect; (4) a limit on the duration of the blocking order; (5) an indication of the "interests", in the sense of one or more of those included in Article 10 § 2 of the Convention, that may justify the blocking order; (6) observance of the criterion of proportionality, which provides for a fair balancing of freedom of expression and the competing "interests" pursued, while ensuring that the essence (or minimum core) of freedom of expression is respected; (7) compliance with the principle of necessity, which enables an assessment to be made as to whether the interference with freedom of expression adequately

> advances the "interests" pursued and goes no further than is necessary to meet the said "social need"; (8) definition of the authorities competent to issue a reasoned blocking order; (9) a procedure to be followed for the issuance of that order, which includes the examination by the competent authority of the case file supporting the request for a blocking order and the hearing of evidence from the affected person or institution, unless this is impossible or incompatible with the "interests" pursued; (10) notification of the blocking order and the grounds for it to the person or institution affected; and (11) a judicial appeal procedure against the blocking order.
>
> ECHR (2012)

In turn, on 25 June 2020, the Economic Community of West African States (ECOWAS) Community Court of Justice ruled that the Togolese government's decision to shut down the internet in 2017 during a wave of protests did not meet their obligations to implement all necessary safeguards about the Togolese people's right to freedom of expression (CCJECOWAS, 2018).

After the outbreak of the pandemic in 2020, the UN Special Rapporteur stated that at the time of its global extent, access to the internet is a critical element of healthcare policy and practice, public information, and even the right to life. Internet shutdowns during the pandemic affect not only citizens in general seeking reliable information about government measures, health recommendations, or health services but also, in particular, healthcare workers who need access to relevant facts regarding the pandemic. Internet access restrictions during a health emergency impact everyone, from the local to the global level (UNHR, 2020).

In turn, the UN Human Rights Council resolution of 16 July 2020 affirmed that states must "refrain from imposing restrictions that are inconsistent with Article 19 of the International Covenant on Civil and Political Rights, including on the free flow of information and ideas, including through practices such as the use of Internet shutdowns to intentionally and arbitrarily prevent or disrupt access to or the dissemination of information online, the banning or closing of publications or other media and the abuse of administrative measures and censorship, and on access to or use of information and communications technology, inter alia radio, television and the Internet" (HRC, 2020b).

Freedom of expression in the digital era

However, the COVID-19 pandemic happened in a very different technological reality to all previous public health crises of this type, that is, in the digital age (Content Regulation, 2018). The technological advances that took place in the media market even before the pandemic significantly impacted the functioning of these markets and entire societies (Allan, 2006; Fenton, 2010; Gates, 2009; Mcnair, 2009; Price, 2015; Salwen et al., 2005; Tewksbury &Rittenberg, 2012). Indeed, digital technologies and internet connectivity became a strategic resource during the pandemic, creating a parallel between public life and individuals in lockdown conditions. This provided a substitute for contacts from the real world.

It is essential to note the remarkable popularity of social media in the second and third decades of the 21st century (Allan, 2006; Fenton, 2010; Gates, 2009; Mcnair, 2009; Price, 2015, p.1; Salwen et al. 2005; Tewksbury & Rittenberg, 2012). This is one excellent typical case of demonstrating how media systems and communication models are undergoing profound changes in the age of the digital revolution. One of their effects is to change the way we use media. These are examples of the concept of the so-called de-massified means of communication and the blurring of boundaries between producers/broadcasters and consumers/viewers/listeners/viewers (Zafarani et al., 2014, p. 1).

In this case, everyone can be not only the recipient of content but also the creator of the content. There are many definitions of this phenomenon in the doctrine. For example, according to one concept, it is "a group of web-based applications, based on the ideological and technological foundations of Web 2.0, that enable the creation and exchange of user-generated content" (Kaplan & Haenlein, 2010, pp. 59–68). A total of 62.5% of the world's population has access to the internet, and just under 58.4% are active social media users (Digital, 2022). As you can see, accessing the internet today is all about using social media.

Thus, while there are many types of social media, it can be argued that they share several common characteristics regardless of their form, platform, ideas, and operating principles. Firstly, it is a type of personal communication, that is personalised. Secondly, content is created when one user communicates with another. Thirdly, they nevertheless offer the possibility of attracting a broad audience. They all allow, among other things, the use of bots, algorithms, and fictitious accounts to distribute content and create, sometimes deliberately and in an entirely intentional way, the illusion of a substantial public interest around a particular issue or person. These networks, which, in essence, enable the sharing of certain content on global circulation, can be used for severe manipulation and disinformation. On the one hand, all this can present a great opportunity, but on the other hand, it can paradoxically be a massive threat to freedom of expression (Briggs, 2018; Palmer, & Eriksen, 1999; Toffler, 2002).

As a result, for some time, even in the pre-pandemic period, calls began to be made for the need for some regulation of the operation of these messages and platforms (Brannon, 2019; Garcia, & Hoffmeister, 2017; Kayode et al., 2018; Scaife 2018; Tan, 2018; Tully, 2014). In doing so, however, several challenges and dilemmas were highlighted (Fox, 2021; Ressa, 2020, p. 17). As emphasised in the doctrine, in the analogue era, the responsibility for guaranteeing freedom of expression was borne by two types of actors: states and international organisations. In contrast, today, in the era of digital platforms, there are, in fact, three actors, in addition to the above two, private corporations creating global communication platforms (Palmer, 2021). States and international organisations played a vital role in the analogue era. However, their role in this field is diminishing in favour of actors who influence the content appearing on global platforms. The latter mainly includes various content aggregators, such as social media platforms, which may restrict certain content and activities due to their internal rules and, as evidenced by practice, their marketing strategies (Ohlheiser & Guo, 2021; Papernik, 2021).

On the other hand, when considering the possibility of introducing appropriate legal regulations in this area, it is argued that the temptation to regulate such platforms' activities may lead to restricting freedom of speech, and the adopted measures will censor and limit public debate.

One must, therefore, fully agree with the position of the Vice President of the European Union, Věra Jourová (Jourová, 2020), already articulated during the pandemic, who stressed that social media platforms must become more accountable for what is published on their sites. Some platforms followed such calls and introduced measures during the pandemic to implement a transparent and consistent moderation policy for discussions. Efforts were also made to promote links to reliable information on the pandemic, such as available on the websites of the WHO and other health institutions. Some social media platforms have also decided to remove harmful or dangerous content, such as advertisements offering fake medicines or overpricing everyday products. For example, instructional material on drinking bleach to kill coronavirus was removed (Jourová, 2020).

As the 2020–2022 pandemic crisis demonstrated, it was crucial to counter disinformation as a toxic driver of secondary, undesirable effects of the pandemic, which can increase the risk of conflict, violence, human rights violations, and mass atrocities. The same applies to the astonishingly famous social media hate speech. It is worth recalling here the UN Secretary-General's statement that "with the spread of COVID-19, a tsunami of disinformation, hatred, scapegoating and causing panic has been unleashed". It is worth clarifying that the WHO defined *infodemic* as "the overabundance of information – some accurate and some not – that occurs during an epidemic. It can lead to confusion and mistrust in governments and public health responses" (WHO, 2023).

Infodemic

In the COVID-19 health crisis, such "infodemics" proliferation has proved as dangerous to human health and safety as the pandemic itself. The WHO emphasised that "the right message at the right time from the right messenger through the right medium can save lives", and therefore "misinformation or mixed messages can cost lives" (WHO, 2023).

An infodemic can cause confusion and risky behaviour that can harm health. It can also lead to a lack of trust in health authorities and weaken the public health response. Information can spread faster with increasing digitalisation – the expansion of social media and internet use. This can help fill information gaps and amplify harmful messages more quickly (Khan, 2021). However, social media has also allowed marginal ideas and social movements to come to the forefront of public debate, introducing polarising rhetoric (WHO, 2023).

However, it is essential to note that the leading social media platforms during the COVID-19 pandemic implemented some self-regulatory measures to combat disinformation (IIGMC, 2020).

The fundamental question, however, is how to combat such a phenomenon. The simplest solution, used in many non-democratic countries but utterly unacceptable from a human rights perspective, is either to shut down social media altogether or to introduce draconian penalties, including imprisonment. It is much more challenging to deal with infodemic through painstaking, patient, and usually very costly information and education efforts (Barata, 2020). The WHO has proposed an infodemic management strategy for this situation (WHO, 2023).

According to this approach, it is necessary to respond relentlessly to any hints of misinformation with an evidence-based narrative that will provide audiences with reliable information in an understandable way. Only such a strategy can stimulate positive health-seeking behaviour. Furthermore, this task is critical. The right message at the right time from the right messenger through a suitable medium can save lives, whereas misinformation or mixed messages can cost lives. Last but not least, the WHO stressed that such a strategy to combat infodemia should be considered a pillar of an integrated approach to public health in knowledge-based societies (WHO, 2023).

The Report of the Special Rapporteur (HRC, 2020a) on promoting and protecting the right to freedom of opinion and expression provides guidelines for combating disinformation concerning the pandemic. As emphasised, everyone, particularly state actors, should act responsibly. Government agencies must refrain from disseminating or endorsing unverified and often reckless claims about the pandemic. Any action by state agencies to counter disinformation should be based on complete, honest communication with the public, the promotion and protection of an independent press, and the careful and public correction of misinformation that may lead to harm to public health. States should support activities that promote media literacy. It is also necessary to be guided by the principle that measures and actions to combat disinformation must not prevent journalists from doing their job or lead to unjustified blocking of content on the internet. It is also necessary to urge social media administrators to take responsibility for disseminating any potentially harmful speech.

The COVID-19 pandemic and media market challenges

Finally, it should be stressed that the time of the COVID-19 pandemic was a challenge for the editors of printed newspapers, as, during lockdown periods, the circulation of magazines dropped significantly, resulting in substantial financial losses and a struggle for survival. This struggle was unsuccessful in many cases, particularly for the local press. Many press offices were closed down and failed to revive after the pandemic. Hence, states should be urged to create a financial support system for these entities.

Conclusions

This crisis has shown, like perhaps none before, how important reliable and responsible journalism and media are for a democratic system, media education, information awareness, and digital skills. Indeed, it also proved that social media is no substitute for quality journalism and mainstream media. However, the COVID-19 pandemic has shown how all-important it is to have responsible and fact-based media to ensure access to information. Providing transparent opportunities to use reliable information on the COVID-19 pandemic in many countries was crucial for preventing the spread of disinformation and creating public trust. It is, therefore, necessary to develop adequate safeguards in access to information, especially in crises and emergencies.

Unfortunately, it is sad to say that this last period has clearly shown that democratic mechanisms to combat fake news and disinformation are not ready. On the other hand, access to reliable, undistorted and independent news is vital and sometimes critical for protecting life and health, especially in periods of uncertainty, threat, and chaos such as pandemics. Taking into account the experience to date, it can be assumed that it will not be possible to develop universal, global, and democratic solutions to combat disinformation quickly, if at all. Yet, every fake news is only dangerous if its recipient believes in the false message. Therefore, the introduction of universal media education should be advocated.

Secondly, it is necessary to ensure appropriate communication models between governments and citizens based on honesty, integrity, and empathy.

References

AP News. (2023). https://apnews.com/search?q=Coronavirus#nt=navsearch

AU. (1979). African charter on human and peoples' rights. https://au.int/sites/default/files/treaties/36390-treaty-0011_-_african_charter_on_human_and_peoples_rights_e.pdf

Barata, J. (2020). *COVID-19: The role of judicial operators in the protection and promotion of the right to freedom of expression: Guidelines*. UNESCO. https://unesdoc.unesco.org/ark:/48223/pf0000374208

Barrett, P. (2020). Regulating social media. https://static1.squarespace.com/static/5b6df958f8370af3217d4178/t/5f58df637cbf80185f372776/1599659876276/NYU+Section+230_FINAL+ONLINE+UPDATED_Sept+8.pdf

Błochowiak, M. et al. (2022). Biała księga pandemii koronawirusa. Fakty i dane ukrywane przed opinią publiczną", Fundacja Ordo Medicus.

Borkowski, L., Drąg, M., Fal, A. M., Flisiak, R., Jemielity, J., Krajewski, J., Mastalerz-Migas, A., Matyja, A., Pyrć, K., Rzymski, P., Sutkowski, M., Simon, K., Wysocki, J., & Zajkowska, J. (2021). Szczepienia przeciw COVID-19. Innowacyjne technologie i efektywność, Warszawa. https://naukaprzeciwpandemii.pl/publikacje/#pas02

Brannon, V. C. (2019). Free speech and the regulation of social media content. https://sgp.fas.org/crs/misc/R45650.pdf

Briggs, S. (2018). The freedom of tweets. The intersection of government use of social media and public forum doctrine. http://blogs2.law.columbia.edu/jlsp/wp-content/uploads/sites/8/2019/04/Vol52-Briggs.pdf.

Content Regulation (2018) in the Digital Age Submission to the United Nations Special Rapporteur on the Right to Freedom of Opinion and Expression by the Association for Progressive Communications (APC) February, https://www.ohchr.org/Documents/Issues/Opinion/ContentRegulation/APC.pdf

CCJECOWAS. (2018). Community court of justice of the economic community of West Africans states, application no. ECW/CCJ/APP/61/18. https://www.accessnow.org/wp-content/uploads/2020/06/KIO_ECOWAS_Togo-Intervention.pdf

CoE. (1950). The European continent, the European convention for the protection of human rights and fundamental freedoms. https://www.echr.coe.int/documents/d/echr/Convention_Instrument_ENG.

CoE. (2001). Convention on cybercrime (ETS No. 185). https://www.europarl.europa.eu/cmsdata/179163/20090225ATT50418EN.pdf
CoE. (2007). Recommendation CM/Rec(2007)16 of the Committee of Ministers to member states on measures to promote the public service value of the Internet (Adopted by the Committee of Ministers on 7 November 2007 at the 1010th meeting of the Ministers' Deputies) https://search.coe.int/cm/Pages/result_details.aspx?ObjectId=09000016805d4a39
CoE. (2008). Recommendation CM/Rec(2008)6 of the Committee of Ministers to member states on measures to promote the respect for freedom of expression and information with regard to Internet filters (Adopted by the Committee of Ministers on 26 March 2008, at the 1022nd meeting of the Ministers' Deputies). https://search.coe.int/cm/Pages/result_details.aspx?ObjectID=09000016805d3bc4
CoE. (2012). Recommendation CM/Rec(2012)3 of the Committee of Ministers to member States on the protection of human rights about search engines. https://search.coe.int/cm/Pages/result_details.aspx?ObjectID=09000016805caa87
CoE. (2016). Recommendation CM/Rec(2016)4[1] of the Committee of Ministers to Member States on the protection of journalism and safety of journalists and other media actors (Adopted by the Committee of Ministers on 13 April 2016 at the 1253rd meeting of the Ministers' Deputies). https://search.coe.int/cm/Pages/result_details.aspx?ObjectId=09000016806415d9#_ftn1
COVID-19 Pandemic: Journalists Attacked and intimidated while Official Threatens Media. HTTPS://MONITOR.CIVICUS.ORG/EXPLORE/COVID-19-JOURNALISTS-ATTACKED-INTIMIDATED-WHILE-OFFICIAL-THREATENS-MEDIA/; HTTPS://WWW.UNESCO.ORG/EN/THREATS-FREEDOM-PRESS-VIOLENCE-DISINFORMATION-CENSORSHIP?TSPD_101_R0=080713870FAB20008FAC1D6CD2C70C05E5F5A2D22EA3B5428B6DB9280A92177B4FCC5FE3BFCECF6B083177A456143000F085E54796EC7250D8C3B7A05178D5E0AA064C68FFDAA7063DC2129DB14827DE21BBD359E5086E1540AB203D54D9E20B
Cyberdefence. (2023). Krótki przewodnik po fake newsach o koronawirusie. https://cyberdefence24.pl/fake-news/krotki-przewodnik-po-aktualnych-fake-newsach-o-koronawirusie
Declaration. (2011). Establishing guidelines for the protection of freedom of expression on the internet. https://www.osce.org/representative-on-freedom-of-media/78309
Deloire, C. (2020). How to address the information chaos. https://informationdemocracy.org/wp-content/uploads/2020/11/ForumID_Report-on-infodemics_101120.pdf
Diaz, J. (2021). Jack Dorsey says Trump's twitter ban was 'right decision' but worries about precedent. https://www.npr.org/2021/01/14/956664893/twitter-ceo-tweets-about-banning-trump-from-site?t=1645378363608
Digital. (2022). Global overview report. https://datareportal.com/reports/digital-2022-global-overview-report
DRIICHPPR. (2021). The domestic, regional and international implications of China's policies and practices Research Paper 17, March HTTPS://WWW.CHATHAMHOUSE.ORG/2021/03/RESTRICTIONS-ONLINE-FREEDOM-EXPRESSION-CHINA
ECHR. (2003). The European court of human rights, case of Times Newspaper Ltd against the United Kingdom, Application nos. 23676/03 and 3002/03, Times Newspaper Ltd against the United Kingdom.
ECHR. (2009). The European court of human rights case of Ku v. Finland.
ECHR. (2011). The European court of human rights, case of editorial board of Pravoye Delo and Shtekel v. Ukraine.
ECHR. (2012). Case of Ahmet Yildirim v. Trukey (Application no. 3111/10). https://hudoc.echr.coe.int/eng#{%22itemid%22:[%22001-115705%22]}
FactCheck.org. (2023). A project of the Annenberg public policy center, a guide to our coronavirus coverage. https://www.factcheck.org/a-guide-to-our-coronavirus-coverage/;
Fagan, F. (2018). "Systemic social media regulation". Duke law & technology review. Retrieved February 25, 2022, from https://scholarship.law.duke.edu/dltr/vol16/iss1/14/

Fox, C. (2021). Social media. How might it be regulated? Retrieved February 20, 2022, from https://www.bbc.com/news/technology-54901083

Garcia, R., & Hoffmeister, T. (2017). "Social media law in a nutshell" School of law faculty publications no 21. Retrieved February 20, 2022, from https://ecommons.udayton.edu/law_fac_pub/2

Global. (2022). Global: Crackdown on journalists weakens efforts to tackle COVID-19. https://www.amnesty.org/en/latest/news/2020/05/global-crackdown-on-journalists-weakens-efforts-to-tackle-covid19/

Google Fact Check Tools. (2023). https://toolbox.google.com/factcheck/explorer/search/Coronavirus;hl=en

Horsley, W. (2020). Safety of journalists, guidebook 3rd edition, office of the representative on freedom of the media, organization for security and co-operation in Europe, A-1010 Vienna, Austria.

HRC. (2016). Human Rights Council. Resolution adopted by the Human Rights Council on 29 September 2016. https://documents-dds-ny.un.org/doc/UNDOC/GEN/G16/226/24/PDF/G1622624.pdf?OpenElement

HRC. (2017). Human rights council. Report of the special rapporteur on the promotion and protection of the right to freedom of opinion and expression, Human Rights Council thirty-fifth session 6–23 June 2017. https://documents-ddsny.un.org/doc/UNDOC/GEN/G17/077/46/PDF/G1707746.pdf?OpenElement

HRC. (2018). Human rights council. The promotion, protection and enjoyment of human rights on the internet: resolution/UN. Human Rights Council (38th sess.: 2018: Geneva)

HRC. (2020a). Human Rights Council. Forty-fourth session 15 June–3 July 2020 Agenda item 3 promotion and protection of all human rights, civil, political, economic, social and cultural rights, including the right to development, Disease pandemics and the freedom of opinion and expression, Report of the Special Rapporteur on the promotion and protection of the right to freedom of opinion and expression. https://www.google.com/url?sa=t&rct=j&q=&esrc=s&source=web&cd=&ved=2ahUKEwjnkZ7H5MGBAxWHIxAIHZkBAp0QFnoECA4QAQ&url=https%3A%2F%2Fwww.ohchr.org%2FDocuments%2FIssues%2FOpinion%2FA_HRC_44_49_AdvanceEditedVersion.docx&usg=AOvVaw1FVfGKomC9wfu6-d5HZqAj&opi=89978449

HRC. (2020b). Human Rights Council resolution adopted by the Human Rights Council on 16 July 2020, Human Rights Council forty-fourth session, 30 June–17 July 2020 Agenda item 3 Promotion and protection of all human rights, civil, political, economic, social and cultural rights, including the right to development. https://documents-ddsny.un.org/doc/UNDOC/LTD/G20/180/77/PDF/G2018077.pdf?OpenElement

Hudson, D. L. Jr. (2017). Hate speech online. Retrieved February 21, 2022, from https://www.freedomforuminstitute.org/first-amendment-center/primers/fake-news-primer/

IACHR. (1985). Inter-American court of human rights, advisory opinion OC-5/85 of 13 November 1985, para. 70. https://www.corteidh.or.cr/docs/opiniones/seriea_05_ing.pdf

IIDEA. (2021). International Institute for Democracy and Electoral Assistance, The Global State of Democracy. Building Resilience in w Pandemic. https://www.idea.int/gsod/sites/default/files/2021-11/the-global-state-of-democracy-2021_1.pdf

IIGMC. (2020). International IDEA's Global Monitor of Covid-19's, Impact on Democracy and Human Rights.

Jourová, V. (2020). Speech of Vice President Věra on countering disinformation amid COVID-19 "From pandemic to infodemic", 4 June 2020. https://ec.europa.eu/commission/presscorner/detail/en/speech_20_1000

Kaplan, A. M., & Haenlein, M. (2010). Users of the world, unite! The challenges and opportunities of social media.

Kayode, A. T., Oyero, O., & Aririguzoh, S. (2018). Regulating the social media for global relationships. https://www.researchgate.net/publication/322531212_Regulating_the_social_media_for_global_relationships

Khan, I. (2021). How can states effectively regulate social media platforms? https://www.law.ox.ac.uk/business-law-blog/blog/2021/01/how-can-states-effectively-regulate-social-media-platforms

Mawarire, T. (2020). COVID-19 effects on freedom of expression in Southern Africa, 2020 research report. https://www.amnesty.org/en/latest/news/2021/10/covid-19-global-attack-on-freedom-of-expression-is-having-a-dangerous-impact-on-public-health-crisis/

OA. (2011). 185 Resolution on the safety of journalists and media practitioners in Africa, adopted by the African Commission at its 49th Ordinary Session, held in Banjul, The Gambia, from 28 April—12 May 2011.

OAS. (1969). Inter-American convention on human rights. https://treaties.un.org/doc/publication/unts/volume%201144/volume-1144-i-17955-english.pdf

OAS. (2017). Resolution of the General Assembly of the OAS (2017) on the right to freedom of thought and expression and safety of journalists and media workers. http://www.oas.org/en/sla/dil/docs/AG-RES_2908_XLVII-O-17.pdf

Ohlheiser, A., & Guo, E. (2021). Twitter locked Trump's account. Insiders say it needs to go further. Retrieved February 18, 2022, from https://www.technologyreview.com/2021/01/06/1015830/twitter-trump-suspension-ban/

Palmer, A. (2021). Facebook will block Trump from posting at least for the remainder of his term. Retrieved February 18, 2022, from https://www.cnbc.com/2021/01/07/facebook-will-block-trump-from-posting-for-the-remainder-of-his-term.html

Palmer, J. W., & Eriksen, L. (1999). Digital news—Paper, broadcast and more converge on the internet. *The International Journal on Media Management*, *1*, 32–40.

Papiernik, O. (2021). Sygnalistka nie zostawia suchej nitki na Facebooku. Zagraża zdrowiu". Dziennik.pl. Retrieved February 23, 2022, from https://technologia.dziennik.pl/sprzet/artykuly/8287958,sygnalistka-facebooku-zagrozenie-zdrowie-zarzuty.html

Paslawsky, A. (2017). The growth of social media norms and the Governments' attempts at regulation. *Fordham International Law Journal. 35*, nr 5, 1486–1539.

Ressa, M. (2020). Working group on infodemics policy framework. Retrieved February 20, 2022, from https://informationdemocracy.org/wp-content/uploads/2020/11/ForumID_Report-on-infodemics_101120.pdf

Roudik, P. (2020). Comparative summary, freedom of expression during COVID-19, the law library of congress, global legal research directorate, September 2020 https://sgp.fas.org/eprint/foe-covid.pdf

Scaife, L. (2018). The effective regulation of social media. Retrieved February 20, 2022, from http://kar.kent.ac.uk/65920

Tan, C. (2018). Regulating content on social media. https://www.uclpress.co.uk/products/95612.

Toffler, A. (2002). Odmasowione środki przekazu. (Maryla Hopfinger Trans.). In M. Hopfinger (Ed.), *Nowe media w komunikacji społecznej w XX wieku* (pp. 441–447). Warszawa.

Tully, S. (2014). People you might know. Social media in the conflict between law and democracy. In G. Patmore & K. Rubenstein (Eds.), *Law and democracy: Contemporary questions* (pp. 53–172). Canberra.

UE. (2000). Charter of fundamental rights of the European Union. https://eur-lex.europa.eu/legal-content/EN/TXT/?uri=CELEX:12012P/TXT

UN. (1948). Universal declaration of human rights. https://www.un.org/en/about-us/universal-declaration-of-human-rights

UN. (1966). The international covenant on civil and political rights. https://www.ohchr.org/en/instruments-mechanisms/instruments/international-covenant-civil-and-political-rights

UN. (2012). UN plan of action on the safety of journalists and the issue of impunity. https://www.ohchr.org/sites/default/files/documents/issues/journalists/2023-01-31/un-plan-on-safety-journalists_en.pdf

UNESCO. (2013). Journalists' safety indicators. https://webarchive.unesco.org/web/20220706081758/https://en.unesco.org/themes/safety-of-journalists/journalists-safety-indicators

UNESCO. (2019). Access to information: A new promise for sustainable development https://unesdoc.unesco.org/ark:/48223/pf0000371485

UNHR. (2020). Disease pandemics and the freedom of opinion and expression. Report of the Special Rapporteur on the promotion and protection of the right to freedom of opinion and expression. https://documents-dds-ny.un.org/doc/UNDOC/GEN/G20/097/82/PDF/G2009782.pdf?OpenElement

Veltman, K. H. (2006). *Understanding new media*. Augmented Knowledge & Culture.

Voorhoof, D. (2022). European court of human rights: Ahmet Yildirim v. Turkey, https://rm.coe.int/16807834d1

Voorhoof, D., McGonagle, T. et al. (2016). Freedom of Expression, the Media and Journalists, Case-law of the European Court of Human Rights: 28, IRIS Themes, vol.III, https://rm.coe.int/16807834d1

Wall, J., Mooppan, H., Joshi, S., Taibleson, R., Mc Intosh, S., & Utrecht, J. (2020). Donald J. Trump, V. Knight, first amendment institute at Columbia University. Retrieved February 20, 2022, from https://www.supremecourt.gov/DocketPDF/20/20-197/150726/20200820102824291_Knight%20First%20Amendment%20Inst.pdf

WHO. (2023). Infodemic management. https://www.who.int/teams/risk-communication/infodemic-management

Zafarani, R., Abbas, M., & Liu, H. (2014). *Social media mining. An introduction*. Cambridge University Press.

Zagórski, J. (2020). Medycy nie chcą szczepić się na COVID. "Nie dam sobie wszczepić chipa, który będzie mnie śledził", OKOpress.pl 16.12.2020. https://oko.press/medycy-nie-chca-sie-szczepic-na-covid-nie-dam-sobie-wszczepic-chipa-ktory-bedzie-mnie-sledzil

9 The Impact of the COVID-19 Pandemic on Changes in the Media Market and Information Pluralism

Wojciech Adamczyk

> "There are decades when nothing happens, and then there come weeks when more is happening than in previous decades."
>
> Vladimir Ilyich Lenin Rajan (2020)

Introduction

National media systems have evolved over the centuries, beginning with the birth of the printed press. Along with the political and economic development of societies and the systematic introduction to modern information technologies, there are changes in the structure of the mass media market and the methods of obtaining, collecting, processing, and distributing information. Journalists' working conditions and the scope of freedom to practise this profession are also changing, impacting the level of information pluralism. Generally, the transformations mentioned above take decades on a global scale. There are, however, extraordinary events that, like a catalyst, change the pace of these alterations, making possible what until recently seemed only a "melody of the distant future". Such a phenomenon on a global scale is undoubtedly the COVID-19 pandemic, which in the years 2019–2021 led to qualitative innovations in media markets in many countries. The pandemic has altered the functioning of all aspects of everyday human life and branches of the economy in the national and global dimensions. Subsequent lockdowns introduced by the governments, which are a reaction to avalanche increases in citizens infected with the SARS-CoV-2 and the consequently growing number of deaths, caused a challenging situation for enterprises in many industries, trade, and services. The restrictions also affected entities operating in the media market, which were pressured to suddenly and, in the vast majority of cases, unintentionally amend the formula of functioning (Adamczyk, 2022).

This chapter aims to demonstrate that, first of all, many transformation processes in the media market have accelerated due to the COVID-19 pandemic. These include, first and foremost, the introduction of a remote and hybrid formula of journalists' work, reduction of employment brought about by the circumstances and the collapse of many editorial offices of traditional media, and relatively serious limitation of the range or frequency of their publications, as well as a visible speed-up of the process of transferring activities to the Internet and popularisation

DOI: 10.4324/9781003482710-10

of new broadcasting formats. Secondly, these alterations harmed media pluralism regarding content, information sources and content providers, and freedom of speech, as many governments decided to use the pandemic period to restrict access to information and even harass journalists.

That issue requires answers to several research questions. How did reporters and employees of traditional media adapt to the new situation, forced by lockdowns introduced by the authorities? How did remote work influence the implementation of new information broadcasting formats and broadcasting? Which media market segments have been most driven to reduce operations and accelerate digitisation? How have the authorities in many countries around the world limited the scope of media pluralism and the freedom of journalists to act?

The author employed the method of source analysis in the research. Especially useful were reports and studies of such scientific units as Pew Research Center, International Press Institute (IPI), NiemanLab, Reuters Institute, Nielsen, and publications of prestigious media, such as *Forbes*, *Time*, *Columbia Journalism Review*, Politico, *Financial Times*, *Press Gazette* and the BBC.

For several decades, media researchers have been considering possible scenarios of the decline of traditional means of communication in the post-press era, resulting, among other things, from the popularisation of the Internet as a source of information, entertainment, and the most crucial channel of daily communication among young generations (Adamczyk, 2013; Dawson, 2010; Lewis, 2020; Mielczarek, 2012; Poulet, 2011; Radcliffe, 2020). However, this process was to be evolutionary, along with changes in the age structure of the reading group (reduction in the number of the oldest recipients with established habits of obtaining information from newspapers for the benefit of young generations looking for interesting content on the Internet and social media) (Coddington & Lewis, 2021; D'Urso, 2020; Fatemi, 2021; How, 2020, September 30; Jones, 2020; Westcott et al., 2021). The forms of editorial functioning were also to be gradually altered. Over time, they were to increasingly convert to modern methods of working with human resources more flexibly. Remote work (homework), so far known mainly from the activities of war correspondents or freelancers, for many media employees, operating for decades in the fossilised structures of traditional editorial offices, seemed a desirable prospect and, at the same time an exciting alternative to the noisy newsroom (Ostwald, 2020). It was primarily perceived as an advantage (flexibility of working time, savings for employees and employers, and less nuisance resulting from the lack of necessity to travel to the editorial office). Hence, this organisational model was implemented, for example in online editorial offices such as ProPublica (Dool, 2020). According to Eurostat, about 10% of EU citizens worked remotely, but in Central and Eastern Europe alone, it was only 1%.

In contrast, in 2020, in the United States, the number of full-time remote workers reached 42% (for comparison, 35% functioned remotely in the same period in Germany; Krzysztoszek, 2020). However, due to the outbreak of the global COVID-19 pandemic, the transition to the new operating and management model had to be implemented instantly, without prepared adaptation plans and procedures. In these extraordinary conditions, not all editorial offices and the journalists working for them have adapted to the new work formula equally. Among the shortcomings of remote work, the following were mentioned:

1 Technical problems (slow Internet connections, unfamiliarity with instant messaging, hardware failures, lack of technical support);
2 Housing problems (lack of own space at home for quiet work);
3 Organisational problems (improper coordination of activities with superiors, lack of supervision over subordinates, inability to properly stimulate creativity among editorial staff, chaos resulting from the need to introduce new formulas for the functioning of the editorial office in remote and hybrid work conditions);
4 Problems of a psychological nature (lack of contact with colleagues, fear of being skipped in the promotion procedure, job insecurity during a recession in the media market, feeling of loneliness, fear of being infected with the virus while performing work, frustration caused by poor organisation of working time at home resulting in delays in preparing materials for publication, inability to adapt to new working conditions, especially by the oldest journalists);
5 Problems related to maintaining work standards (young adepts of journalism, deprived of daily contact with experienced reporters, had no one to learn their profession from, the risk of an avalanche increase in the amount of disinformation content, difficult to verify quickly in pandemic conditions);
6 Problems with access to confidential informants (restrictions on free movement resulted in difficulties in contact with secret sources of information using instant messaging and telephones – informants were afraid of disclosing their identity to undesirable persons or institutions) (Baker, 2020; Balakrishnan, 2021; ICFJ, 2020; Garthwaite; 2020; Majid, 2021; Margalit, 2020; McGarvey, 2020; Newman, 2021; Stopka, 2020; Tobitt, 2021; Waterson, 2021).

At the same time, many researchers noticed several positive consequences of the accelerated implementation of remote and hybrid work. Experience in online work of media employees shows the few primary advantages of this way of organising work and managing human resources. They mainly include:

1 Greater flexibility at work thanks to communication tools;
2 Reporters are more often involved in new journalistic formats;
3 saving time and money (commuting);
4 Greater chances of journalists from the local newsrooms appearing in the national media;
5 More effective protection against infection (Adamczyk, 2022; Hale; 2021).

There were also other significant forms of the impact of the COVID-19 pandemic on the media market. The latter's financial situation caused by the pandemic chiefly resulted from a serious decrease in advertising revenues. For example, a report prepared by the British Advertising Association and WARC revised their forecasts for advertising spending in 2020 downward to £21.13 billion, which meant a 16.7% decrease year-on-year, that is £4.23 billion. In the meantime, advertising spending in 2021 is expected not to exceed the total amount of 2019 (bcz, 2020; *How,* 2020; Mayhew, 2020). The European media has also suffered a significant decline in advertising revenues. According to Anda Rožukalne, professor of communication sciences at Stradins University in Riga, Latvia, lower incomes reduced the diversity of content, as some editorial offices, seeking to save money, resigned from collaborating with freelancers or reduced the frequency of publications.

For the same reason, the use of ready-made information provided by the authorities but devoid of critical editorial evaluation has also increased (Krūtaine, 2020). In its annual State of the News report, Pew Research Center presented the latest press trends. In 2020, the circulation (print and digital) of daily newspapers was 24.3 million, and for Sunday newspapers, 25.8 million (down 6% year-on-year; in 1990, the circulation of newspapers on weekdays was 63.2 million, and the circulation of Sunday newspapers was 62.6 million). The recent decline of the circulations has been marked, but 2020 was a record year in this respect. At the same time, subscription and sales prices at kiosks were rising. According to estimates by the Pew Research Center, revenues from circulation in 2020 amounted to USD 11.1 billion, slightly more than in the previous year (USD 11.0 billion). The pandemic also led to a significant drop in newspaper advertising incomes. The Pew Research Center report brought interesting information – for the first time in 2020, newspapers generated more revenue from circulation than from advertising (Adgate, 2021; Pew, 2021).

According to the Poynter Institute report, the most common consequences of the pandemic for the functioning of editorial offices were (1) merging editorial offices, (2) forced salary reduction, (3) suspending the publication of press titles, (4) reducing newspaper editions publication frequency (from five to three per week or from six to four), (5) unavoidable leave of editorial staff, (6) collapse of press titles, (7) closing printing houses, (8) merging branches, (9) selling offices, resigning from renting, and moving to cheaper locations, (10) resigning from the paper version in favour of online, or (11) shifting employees to remote work. These activities have been implemented by large corporations, publishing houses, or well-known editorial offices – Gannett, McClatchy, Tribune Publishing, Meredith, News Corp., The New York Times Company, CNN, Bloomberg News, NBC Universal, CBS, Fox News, NPR, or BuzzFeed (Barthel et al., 2020, Hare, 2021a; Tracy, 2020; Waterson, 2021).

The drop in newspaper revenues was one of the fundamental reasons for the decline in media employment. In 2020, the press industry numbered 30,820 employees (74,410 in 2006). According to a report prepared by the Pew Research Center, in 2020, layoffs occurred in as many as one-third of all newspapers. Interestingly, job cuts were more frequent in newspapers with a large circulation, while small editorial offices used this instrument less frequently. The economically tricky situation in the press industry often resulted in newspapers' closing. According to the Poynter report, more than 100 local newsrooms were permanently closed during the pandemic (this worrying trend has continued since 2004, with an average of 100 newspapers closed each year) (Hare, 2021a; Hare, 2021b). As Rick Ducey, Managing Director, BIA Advisory Services, notes, "There are three trends in the local newspaper industry that are converging in meaningful ways that could reshape community news. First, after waves of consolidation of newspapers and chains by private equity and larger publishers into larger and, in theory, more efficient operations, there's a new trend of returning some smaller newspapers back to local owners. Second, the value of local newspapers to local communities and their citizens and businesses has not been lost on Capitol Hill, where the Local Journalism Sustainability Act has been introduced in both the House and the Senate. The third trend is the continuation of declining economics in local newspapers (revenues in print advertising are falling faster than digital)" (Adgate, 2021). The phenomenon of closing more newspapers has led, for example in the United States, to the emergence of so-called information deserts. This term describes communities where the inhabitants do not have a local newspaper or access to information necessary for a democracy is severely limited. Of the 3,143 counties in the United States with a population of approximately 3.2 million, 200 no longer have a daily newspaper or weekly magazine. In addition, 1,449 counties have only one newspaper, usually published weekly. There is no daily newspaper in 2,000 counties. These informational deserts are mainly inhabited by elderly, poorer, and less educated persons (Adgate, 2021).

The coronavirus pandemic turned out to be a perfect time for online media, while traditional print media experienced a severe crisis (Fisher, 2021; Meyer, 2009). It was manifested, for example in the Czech Republic by a decrease in sales or even a suspension of publications (Gosling, 2020). More than 200 regional newspapers in Australia were closed or temporarily suspended in 2020 (Hess & Waller, 2021). Another adverse effect of the crisis in this media segment was the layoffs of journalists and publishing house employees. In 2020 alone, the prestigious British daily *The Guardian* laid off 180 employees – 70 in editorial positions, and the public broadcaster BBC announced 520 layoffs. Employment reductions also affected McClatchy and Vox (Adgate, 2021; Harris, 2020a; Nicolaou & Barker, 2020; Vogt, 2020). One of the effects of the crisis in the print media was wage cuts. They particularly affected journalists from local media and freelancers, where salary cuts ranged from 5 to 25% in Croatia (Prtorić, 2020). Publishers in the more developed media markets of the United States, Great Britain, and Italy also offered their employees lower salaries (Cruciata, 2020a; Law, 2021; Rajan, 2020). In search of savings, in some publishing groups, mergers of editorial teams were introduced, the number of editions per week was reduced, the frequency of publication of the title from daily to weekly was changed, or even the paper version was abandoned in favour of online. The layoffs of staff and the introduction of the remote work model necessitated some publishing houses to sell editorial facilities and move to other, cheaper ones to rent (Harris, 2020a; Hare, 2021a).

The COVID-19 pandemic had a negative impact not only on the economic aspect of media operations but also on their freedom. The extraordinary conditions of the functioning of societies in this period were used by the authorities of many countries to introduce restrictions that hampered the free operation of the media. The most serious threats to the flow of information negatively affected pluralism in three aspects: content, information sources, and content providers. In terms of content, one of the more frequently cited consequences was the deluge of disinformation regarding the coronavirus. The so-called infodemic was used to disseminate, in particular via social media, conspiracy theories about the alleged ineffectiveness of vaccines or even to question the existence of the pandemic itself (German Širotníková, 2020; Scott & Wheaton, 2021). To some extent, this was because many editorial offices were not professionally prepared to inform reporters about health-related issues. Therefore, during the initial period of the pandemic, the information provided to the public was often inconsistent, unverified, and incomprehensible to the average recipient, who was concerned about the development of the epidemiological situation and the direct threat to life and health (Natividad, 2020). According to Nielsen, the necessity to stay at home longer than usual for whole family members has contributed to a significant increase in video streaming, news consumption, and radio listening. The most popular TV news sources were local TV, national cable news, and national TV news (Adgate, 2020). The issue, as mentioned earlier, was also the transmission of government communications, mainly in the initial period of the pandemic, without journalistic verification and a critical view. In addition, reporters in some countries faced a wave of hate after publicising violations of sanitary restrictions introduced by the authorities due to COVID-19. This was the case in Croatia (in March 2020, it introduced a state of emergency and a ban on assembly), where on Easter Sunday, 14 April, a reporter from the local news portal Dalmatinski Portal and a camera operator from the N1 TV station informed about a mass (chyba mess? albo mass gathering) in the suburbs of Split. Media representatives were first physically attacked, and later, during an illegal demonstration supporting the priest, masked men carried a banner with the words "Journalists are worms" (Prtorić, 2020). As reported by the IPI, in early 2020, many European governments, especially in Eastern and Central Europe, used the ongoing health crisis as an excuse to restrict the free flow of information. In Hungary and Russia, control of pandemic information has been tightened, while in Bulgaria and Romania, the authorities imposed excessive penal sanctions for "fake news" about the virus. In Serbia and Moldova, governments tried to control COVID-19 reporting and banned the publication of opinion makers' articles. An emergency decree has been issued in Moldova prohibiting all media from printing and disseminating any "personal opinions" about the disease during the state of emergency. Instead, reports on the virus were to convey only the official position of the authorities. In Serbia, on the other hand, a decree issued by the administration provided penalties for local institutions for disclosing to the media information about new places of coronavirus outbreaks that were not "authorised" by the Belgrade officialdom. The Belarusian authorities went to extreme lengths in "disciplining" unruly journalists, where the editor of the news website Jeżedniewnik was arrested for critical comments on the government's actions during the pandemic (Bede, 2020; Wiseman, 2020). This particular period in Hungary was also used to destroy one of the last strongholds of free media. The authorities forced the resignation of the editorial staff of Index.hu, the country's largest news site (Bede, 2020).

Journalists from media independent of the establishment were also limited in access to information on the epidemiological situation at conferences of government representatives. In Austria, problems of this type appeared as early as March 2020, with fewer reporters participating in government press events. Only journalists from the public service broadcaster ORF and the Austrian Press Agency (APA) were granted access; others were encouraged to submit questions to the APA earlier (Vogt, 2020). In Spain, on the other hand, the organisers of the prime minister's press conferences tried to censor uncomfortable questions asked by correspondents, and national and regional governments also limited press access to hospitals, retirement homes, and official institutions – including the regional parliament in Madrid. In the Czech Republic, Bosnia and Herzegovina, and Slovenia, the authorities tried to limit the media's ability to question the actions of policymakers in the fight against the virus. Emergency regulations were enacted to make it more difficult for reporters to access information in Romania and Bulgaria, giving government institutions twice as long to answer corespondents' questions (Velasco, 2020; Wiseman, 2020). On the other hand, in Hungary, during press conferences, journalists could only ask the authorities' representatives about the pandemic's development by e-mail (Bede, 2020). In Romania, the administration made access to information difficult by abusing the Personal Data Protection Regulation (GDPR) provisions, which led to incomplete replies, long delays, or even refusal to disclose information (Holdiş, 2020).

During COVID-19, the authorities of various countries tried to subjugate the media, gaining their favour by providing financial support. The Greek government has allocated EUR 20 million to the media to cover public health news. The data released by the establishment showed that the media critical of the government's actions received less than 1% of this sum, and the criteria for granting support were vague and non-transparent (The Manifold, 2020). In Malta, the authorities introduced a non-transparent system allowing public aid to the media. The government has often suspended or offered publicly funded advertising to put pressure on the media (The Shift News, 2020). In Central and Eastern Europe, research conducted by N-Ost and the Friedrich Ebert Stiftung found widespread fears in the region that "the crisis posed an existential threat to financially vulnerable critical media, and that it would further accelerate market concentration among media moguls who pursue political interests" (Berger et al., 2020, p. 4; Carlini & Bleyer-Simon, 2021, p. 5).

Conclusions

The COVID-19 pandemic was undoubtedly an extraordinary and tremendous challenge to societies worldwide. Its consequences had multi-level effects in various spheres of life. It has also left its mark on the media market and the freedom of journalists to act. Some of the described phenomena can be considered catalysts of change, speeding up specific transformation processes in how the editorial office and reporters perform (remote operation and the hybrid formula of editorial work). Other phenomena, such as the inescapable reduction of employment, the collapse of many editorial offices of traditional media, or a relatively severe limitation of the range or frequency of their publication, constitute a painful experience for the media community. In a sense, the pandemic benefitted online media, which have adapted very well to operating in COVID-19 sanitary conditions and profited from the high demand for information about the coronavirus. However, the disease has also been used by the governments of many countries to try to limit media pluralism in terms of content, information sources, and content providers, which has had a harmful impact on the level of freedom of speech. In many of the countries described, the political officialdom introduced states of emergency, with emergency regulations, which restrictively limited access to information to hide their mistakes and omissions, and they even harassed reporters who were critical of these actions. The task of the journalistic community in these countries will be to exert pressure on the authorities to withdraw from the transitional regulations and bad practices applied to independent media after the pandemic ends.

Functioning during the pandemic restrictions also brings essential lessons for the future. Editors and journalists gained the necessary experience that will be useful in the event of another pandemic or terrorist threats in the future. The developed remote work procedures will then facilitate a quick and seamless transition to operate during the crisis. Remote work, despite some drawbacks, has become a leading solution in editorial management after the pandemic (in Poland, e.g. in local branches of the national daily *Gazeta Wyborcza* and the tabloids *Fakt* and *Super Express*).

Bibliography

Adamczyk, W. (2013). *Przyszłość prasy lokalnej w "epoce śmierci gazet"*. In R. Kowalczyk, W. Machura, & J. Sobczak (Eds.), *Pomiędzy wolnością a odpowiedzialnością. Problemy współczesnych mediów* (vol. II). Scriptorium. Wydawnictwo Naukowe, Opole

Adamczyk, W. (2022). *A road of no return? Media and journalism "Remotely" during and after the pandemic*. In K. Hajder, Ł. Donaj, & T. Herzog (Eds.), *Economy 4.0 and the COVID-19 pandemic – A review of research*. Logos Verlag Berlin GmbH.

Adgate, B. (2020, August 21). *Nielsen: How The pandemic changed at home media consumption*. Nielsen 21.08.2020. Retrieved October 17, 2021, from https://www.forbes.com/sites/bradadgate/2020/08/21/nielsen-how-the-pandemic-changed-at-home-media-consumption/?sh=430979085a28

Adgate, B. (2021, August 20). *Newspapers have been struggling and then came the pandemic*. "Forbes". Retrieved October 17, 2021, from https://www.forbes.com/sites/bradadgate/2021/08/20/newspapers-have-been-struggling-and-then-came-the-pandemic/?sh=65013ac112e6

Baker, M. (2020, April 14). *Gartner HR survey reveals 41% of employees likely to work remotely at least some of the time post coronavirus pandemic*. Retrieved May 23, 2020, from https://www.gartner.com/en/newsroom/press-releases/2020-04-14-gartner-hr-survey-reveals-41–of-employees-likely-to-

Balakrishnan, A. (2021, March 22). *Canadian news outlets close physical offices, codifying remote work*. Retrieved April 17, 2021, from https://www.orilliamatters.com/national-business/canadian-news-outlets-close-physical-offices-codifying-remote-work-3564566

Barthel, M., Matsa, K. E., & Worden, K. (2020, October 29). *Coronavirus-driven downturn hits newspapers hard as TV news thrives*. Pew Research Center. Retrieved October 16, 2021, from https://www.pewresearch.org/journalism/2020/10/29/coronavirus-driven-downturn-hits-newspapers-hard-as-tv-news-thrives/

bcz. (2020, May 4). *Rynek reklam w Wielkiej Brytanii skurczy się o 4,2 mld funtów*. WirtualneMedia. Retrieved May 5, 2020, from https://www.wirtualnemedia.pl/artykul/rynek-reklam-w-wielkiej-brytanii-skurczy-sie-o-4-2-mld-funtow

Bede, M. (2020, September 23). *In Hungary a government rattled by the pandemic finds new ways to suppress independent media*. International Press Institute. Retrieved October 22, 2021, from https://ipi.media/in-hungary-a-government-rattled-by-the-pandemic-finds-new-ways-to-suppress-independent-media/

Berger, V. et al. (2020). *A lockdown for independent media? Effects of the COVID–19 pandemic on the media landscape and press freedom in Central and Southeast Europe*. Working Paper. Retrieved October 20, 2021, from https://www.fes-budapest.org/fileadmin/user_upload/dokumente/pdf-dateien/A_Lockdown_for_Independent_Media_Report_Final.pdf

Carlini, R., & Bleyer-Simon, K. (2021, April). *Media economy in the pandemic: A European perspective*. European University Institute Technical Report.

Coddington, M., & Lewis, S. (2021, August 24). *How the pandemic (sort of) changed the way we consume news*. NiemanLab. Retrieved October 11, 2021, from https://www.niemanlab.org/2021/08/how-the-pandemic-sort-of-changed-the-way-we-consume-news/

Cruciata, G. (2020a, September 29). *Covid-19 intensifies challenges for freelance journalists in Italy*. International Press Institute. Retrieved October 22, 2021, from https://ipi.media/covid-19-intensifies-challenges-for-freelance-journalists-in-italy/

Cruciata, G. (2020b, December 10). *Successful models of local journalism blossom in Italy despite pandemic challenges*. International Press Institute. Retrieved October 22, 2021, from https://ipi.media/successful-models-of-local-journalism-blossom-in-italy-despite-pandemic-challenges/

D'Urso, J. (2020, July 6). *How the coronavirus pandemic is changing social media*. Reuters Institute. Retrieved June 27, 2021, from https://reutersinstitute.politics.ox.ac.uk/risj-review/how-coronavirus-pandemic-changing-social-media

Dawson, R. (2010). *Newspaper Extinction Timeline. When newspapers in their current form will become insignificant*. Future Exploration Network.

Dool, G. (2020, September 17). *The future of the newsroom post-pandemic*. Digital Content Next. Retrieved February 15, 2021, from https://digitalcontentnext.org/blog/2020/09/17/the-future-of-the-newsroom-post-pandemic/

Fatemi, F. (2021, February 1). *How the pandemic has changed video content and consumption*. "Forbes". Retrieved March 29, 2021, from https://www.forbes.com/sites/falonfatemi/2021/02/01/how-the-pandemic-has-changed-video-content-and-consumption/?sh=5b7760446ec0

Fisher, S. (2021, March 14). *How COVID changed media consumption in America*. Retrieved June 28, 2021, from https://www.axios.com/pandemic-media-streaming-podasts-cable-news-966f4b15-60c5-45c2-a6ba-f5d77febda13.html

Garthwaite, A. (2020, April 29). *"Adapt or die": Newsrooms amid COVID-19 pandemic*. World Association of News Publishers. Retrieved June 6, 2020, from https://wan-ifra.org/2020/04/adapt-or-die-newsrooms-amid-covid-19-pandemic/

German Širotníková, M. (2020, October 13). *As pandemic grows, Slovak media struggle to fight the infodemic*. International Press Institute. Retrieved May 19, 2021, from https://ipi.media/as-pandemic-grows-slovak-media-struggle-to-fight-the-infodemic/

Gosling, T. (2020, October 16). *A model for survival? Online subscriptions help Denník N weather pandemic*. International Press Institute. Retrieved May 21, 2021, from https://ipi.media/a-model-for-survival-online-subscriptions-help-dennik-n-weather-pandemic-in-czech-republic/

Hale, S. (2021, March 23). *Five ways Covid-19 has changed media for good*. Retrieved April 15, 2021, from https://www.fipp.com/news/five-ways-covid-19-has-changed-media-for-good/#

Hare, K. (2021a, March 2021). *Here are the newsroom layoffs, furloughs and closures that happened during the coronavirus pandemic*. Poynter. Retrieved April 7, 2021, from https://www.poynter.org/business-work/2021/here-are-the-newsroom-layoffs-furloughs-and-closures-caused-by-the-coronavirus/

Hare, K. (2021b, December 2). *More than 100 local newsrooms closed during the coronavirus pandemic*. Poynter. Retrieved December 10, 2021, from https://www.poynter.org/locally/2021/the-coronavirus-has-closed-more-than-100-local-newsrooms-across-america-and-counting/

Harris, L. (2020a, July 22). *Will changes to print outlast the pandemic?*, Columbia Journalism Review. Retrieved August 27, 2021, from https://www.cjr.org/business_of_news/will-changes-to-print-outlast-the-pandemic.php

Harris, L. (2020b, July 28). *How the pandemic may change the way we get our news*. Retrieved August 23, 2021, from https://billmoyers.com/story/will-changes-to-print-outlast-the-pandemic/

Hess, K., & Waller, L. J. (2021). Local newspapers and coronavirus: Conceptualising connections, comparisons and cures. *Media International Australia*, *178*(1), 21–35.

Holdiş, D. (2020, October 20). *Right to information suffers further in Romania during pandemic*. International Press Institute. Retrieved August 23, 2021, from https://ipi.media/right-to-information-suffers-further-in-romania-during-pandemic/

How Does the Media Industry Change During Pandemic? (2021, February 19). Retrieved March 2, 2021, from https://www.bsgroup.eu/blog/how-does-the-media-industry-change-during-pandemic/

How has Covid-19 Changed Media Consumption? (2020, September 30). Retrieved June 12, 2021, from https://oxfordbusinessgroup.com/news/how-has-covid-19-changed-media-consumption

ICFJ. (2020, October 13). *New global survey raises red flags for journalism in the COVID-19 era*. International Center for Journalists. Retrieved November 15, 2020, from https://www.icfj.org/news/new-global-survey-raises-red-flags-journalism-covid-19-era

Jones, K. (2020, April 9). *This is how COVID-19 has changed media habits in each generation*. Retrieved March 5, 2021, from https://www.weforum.org/agenda/2020/04/covid19-media-consumption-generation-pandemic-entertainment/

Krūtaine, A. (2020, October 29). *Baltic media, reinvigorated in their mission, buckle up for tough ride under COVID-19*. International Press Institute. Retrieved October 17, 2021, from https://ipi.media/baltic-media-reinvigorated-in-their-mission-buckle-up-for-tough-ride-under-covid-19/

Krzysztoszek, A. (2020). *Praca zdalna nie tylko w czasie pandemii. Czeka nas era home office?*, Euractiv.pl 1.08.2020. Retrieved September 2, 2020, from https://www.euractiv.pl/section/praca-i-polityka-spoleczna/news/google-praca-zdalna-koronawirus-pandemia-covid19-homeoffice/

Law, T. (2021, January 22). *COVID-19 is ravaging local newspapers, making it easier for misinformation to spread*. "Time". Retrieved March 1, 2021, from https://time.com/5932520/covid-19-local-news/

Lewis, P. (2020, June 15). *COVID-19 has changed the media landscape—maybe forever*. Retrieved March 1, 2021, from https://www.mower.com/news/covid-19-has-changed-the-media-landscape-maybe-forever/

Majid, A. (2021, March 18). *One year since lockdown news industry survey: Business confidence returning but few plan full-time office return*. "Press Gazette". Retrieved March 27, 2021, from https://www.pressgazette.co.uk/one-year-lockdown-how-pandemic-affected-media-work/

Margalit, R. (2020). *Out of nowhere. What's lost and won as newsrooms close their offices for good*. "Columbia Journalism Review" Winter 2020. Retrieved February 27, 2021, from https://www.cjr.org/special_report/out-of-nowhere.php

Mayhew, F. (2020, June 12). *Journalism after Covid-19: 'It's not an extinction-level event'*. "Press Gazette". Retrieved November 9, 2020, from https://www.pressgazette.co.uk/journalism-after-covid-19-its-not-an-extinction-level-event/

McGarvey, E. (2020, June 1). *Coronavirus: How a pandemic changed our newspaper industry*. BBC News. Retrieved July 25, 2021, from https://www.bbc.com/news/uk-northern-ireland-52807646

Meyer, P. (2009). *The vanishing newspaper: Saving journalism in the information age*. University of Missouri Press.
Mielczarek, T. (2012). *Raport o śmierci polskich gazet*. Warszawa.
Natividad, I. (2020, May 6). *COVID-19 and the media: The role of journalism in a global pandemic*. Retrieved July 26, 2021, from https://news.berkeley.edu/2020/05/06/covid-19-and-the-media-the-role-of-journalism-in-a-global-pandemic/
Newman, N. (2021, January 7). *Journalism, media, and technology trends and predictions 2021*. Reuters Institute. Retrieved January 22, 2021, from https://reutersinstitute.politics.ox.ac.uk/journalism-media-and-technology-trends-and-predictions-2021
Nicolaou, A., & Barker, A. (2020, June 25). *Coronavirus rips a hole in newspapers' business models*. "Financial Times". Retrieved September 2, 2021, from https://www.ft.com/content/b6fdec4c-e3e7-43b9-a804-03c435de65bb
Ostwald, P. (2020, October). *COVID changing the classical newsroom: How could the future of journalism look like?*, "What's new in publishing".
Pew Research Center. (2021). *State of the News Media. Data and trends about key sectors in the US news media industry*. Retrieved October 4, 2021, from https://www.pewresearch.org/topic/news-habits-media/news-media-trends/state-of-the-news-media-project/
Poulet, B. (2011). *Śmierć gazet i przyszłość informacji*, Wołowiec.
Prtorić, J. (2020, October 2). *Covid-19 lays bare precarious working conditions of Croatian journalists*. International Press Institute. Retrieved July 26, 2021, from https://ipi.media/covid-19-crisis-lays-bare-dire-working-conditions-of-journalists-in-croatia/
Radcliffe, D. (2020, October 14). *COVID-19's impact on the media, in 10 charts*. Retrieved May 18, 2021, from https://whatsnewinpublishing.com/covid-19s-impact-on-the-media-in-10-charts/
Rajan, A. (2020, April 16). *How coronavirus infected publishing*. BBC. Retrieved May 19, 2021, from https://www.bbc.com/news/entertainment-arts-52299925
Scott, M., & Wheaton, S. (2021, July 21). *Social media's coronavirus challenge: Responsibility*. "Politico". Retrieved September 17, 2021, from https://www.politico.eu/article/coronavirus-pandemic-misinformation-facebook-google-twitter/
Stopka, A. (2020, December 18). *Dziennikarz zdalny*, Stowarzyszenie Dziennikarzy Polskich. Retrieved January 6, 2021, from https://sdp.pl/ks-artur-stopka-dziennikarz-zdalny/
The Manifold. (2020, August 6). *The Covid-19 crisis highlights Greece's media problem*. International Press Institute. Retrieved September 15, 2021, from https://ipi.media/the-covid-19-crisis-highlights-greeces-media-problem/
The Shift News. (2020, November 20). *COVID-19 adds to press freedom challenges in Malta*. International Press Institute. Retrieved September 15, 2021, from https://ipi.media/covid-19-funds-threaten-media-independence-in-malta/
Tobitt, C. (2021, March 18). *"Swings and roundabouts": What Covid-19 remote working has done to newsroom productivity*. "Press Gazette". Retrieved March 22, 2021, from https://www.pressgazette.co.uk/what-covid-19-remote-working-has-done-to-newsroom-productivity/
Tracy, M. (2020, April 10). *News media outlets have been ravaged by the pandemic*. "The New York Times". Retrieved April 21, 2020, from https://www.nytimes.com/2020/04/10/business/media/news-media-coronavirus-jobs.html
Velasco, P. (2020, November 24). *Spain's free press put to test under COVID-19 restrictions*. International Press Institute. Retrieved September 15, 2021, from https://ipi.media/spains-free-press-put-to-test-under-covid-19-restrictions/
Vogt, J. (2020, October 22). *New problems and some old ones: Austria's media landscape under the pandemic*. International Press Institute. Retrieved September 16, 2021, from https://ipi.media/new-problems-and-some-old-ones-austrias-media-landscape-under-the-pandemic/
Waterson, J. (2021, March 19). *Mirror owner to tell most journalists to permanently work from home*. "The Guardian". Retrieved March 24, 2021, from https://www.theguardian.com/business/2021/mar/19/mirror-owner-tell-most-journalists-permanently-work-from-home-reach

Westcott, K., Arbanas, J., Downs, K., Arkenberg, C., & Jarvis, D. (2021, April 16). *Digital media trends, 15th edition. Courting the consumer in a world of choice*. Retrieved May 14, 2021, from https://www2.deloitte.com/us/en/insights/industry/technology/digital-media-trends-consumption-habits-survey/summary.html

Wiseman, J. (2020, April 10). *European media freedom suffers under COVID-19 response*. International Press Institute. Retrieved September 15, 2021, from https://ipi.media/european-media-freedom-suffers-covid-19-response/

10 The COVID-19 Pandemic as Another Pretext for Information Control

Case Studies of Belarus and Ukraine

Vladyslav Zinichenko

Introduction

The beginning of 2020 was marked by reports of "atypical pneumonia cases" in Wuhan, China (World Health Organization, 2020). At that time, the issue seemed distant and unimportant to the inhabitants of Eastern Europe. However, the situation began to change on 27 February, when the first case of the disease was recorded in Belarus. It was brought to the country by a student from Iran (Ministry of Health of the Republic of Belarus, 2020). Five days later, a similar situation occurred in Ukraine. In this case, the patient returned from Italy (Ukrinform, 2020). Since the circumstances in the world only worsened, the World Health Organisation declared the coronavirus a global pandemic (World Health Organization, 2020).

The political establishment was confused due to insufficient information about the new disease. The main task was to limit its spread. However, this pandemic has become more than just a responsibility for them. It gave authorities new opportunities to control media and society. Freedom of information has been limited not only in authoritarian but also in democratic countries. The crisis also benefitted some other interest groups. "We could have a parallel epidemic of authoritarian and repressive measures following close if not on heels of a health epidemic", the United Nations Special Rapporteur on counter-terrorism and human rights Fionnuala D. Ní Aoláin stated (Gebrekidan, 2020).

The main aim of this chapter is to analyse the use of the COVID-19 pandemic as a new pretext for information control, specifically in Belarus and Ukraine. This is important for several reasons. Firstly, the two Eastern European countries have different political systems. According to the Freedom House report, Belarus is a consolidated authoritarian regime with a democracy score of 1.18 (fourth from the bottom). At the same time, Ukraine is a transitional or hybrid regime with a score of 3.36 (Freedom House, n. d.). Secondly, they differ in terms of political direction. If the Belarusian regime entirely depends on Russia, then the Ukrainian people intend to become members of the European Union. Thirdly, the active period of the pandemic was very difficult for both countries. Ukraine ranked 26th in morbidity among 231 world countries as of 20 February 2023 (Worldometr, n. d.). Although Belarus was in 74th place according to the official data (Worldometr, n. d.), the government could hide the real figures. The country did not introduce strict quarantine

DOI: 10.4324/9781003482710-11

measures. Finally, the scientific literature has understudied the pandemic in Belarus and Ukraine. At the same time, authors included Armenia and Moldova in their academic papers (Eck & Hatz, 2020; Papadopoulou & Maniou, 2021).

It is necessary to conduct an exploratory study on the topic. Its aim is transformed into the following research question:

RQ. What options were used to limit media freedom in Belarus and Ukraine during the COVID-19 pandemic?

A potential reason for the increase in morbidity could be the lack of transparency on the coronavirus. These actions also contributed to the spread of rumours and fake news. The so-called "infodemic" developed parallel to the pandemic (World Health Organization, n. d.). Thus, it is essential to focus on the restrictions of media representatives as a core issue. The author has an advantage in knowledge of the Ukrainian language and understanding of the Belarusian language. It allows this research to cover violations not presented in general international reports.

Definition of media freedom

The concept of media freedom has changed several times throughout history. Richter (2016) identified at least three periods of its development. In particular, the time interval from 1945 to the 1960s was called "freedom of information". The lack of freedom of speech and information during WWII and the desire of people to gain new knowledge led to the establishment of this provision in international law. The 1945 Constitution of UNESCO, the Universal Declaration of Human Rights, the International Covenant on Civil and Political Rights, and the European Convention for the Protection of Human Rights and Fundamental Freedoms were among the main documents.

The growing popularity of television and the need of society to access and gather information about various areas of a country's life marked the beginning of the second stage, or "freedom of the mass media period". It lasted from 1970 to the mid-1990s. Journalists and media were then recognised as information mediators (Richter, 2016). They had to be autonomous to perform this socially important function. The other main criteria were the ability to control authorities' actions, the absence of restrictions from governmental and non-governmental actors, and the presence of favourable conditions for spreading diverse thoughts (Papadopoulou & Maniou, 2021, p. 3). Therefore, the corresponding right to mass media freedom was secured in the documents of the Parliament Assembly of the Council of Europe, the Committee of Ministers of the Council of Europe, and UNESCO (Richter, 2016).

"Freedom of the mass media period" transformed into "freedom of the media period" in the mid-1990s. The reason for the name change was the advent of social media, which are more individualised tools than traditional media. They ensured the pluralism of opinions in the information space. This category played a significant role in determining the place of media freedom in international law. The latter began to develop separately from freedom of speech and freedom of information in the terminology of international organisations (Richter, 2016). After all, the most

Environment		*Description*
Legal	1	Protection of media freedom by the constitution.
	2	Absence of laws that can limit the professional work of the media.
Political	1	Absence of state censorship.
	2	Open access to diverse sources of information.
	3	No cases of physical or other violence against journalists.
Professional	1	Journalists as the Fourth Estate (watchdogs).
	2	Media as the voice of the marginalised.
	3	Prefers controversial stories and disputes.
	4	Prevents self-censorship.
Economic	1	Contributes to the dissemination of information to the audience.
	2	Encourages competition and ownership by several people or other entities.
	3	Exclusion of financial manipulations on the part of the government.

Figure 10.1 Criteria that influence media freedom

Source: From Whitten-Woodring (2009). Watchdog or Lapdog? Media Freedom, Regime Type, and Government Respect for Human Rights. *International Studies Quarterly*, 53(3): 598.

applicable definition of media freedom is "the degree of freedom enjoyed by the media to publish news and the degree of freedom and access of citizens to public information" (McQuail, 2003 in Masduki 2022, p. 221). Figure 10.1 shows the criteria that make media free. The list was expanded by Whitten-Woodring.

State of media freedom in Ukraine and Belarus

Since the two countries have different political systems, it affects the level of media freedom. One of the confirmations is the annual ranking of Reporters Without Borders. According to the data in 2019, Ukraine took the 102nd position, corresponding to formulating the transitional regime mentioned above. As an authoritarian country, Belarus reached only 153rd place out of 180 countries (Reporters Without Borders, 2019). If the former country improved the situation as of 2021, the latter dropped to 158th place (Reporters Without Borders, 2021). The reason for this was not only the authorities' actions during the pandemic but also numerous suppressed protests.

In theory, the national legislation of both countries guarantees the necessary rights and freedoms to journalists. Specifically, they are ensured by two laws of Belarus, as well as five laws of Ukraine and the Civil Code of Ukraine as of 2021 (Figure 10.2). The most important provisions are outlined in their constitutions. Article 33 of the Belarusian Constitution states[1]:

- "Everyone is guaranteed freedom of thought and beliefs and their free expression",
- "No one can be forced to express one's beliefs or to deny them",
- "Monopolisation of the mass media by the State, public associations or individual citizens and also censorship is not permitted".

Belarus	Ukraine
1 Law of the Republic of Belarus "On Mass Media" (2008). 2 Law of the Republic of Belarus "On Information, Informatization and Protection of Information" (2008).	1 Law of Ukraine "On Information" (1992). 2 Law of Ukraine "On Printed Mass Media (Press)" (1993). 3 Law of Ukraine "On Television and Radio Broadcasting" (1994). 4 Law of Ukraine "On News Agencies" (1995). 5 Law of Ukraine "On Access to Public Information" (2011). 6 Civil Code of Ukraine (2003).

Figure 10.2 National legislation of Belarus and Ukraine in the context of media freedom

Source: Own elaboration based on Kalitenko, O. M., Anikina, H. V., Anikina, G., Spasova, K. I., Spasova, E., & Shahaka, O. V. (2021). The restrictions of the freedom of information during the Covid-19 pandemic. *Cuestiones Politicas*, 39(70): 426–445.

Article 34 of the Ukrainian Constitution states[2]:

- "Everyone is guaranteed the right to freedom of thought and speech, and to the free expression of his or her views and beliefs",
- "Everyone has the right to freely collect, store, use and disseminate information by oral, written or other means of his or her choice",
- "The exercise of these rights may be restricted by law in the interests of national security, territorial indivisibility or public order, with the purpose of preventing disturbances or crimes, protecting the health of the population, the reputation or rights of other persons, preventing the disclosure of information received confidentially, or supporting the authority and impartiality of justice".

Examining the two articles, one can find a significant difference between the two countries. Although the Belarusian document includes a provision prohibiting censorship, the authorities do not follow it in practice. The situation in Ukraine is the opposite, despite the article specifying permissible cases of restriction of freedom of speech.

The concept of digital authoritarianism can be applied to Belarus as well. It refers to using digital technologies to control and restrict citizens, including media workers (Masduki, 2022, p. 220). Among other things, the authorities created a Ministry of Information. One of the tasks of this governmental body is to prepare a list of so-called "extremist" Telegram channels and social media accounts. It also blocks "inappropriate" websites. All of them are oppositional.

The same claims cannot be addressed in Ukraine. The country indeed has a Ministry of Culture and Information Policy, but its work is not sufficiently visible. Their affiliation with pro-Russian forces justifies the blocking of websites and social media. For example, the popular VK was a source of disinformation and information-psychological operations in Ukraine. User data could easily be transferred to Russian special services. Therefore, former president Petro Poroshenko implemented the decision of the National Security and Defence Council to restrict access to this website in 2017[3].

In general, Belarus and Ukraine differ in the level of media freedom. However, this research goes further and offers a specific analysis of exceptional circumstances, namely the COVID-19 crisis. The author considers it essential to enrich international scientific literature with knowledge about two key Eastern European countries.

Methodology

This research is qualitative in nature. It is designed to create a picture of the main trends regarding restrictions on media freedom in Belarus and Ukraine. It uses secondary sources for data collection and covers the period of 2020–2021. The sample is drawn from two local monitoring tools/platforms: (1) the Belarusian Association of Journalists (BAJ; Belarus) and (2) the Institute of Mass Information (IMI; Ukraine). They provided significantly more results than worldwide monitoring tools/instruments. Specifically, the author searched for materials using the keyword "COVID-19" on the Belarusian website[4] and analysed materials under the name "Freedom of Speech Barometer" (*Барометр свободи слова*) on the Ukrainian website[5]. He also added several cases from his own knowledge. The study is expected to be one of the most accurate.

The BAJ is a complete counterweight to the pro-government Belarusian Union of Journalists. The former describes itself as a "voluntary, non-governmental, non-partisan association of citizens". It has been operating since 1995 and has already managed to become a member of the International Federation of Journalists and the European Federation of Journalists. The main tasks are media monitoring, protection of the rights and interests of reporters, development of media skills, and cooperation with journalistic organisations worldwide. Among other things, it received the National Prize of Ukraine for the defence of freedom[6].

The IMI was founded in 1995 as well. It does not represent any political or commercial power and operates based on voluntary donations from other NGOs and citizens. The main objectives are "the development of socially responsible journalism and the improvement of media literacy of the population" in accordance with European values. It is important to note that the IMI is an official partner of Reporters Without Borders[7].

The sample resulted in 25 cases of media violations from the Belarusian side and 95 cases from the Ukrainian side. Each situation is analysed through the prism of possible options for limiting media freedom. The classification is based on the scientific article by Papadopoulou and Maniou (2021) and the one by Eck and Hatz (2020), with some modifications. This study attempts to cover both online and offline cases. It consists of the following points:

- Among *political options* are censorship and barriers to access public information implemented by authorities or other state political representatives.

They can include information manipulation and revocation of accreditations. Moreover, they can provoke self-censorship on the part of journalists and other representatives of a media community;

- *Popular options* are barriers to access information set by random individuals, including entrepreneurs, clergy, and other members of society;
- *Legal options* include arbitrary use of laws and "coronavirus" regulations by judges, detention and criminal proceedings against reporters, and formal warnings;
- *Economic options* encompass fines, cuts in media funding, and refusal to rent space for work;
- Among *physical options* are the destruction of journalistic equipment, physical attacks on media representatives by the police and random individuals, deliberate attempts to affect reporters with the coronavirus, and killings;
- Smear campaigns, threats, and online harassment are attributes of *psychological options*;
- *Technological options* equal digital tracking practices.

Results

The general picture of the analysed cases of media freedom violations in Belarus and Ukraine is presented in Figure 10.3. Although the numbers cannot be exhaustive, they are intended to give an idea of the preference for certain options over others. Their examples with crucial additional information are described below.

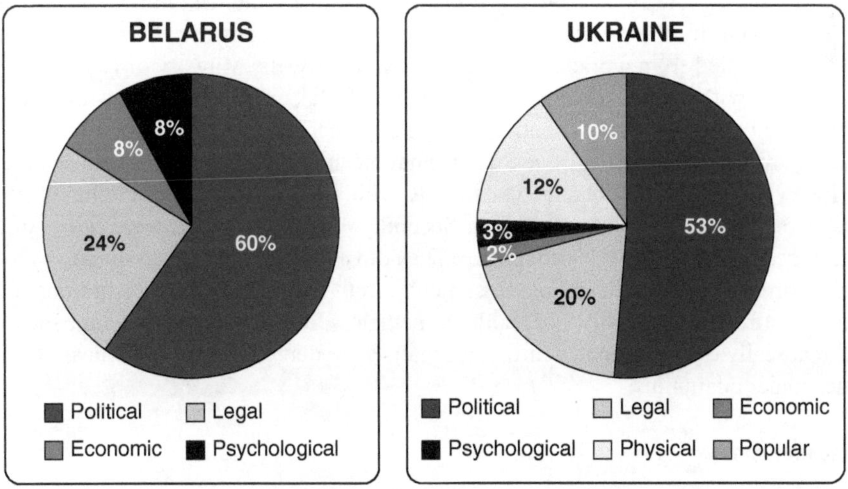

Figure 10.3 Use of various options for information control in Ukraine and Belarus

Source: Own elaboration.

Political options

The Belarusian authorities have created all the conditions for self-censorship of medical workers. For example, the head doctor of a hospital in Vitebsk was fired after a critical review regarding the authorities' actions during the pandemic (Korovenkova, 2021). Therefore, media requests for information were rejecte, with some of them remained unanswered. Journalists were advised to contact the Ministry of Health's press service. The latter, in turn, tried to hold press briefings as rarely as possible. Its representatives selectively answered questions from reporters and manipulated data (Nasha Niva, 2020).

If independent media managed to publish certain information, it was called "fake" and demanded to be removed (Monitoring Service of the Civil Organization "Belarusian Association of Journalists", 2020). The authorities even revoked the accreditation of a journalist from "friendly" Russia due to a news story about the coronavirus situation in Belarus. Aleksei Kruchinin was expelled from the country (Tolkacheva, 2020).

Compared to the Belarusian violations, the Ukrainian ones were slightly different. Regional councils, city councils, and village councils were the entities that limited access to their meetings under the guise of quarantine restrictions. The same measures were used during the Congress of the Servant of the People party (*Слуга народу*) in Lutsk (Institute of Mass Information, 2020a). However, the biggest surprise was the restriction on the press conference of Ukrainian President Volodymyr Zelenskyy. The press service accredited only 30 reporters from all over the country. Many "non-leading" media were left without the opportunity to ask questions (Hryhorska, 2021). A similar situation was repeated with the opposition media during the visits of the presidents of Poland and Israel (Institute of Mass Information, 2020b; 2021a).

As for healthcare system representatives, one of the Ukrainian journalists agreed to clarify the situation in a comment based on anonymity. Three problems were identified from a practical point of view. Firstly, the Ministry of Health's cooperation with the media under the leadership of Maksym Stepanov was limited. It happened at a time when attention to medicine increased significantly. For example, they asked to send requests for information and could leave them unanswered. However, the situation changed positively with the appointment of the new Minister of Healthcare, Viktor Lyashko. Secondly, medical workers were noticeably engaged in preventive self-censorship. They did not want to complain due to fear of a reprimand from the head doctor, someone from the regional administration, and directly from the Ministry of Health. Nonetheless, it is not known whether such a threat really existed or not. Thirdly, journalists are denied access to medical facilities under quarantine.

Popular options

If censorship was the exclusive tool of the authorities in Belarus, various representatives of society introduced barriers to access to information in Ukraine. For instance, parishioners prevented reporters from checking compliance with quarantine measures in one of the churches in Chernivtsi (Institute of Mass Information, 2020c). Furthermore, security did not allow media representatives to attend the election of the rector of Odesa National Medical University (Institute of Mass Information, 2020d).

Legal options

One of the most severe forms of limiting media freedom was the imprisonment of journalists. The detention of Sergei Satsuk, who investigated corruption in Belarus's healthcare system, became a high-profile case. His previous materials have already caused threats from unknown people. In the most recent article, the reporter questioned the reliability of official statistics regarding the COVID-19 pandemic. As a result, he was detained on the charge of accepting bribes for the publications. In 2022, the court sentenced Satsuk to eight years in prison (Monitoring Service of the Civil Organization "Belarusian Association of Journalists", 2022).

The nature of violations was weaker in Ukraine. All of them were related to decisions barring journalists from attending court sessions. Quarantine measures were the primary justification, although they could not be applied to reporters' activities (Institute of Mass Information, 2020b). Moreover, courts continued to deny access even after restrictions on the number of people on the premises were lifted (Institute of Mass Information, 2021b).

Economic options

The Belarusian government strengthened information control through fines. The head of the Belarusian Union of Journalists, Andrew Krivosheev, also spoke in favour of this step (Press Service of the "Belarusian Association of Journalists", 2020a). Among other things, Media-Paliessie (*Медыя-Палессе*) published news material about the death of a patient from the coronavirus in the Brest region. Since it turned out to be false, the website removed this information after 15 minutes. The patient had no complaints. However, this was not enough. The court imposed a fine of approximately 1,250 euros on the media. The judge argued that the publication harmed Belarus's national interests (Press Service of the "Belarusian Association of Journalists", 2020b).

In Ukraine, the Cabinet of Ministers cut funding to the Public Broadcaster during the review of the state budget due to the COVID-19 pandemic (Zakusylo, 2020). The decision could endanger its functioning. Fortunately, the National Public Broadcasting Company was able to survive this period.

Physical options

The circumstances proved the fact that journalism is a dangerous profession. One of the locations for attacks on them was a sports ground in the Kyiv district of Hydropark. Firstly, random youths beat the "ZIK" TV channel team. Secondly, an unknown man took Espeso's camera and mobile phone and threw them into the

Dnipro River (Institute of Mass Information, 2020e). In another situation, an attempt to record violations of quarantine measures at one of the parties in Vinnytsia resulted in a broken finger for journalist Andriy Kachor (Institute of Mass Information, 2021c). Surprisingly, this tendency was typical only for Ukraine.

Psychological options

One of the Belarusian smear campaigns against media representatives was organised not by government officials but by the president himself. Aliaksandr Lukashenka indirectly compared independent reporters to "scumbags" who spread "fake stories" about the COVID-19 pandemic and instructed the head of the KGB to deal with them (BELTA, 2020). This move was supposed to affect the coverage of these media and reduce public trust in them.

Ukrainian media also received threats. In particular, the personal life of Hromadske journalist Alina Sheremeta began to be actively discussed on the Internet after she reported on the work of Kyiv bars during the COVID-19 pandemic. Unknown people sent her harassing messages through Facebook (Institute of Mass Information, 2021d). Additionally, the mayor of Cherkasy threatened to "twist the hands" of the reporters from the VIKKA TV channel. The reason was the professional gestures of media representatives during one of the meetings (Institute of Mass Information, 2020e).

Technological options

The Ministry of Digital Transformation of Ukraine has developed the "Act at Home" (*Дій вдома*) application to monitor compliance with self-isolation by any citizen, including journalists. Its installation was not mandatory. According to the amended legislation, it could collect the following data: (1) first name and last name; (2) date of birth; (3) sex; (4) phone number; (5) address of self-isolation; (6) residential address; (7) places of work, study, children's institution and their addresses; (8) information about the ability to self-care; (9) health status; (10) contact people (if provided); (11) period of self-isolation; (12) location; and (13) photo of the person. Some were sent to the police if the user did not comply with self-isolation requirements (Communications Department of the Secretariat of the Cabinet of Ministers of Ukraine, 2020)[8]. Although there were no reports of surveillance, the app raised some concerns. For example, it is not known for certain whether this data was used by the police only for verification purposes (Internet Freedom, 2020). After all, this case still cannot be included in Figure 10.3, but it must be mentioned.

Conclusions

There were significant violations of media freedom in both countries. Belarusian authorities resorted to political, legal, economic, and psychological options, while various actors from Ukraine used a much more comprehensive range of options. Although some of these categories overlapped, their nature was slightly different.

For instance, Belarusian journalists were often fined for trying to cover the COVID-19 pandemic. It is important to note that they were not afraid to publish the truth in conditions of complete censorship. Perhaps the upcoming presidential election and further protests influenced their decisions. In turn, Ukrainian colleagues could lose their jobs due to funding cuts or attempts to take away their workspace. While the reporter was sentenced to prison in Belarus, media representatives were beaten for performing their professional duties in Ukraine. In the latter country, journalists received threats via social media platforms. To summarise, these actions can be explained by the difference in the political systems of the two countries, which affected citizens' awareness of the coronavirus.

The Russian–Ukrainian war, which also influenced Belarus, did not fundamentally change the situation with freedom of information. The majority of Belarusian independent journalists work from abroad. Those who remain in Belarus are subjected to searches by law enforcement agencies, detentions, and other forms of repression. The country is called a "black hole" for media freedom (United Nations, 2021). Lukashenka has no so-called "red lines". The story of the forced landing of the Ryanair plane in Minsk is well known. One of the passengers, who turned out to be the opposition journalist Roman Protasevich, was detained together with his girlfriend (BBC, 2021). At the same time, the television marathon "The Only News" (*Єдині новини*) was launched in Ukraine. It was supposed to become a single and continuous source of information for the population during the war. However, the authorities stopped broadcasting some opposition TV channels (Pryamiy, Espreso.TV, and 5 Kanal). Moreover, military censorship was introduced. As of December 2023, Belarus fell to 157th, and Ukraine rose to 79th spot in the World Press Freedom Index (Reporters Without Borders, 2023).

Further studies should focus on more countries from Eastern Europe. Reading analysis prepared by local scholars who understand the context would be interesting.

One of the limitations of this research is the inability to cover all cases of media freedom violations in Belarus and Ukraine. It is assumed that the Belarusian numbers are much higher. Unfortunately, it is impossible to analyse all of them due to the problematic reporting conditions in this country.

Notes

1 See: Constitution of the Republic of Belarus (1996) https://constitutionnet.org/sites/default/files/Belarus%20Constitution.pdf, accessed on 18.02.2023.
2 See: Constitution of Ukraine (1996). https://www.refworld.org/pdfid/44a280124.pdf, accessed on 18.02.2023.
3 See: Decree of the President of Ukraine No. 133 (2017). https://www.president.gov.ua/documents/1332017-21850, accessed on 18.02.2023.
4 See: Belarusian Association of Journalists. https://baj.by/be, accessed on 02.02.2023.
5 See: Institute of Mass Information. https://imi.org.ua/monitorings/barometr-svobody-slova, accessed on 03.02.2023.
6 See: Belarusian Association of Journalists. https://baj.by/en/aboutbaj, accessed on 10.02.2023.
7 See: Institute of Mass Information. https://imi.org.ua/en/about, accessed on 03.02.2023.

8 See: Resolution of the Cabinet of Ministers No. 291 (2020). https://zakon.rada.gov.ua/laws/show/291-2020-п#Text, accessed on 25.02.2022.

Bibliography

BBC. (2021). *Roman Protasevich: Belarus dissident seized from Ryanair plane*. Retrieved December 20, 2023, from https://www.bbc.com/news/world-europe-57229635

BELTA. (2020). *Lukashenko demands to tackle spread of fake news about coronavirus deaths*. Retrieved February 24, 2023, from https://eng.belta.by/president/view/lukashenko-demands-to-tackle-spread-of-fake-news-about-coronavirus-deaths-129197-2020

Communications Department of the Secretariat of the Cabinet of Ministers of Ukraine. (2020). *Yak pratsyuye zastosunok "Diy vdoma"*. Government portal. Retrieved February 25, 2022, from https://www.kmu.gov.ua/news/yak-pracyuye-zastosunok-dij-vdoma

Eck, K., & Hatz, S. (2020). State surveillance and the COVID-19 crisis. *Journal of Human Rights*, *19*(5), 603–612. https://doi.org/10.1080/14754835.2020.1816163

Freedom House. (n. d.). *Countries and territories. Democracy scores*. Retrieved February 15, 2023, from https://freedomhouse.org/countries/nations-transit/scores?sort=asc&order=Country

Gebrekidan, S. (2020). *For autocrats, and others, coronavirus is a chance to grab even more power*. The New York Times. Retrieved February 15, 2023, from https://www.nytimes.com/2020/03/30/world/europe/coronavirus-governments-power.html

Hryhorska, N. (2021). *"Pryvit, Viktore Fedorovychu". Zhurnalisty povidomyly pro pidhotovku protestu na mistsi provedennya presmarafonu Zelens'koho*. NV.ua. Retrieved February 22, 2023, from https://nv.ua/ukr/ukraine/politics/preskonferenciya-zelenskogo-26-listopada-zhurnalisti-gotuyut-protest-novini-ukrajini-50198352.html

Institute of Mass Information. (2020a). *Barometr svobody slova za veresen' 2020 roku*. Retrieved February 22, 2023, from https://imi.org.ua/monitorings/barometr-svobody-slova-za-veresen-2020-roku-i35457

Institute of Mass Information. (2020b). *Barometr svobody slova za zhovten' 2020 roku*. Retrieved February 22, 2023, from https://imi.org.ua/monitorings/barometr-svobody-slova-za-zhovten-2020-roku-i36006

Institute of Mass Information. (2020c). *Barometr svobody slova za berezen' 2020 roku*. Retrieved February 23, 2022, from https://imi.org.ua/monitorings/barometr-svobody-slova-za-berezen-2020-roku-i32469

Institute of Mass Information. (2020d). *Barometr svobody slova za lystopad 2020 roku*. Retrieved February 23, 2022, from https://imi.org.ua/monitorings/barometr-svobody-slova-za-lystopad-2020-roku-i36524

Institute of Mass Information. (2020e). *Barometr svobody slova za kviten' 2020 roku*. Retrieved February 24, 2023, from https://imi.org.ua/monitorings/barometr-svobody-slova-za-kviten-2020-roku-i32940

Institute of Mass Information. (2021a). *Barometr svobody slova za zhovten' 2021 roku*. Retrieved February 22, 2023, from https://imi.org.ua/monitorings/barometr-svobody-slova-za-zhovten-2021-roku-i42108

Institute of Mass Information. (2021b). *Barometr svobody slova za cherven' 2021 roku*. Retrieved February 23, 2023, from https://imi.org.ua/monitorings/barometr-svobody-slova-za-cherven-2021-roku-i40149

Institute of Mass Information. (2021c). *Barometr svobody slova za lyutyj 2021 roku*. Retrieved February 24, 2023, from https://imi.org.ua/monitorings/barometr-svobody-slova-za-lyutyj-2021-roku-i37963

Institute of Mass Information. (2021d). *Barometr svobody slova za berezen' 2021 roku*. Retrieved February 23, 2023, from https://imi.org.ua/monitorings/barometr-svobody-slova-za-berezen-2021-roku-i38469

Internet Freedom. (2020). *Dodatok "Diy vdoma": yak uryad namahayet'sya kontrolyuvaty ukrayintsiv pid chas poshyrennya COVID-19*. Retrieved February 25, 2023, from https://netfreedom.org.ua/article/dodatok-dij-vdoma-yak-uryad-namagayetsya-kontrolyuvati-ukrayinciv-pid-chas-poshirennya-covid-19

Kalitenko, O. M., Anikina, H. V., Anikina, G., Spasova, K. I., Spasova, E., & Shahaka, O. V. (2021). The restrictions of the freedom of information during the covid-19 pandemic. *Cuestiones Politicas*, *39*(70), 426–445.

Korovenkova, T. (2021). Human Rights Watch: *Vlasti Belarusi razvyazali bespretsedentnyye repressii*. Belarusian Association of Journalists. Retrieved February 22, 2023, from https://baj.by/be/analytics/human-rights-watch-vlasti-belarusi-razvyazali-besprecedentnye-repressii

Masduki. (2022). Cyber-troops, digital attacks, and media freedom in Indonesia. *Asian Journal of Communication*, *32*(3), 218–233. https://doi.org/10.1080/01292986.2022.2062609

McQuail, D. (2003). *Media accountability and freedom of publication*. Oxford University Press.

Ministry of Health of the Republic of Belarus. (2020). *V Belarusi zaregestrirovan zavoznyy sluchay koronavirusa*. Retrieved February 15, 2023, from https://minzdrav.gov.by/ru/sobytiya/v-belarusi-zaregistrirovan-zavoznoy-sluchay-koronavirusa/

Monitoring Service of the Civil Organization "Belarusian Association of Journalists". (2020). *Babruyski sayt prymusili vydalits' interv"yu z myedsyastroy, yakaya raspavyala pra pratsu z COVID-19*. Belarusian Association of Journalists. Retrieved February 22, 2023, from https://baj.by/be/content/babruyski-sayt-prymusili-vydalic-intervyu-z-medsyastroy-yakaya-raspavyala-pra-pracu-z-covid

Monitoring Service of the Civil Organization "Belarusian Association of Journalists". (2022). *8 hadow znyavolyennya: vynyesli prysud zhurnalistu-rasslyedaval'niku Syarhyeyu Satsuku*. Belarusian Association of Journalists. Retrieved February 23, 2023, from https://baj.by/be/content/8-gadou-znyavolennya-vynesli-prysud-zhurnalistu-rassledavalniku-syargeyu-sacuku

Nasha Niva. (2020). *"Usye raz'yekhalisya. Nyama kamu pravodzits'". Minzdarowya nye sustrakalasya z zhurnalistami z 24 krasavika, nye adkazvala na pytanni z 17 krasavika*. Belarusian Association of Journalists. Retrieved February 22, 2023, from https://baj.by/be/content/use-razehalisya-nyama-kamu-pravodzic-minzdarouya-ne-sustrakalasya-z-zhurnalistami-z-24

Papadopoulou, L., & Maniou, T. A. (2021). Lockdown' on digital journalism? Mapping threats to press freedom during the COVID-19 pandemic crisis. *Digital Journalism*, *9*(9), 1–23. https://doi.org/10.1080/21670811.2021.1945472

Press service of the "Belarusian Association of Journalists". (2020a). *Andrey Krivosheyev rekomenduyet shtrafovat' SMI za rasprostraneniye nedostovernoy informatsii o Covid-19*. Belarusian Association of Journalists. Retrieved February 24, 2023, from https://baj.by/be/content/andrey-krivosheev-rekomenduet-shtrafovat-smi-za-rasprostranenie-nedostovernoy-informacii-o

Press service of the "Belarusian Association of Journalists". (2020b). *Masmyedyya w Byelarusi, №2 (61), 2020. SMI BYELARUSI PADCHAS KARANAVIRUSA*. Belarusian Association of Journalists. Retrieved February 24, 2023, from https://baj.by/be/analytics/masmedyya-u-belarusi-no2-61-2020-smi-belarusi-padchas-karanavirusa

Reporters Without Borders. (2019). *World press freedom index*. Retrieved February 17, 2023, from https://rsf.org/en/index?year=2019

Reporters Without Borders. (2021). *World press freedom index*. Retrieved February 17, 2023, from https://rsf.org/en/index?year=2021

Reporters Without Borders. (2023). *World press freedom index*. Retrieved December 20, 2023, from https://rsf.org/en/index

Richter, A. (2016). Defining media freedom in international policy debates. *Global Media and Communication*, *12*(2), 127–142. https://doi.org/10.1177/1742766516652164

Tolkacheva, E. (2020). *"Pokinut' stranu do polunochi". Zhurnalista "Pervogo kanala" vyslali iz Belarusi*. Belarusian Association of Journalists. Retrieved February 22, 2023, from https://baj.by/be/content/pokinut-stranu-do-polunochi-zhurnalista-pervogo-kanala-vyslali-iz-belarusi

Ukrinform. (2020). *V Ukrayini zareyestruvaly pershyy vypadok koronavirusu*. Retrieved February 15, 2023, from https://www.ukrinform.ua/rubric-society/2888412-v-ukraini-zareestruvali-persij-vipadok-koronavirusu.html

United Nations. (2021). *Belarus: 'Black hole' for media freedoms after egregious attacks, say UN experts*. Retrieved December 20, 2023, from https://www.ohchr.org/en/press-releases/2021/06/belarus-black-hole-media-freedoms-after-egregious-attacks-say-un-experts

Whitten-Woodring, J. (2009). Watchdog or lapdog? Media freedom, regime type, and government respect for human rights. *International Studies Quarterly*, *53*(3), 595–625. https://doi.org/10.1111/j.1468-2478.2009.00548.x.

World Health Organization. (n. d.). *Infodemic*. Retrieved February 15, 2023, from https://www.who.int/health-topics/infodemic#tab=tab_1

World Health Organization. (2020). *Listings of WHO's response to COVID-19*. Retrieved February 15, 2023, from https://www.who.int/news/item/29-06-2020-covidtimeline#cms

Worldometr. (n. d.). *Covid-19 coronavirus pandemic*. Retrieved February 15, 2023, from https://www.worldometers.info/coronavirus/#countries

Zakusylo, M. (2020). *Rada ukhvalyla novyy byudzhet: 1,5 mlrd dlya Suspil'noho, 455 mln dlya kino, 400 mln dlya UKF, 100 mln dlya Instytutu knyhy*. Detector media. Retrieved February 24, 2023, from https://detector.media/rinok/article/176326/2020-04-13-rada-ukhvalyla-novyy-byudzhet-15-mlrd-dlya-suspilnogo-455-mln-dlya-kino-400-mln-dlya-ukf-100-mln-dlya-instytutu-knygy/

11 Grassroots Activity of Russian Citizens in Response to the Worsening Pandemic-Related Crisis of the State

Anna Jach

Introduction

The grassroots activity of citizens is one of the indicators of a functioning civil society, in which people voluntarily self-organise to fulfil everyday needs and promote common interests. The concept of a civil society, whose development is based on human capital, should be understood as a sum of social relations and institutions distinct from the state and business sectors. It comprises a variety of non-governmental organisations and public actions connected by specific goals and principles that determine their activities focused on serving the interests they declare (Grudtsyna & Petrov, 2012).

The demands of civic activists can be fulfilled by making civic participation a governing principle. It is a crucial factor as it influences society's modernisation, the emergence of leaders, and the shape and outcomes of political decisions. It also expresses social acceptance or rejection of decision-makers' core strategies. As it means citizens' participation in the process of governance, it has several constituting elements: (1) activity/actions undertaken by (2) people (i.e. ordinary citizens, not politicians or state officials) in the sphere of (3) politics, which is not limited to one institution type but refers to the entire political system; their essential function is to pass opinions and suggestions to the power centre to (4) influence the shaping of desirable solutions and political decisions (Garlicki, 2016, p. 457). This approach illustrates several levels of participation that guarantee the functioning of civil society in contemporary Russia regarding the relations between the state and the citizens under conditions that enable it to continue to function. The model to which advocates of democratic change aspire is the type of participation presented below. As long as the state did not start to combat this type of social activism after 2018, they could be encountered in many places. They became the leaven for the realisation of the principles of association and citizens' association in practice before the outbreak of full-scale war in 2022. It is also hoped that, once this devastating hecatomb is over, they can become the seedbed for the rebirth of civil society.

1 Community participation, also called "horizontal" or "social", assumes citizens' participation and involvement in group activities undertaken within their communities. It is characterised by active and voluntary engagement in creating and functioning local citizens' groups and non-governmental structures.

DOI: 10.4324/9781003482710-12

2 Participatory governance, also called "civic", "vertical", and "public" – assumes participation in political activity. Citizens' actions within structures and institutions of a democratic state focus on participating in elections or consultations organised by public governance bodies and informing the authorities about the local community's expectations.
3 Individual – It refers to activities expressing everyday choices made by citizens, considering their expectations as to the character of the society they belong to. Activities in this field include following the principles of socially responsible consumption, financial support of charities, and participation in social movements (Kaźmierczak, 2011)

Source: own research based on Kaźmierczak (2011).

Shaped by over 30 years of modernisation, the Russian socio-political system and the society functioning in these specific conditions can offer numerous insights for researchers. Firstly, it helps explain the processes of social initiative formation, self-education of interest groups, and rapid change of social identification in a country with solid statehood traditions. Secondly, it allows research of the non-governmental sphere in a state with poorly developed property rights and a small-scale middle class. Thirdly, the civic organisations and civil society operating in Russia demonstrate the specifics of the fight against the omnipotence of political power – a grassroots battle initiated by non-commercial structures and social groups. Fourthly, the growing interest in internal transformations within the country, particularly in the aspect of studies of the non-governmental, non-commercial sector, opens a new direction in research on liberalism and reforms in a state whose tradition of grassroots citizen activity is entirely different from the Western one (Jach, 2019, pp. 69–70).

In the diagnosed picture of Russian reality, we can point to civil society institutions – both traditional and specifically Russian. The former group comprises citizens, local communities, religious organisations, and civic associations, including political parties, trade unions, social movements, as well as social initiatives, charities, and the media. Besides ongoing processes of society's self-organisation, the latter group comprises intermediary institutions. In practice, they are responsible for the top-to-bottom organisation of social engagement in grassroots participation processes. They include the Civic Chamber of the Russian Federation (RF), chambers and civic councils of the RF subjects, and civic councils at individual ministries, departments, and government institutions at regional and municipal levels.

In this shape, the system still allows the grassroots activity of its citizens, particularly in the face of serious crises such as the SARS-CoV-2 pandemic, which has been ongoing since 2019. In all the afflicted societies, the pandemic has been an impulse to initiate a number of activities that otherwise would have appeared later and been much less extensive. Considering the grassroots activity of Russian citizens during the pandemic-related state crisis, it is worth noting that social engagement can take different forms. The analysis will focus on the following questions: (1) can the coronavirus pandemic strengthen civil society? (2) To what extent will the institutional social activity stimulated from the top translate into the development of grassroots civic activity? (3) To what extent can the support from the business sphere strengthen the social structures of grassroots activity?

Coronavirus will strengthen the Russian civil society

During the coronavirus pandemic, Russia found itself in a unique situation. On the one hand, there is a dominant, widespread conviction that in any crisis, there will be an appropriate structure that will ensure a sense of safety when people experience its loss. Since Gorbachev's perestroika, the ability to bear responsibility for one's choices has become marginalised. Independent thinking and the ability to undertake civic activity without an impulse from the top are not very common in today's Russia. However, the pandemic crisis changed how people perceive themselves and their needs, as well as the role of the state and the tasks performed by its institutions. Hopes have risen that this crisis will finally lead to the rebirth of a civil society that will not only inspire changes in the Russian population but also find in itself a potential for more decisive involvement in political activities.

The first to react to these social expectations were Moscow authorities. Counting on citizens' involvement, the mayor proposed that the residents decide whether they wanted to self-isolate or not. This offer was made due to the increasing number of infected individuals and the lack of central-level decisions about introducing even a partial lockdown. The state authorities stopped issuing numerous recommendations, pointing to various possible activities. As Elena Kondratyeva (2020) stresses, many of those brave enough to criticise the Mayor of Moscow or shout at anti-Putin demonstrations, "We are the power" and "We will be the ones to act", were not ready to make independent decisions about themselves. This crisis of consciousness was exemplified by their inability to finally take responsibility for their lives and decide what they wanted – get dressed, eat dinner, self-isolate at home, or go to shopping malls (Kondratyeva, 2020).

The attitudes in Russia towards the spreading coronavirus pandemic are not uniform. There are individuals, groups, and politicians who think that the enemies of the Russian state have engineered the pandemic; besides, they do not consider it necessary to resort to methods as strict as those introduced in the West, that is total or partial lockdown. However, other individuals, groups, and politicians are aware of the constantly growing danger, and they attempt to convince others that not just the authorities but Russians themselves should become actively involved in counteracting the worsening crisis.

The Internet is a platform that can mobilise society for grassroots activity during the pandemic – a tool used to shape attitudes and run pro-social actions. It also reveals the progress of sociopolitical socialisation, replacing the mood of alienation concerning decision-makers' actions. This new reality, stemming from the discrepancy between strict preventative police measures and the pandemic-caused crisis, offers Russian citizens a chance to learn more about themselves and define their relations with others and the world.

In different times and places, the grassroots activities undertaken during a crisis were a real test for civil society. In such a situation, volunteer activity may intensify; some people abandon their interest in helping those in need. However, others consider a worsening crisis a perfect opportunity to increase their assets by, such as raising prices of basic necessities or high-demand goods. Russia during the COVID-19 pandemic is no different, as illustrated by several examples presented below.

Companies offering and supporting online educational services waived regular fees for using their educational and entertainment programmes. Nevertheless, the number of children and young people visiting shopping centres or staying outside their homes increased dramatically during the first days of free online education – it was perceived as a holiday time, perfect for entertaining and visiting each other, not as a measure to prevent further virus transmission.

Some web services announced their intention to dissolve contracts with those who would profiteer during the pandemic. Ordinary medical masks (about 10 rubles in drugstores) were sometimes offered for 100 rubles apiece. The price of infrared thermometers has risen to 20,000 rubles. The situation was unlikely to change without an official intervention (Kondratyeva, 2020).

What has helped the citizens maintain self-isolation were numerous films, series, and cultural events available on home screens as an alternative to the majority of theatres, museums, and other cultural institutions that were closed in compliance with quarantine rules. After closing, the institutions refunded money to the ticket holders and wished their audiences minimal damage caused by separation from culture. However, some establishments decided to continue their operations. Teatr.doc announced they would not close but limit the number of seats to 40. Some cinema chains followed this example ("Kino Okko", 2020).

Ultimately, the audience decided whether to go to the cinema, theatre, etc. However, some cultural personalities spoke against the guidelines issued by the authorities. Nikolai Kolyada, the director of the Kolyada Theatre, publically described the restrictive measures as an "incredible, unbelievable and unthinkable" deception and promised that the number of performances would not change. In an official statement, Teatr.doc explained that, according to doctors, positive emotions help strengthen the immune system, and their theatre was a place where the audience and actors would experience many positive emotions (Kuznetsov, 2020).

Unlike the faithful visiting John the Baptist's relics brought to the Kazan Cathedral in St. Petersburg, this explanation was not met with the derision of Internet users. What fueled the public outcry was the controversial decision of the Russian Orthodox Church to allow the relics worship ("Potok k moshcham", 2020). Internauts saw the queue of waiting people, primarily elderly, as a testament to the irresponsibility of the Church authorities. Although the latter promised to improve the sanitary condition of the reliquaries, Facebook users pointed out that this problem was not as dangerous to the population as people's belief in the healing power of the relics (Baranyuk, 2020). Boris Vishnevsky, a St. Petersburg deputy to the Duma, openly expressed his indignation and demanded a ban on kissing Orthodox relics (Troyanskaya, 2020).

Another type of civic activity is mutual assistance. Every day, in social media groups that unite inhabitants of particular neighbourhoods, offers of help appear for people who have gone into voluntary self-isolation in their apartments. The volunteers provide care, in particular to senior citizens. The neighbours offer to bring each other food, take out the garbage, or walk the dog. People share medicines and protective masks with other home residents – and the key word here is sharing, not selling.

As Elena Kondratyeva (2020) concludes, when the state does not hang a Damocles sword of law over the citizens' heads, it is possible to notice all our neighbours. When actions are dictated by conscience, not fear, people become closer to each other. Yet there are still malcontents who passively wait for someone or something (the state) to tell them what to do (Kondratyeva, 2020).

The COVID-19 pandemic phenomenon was an experience for which no one was prepared, least of all any state. While states that adhere to democratic solutions tend to cope with crises of various kinds to a greater or lesser extent than authoritarian states, the peri-pandemic crisis triggered in 2019 took everyone by surprise without exception. For this reason, authoritarian or dictatorial governments also give wide latitude to structures that are able to take effective and efficient measures to bring society or the state out of this condition. This was also the case in Russia, which, by militarising itself, could not bear the burden of fighting the pandemic. There was, therefore, a real opportunity to strengthen the institutions of civil society, which took up the fight against the consequences of the spread of the coronavirus from the bottom up, spontaneously. State structures provided relatively little assistance but did not stand in the way of these efforts. The situation changed dramatically in 2022 when the Russian state launched an armed invasion of its neighbour Ukraine.

Has the coronavirus pandemic limited human rights in Russia?

The COVID-19 pandemic has posed questions about whether the authorities do not violate civil rights by taking extraordinary measures to combat the spread of the virus and where the line should be drawn ensure these measures do not overstep bounds. Those issues have become vital also for the citizens of the RF. As an autonomous non-commercial organisation aimed at conducting socially significant litigations, legal education, research, and publishing, the Institute for Law and Public Policy (ILPP) (https://academia.ilpp.ru/) is one of the institutions that decided to take a closer look at these issues.

Among other ILPP analysts, Ekaterina Zvorykina and Valentina Putresha conducted a series of interviews with ordinary citizens, activists, entrepreneurs, doctors, and experts in constitutional law to reveal how the pandemic affected their lives and to what extent the introduced restrictive measures were necessary and compliant with the law (Zvorykina & Putresha, 2020). The following issues raised concern among the volunteers associated in this non-governmental organisation.

Infringement of labour rights

The number of people who lost their jobs was one of the symptoms of the deteriorating social and economic situation. The deepening recession in the labour market was illustrated by Rosstat's report for the period from January to August 2020, which showed that the number of unemployed increased by as much as 1.3 million. While the redundancies were consistent with the binding regulations, the fact that the dismissed employees were made to work for the remaining days of their contract without being paid was absolutely against the labour law as employers asked their workers to perform their duties remotely.

The above practices adopted by employers were to be hindered by the so-called paid days off introduced by RF authorities. These additional 35 days in a year were neither holidays nor working days as stipulated in articles 111–112 of the Labour Code of the Russian Federation. During this period (30 March–30 April, 6–8 May) (Ukaz Prezidenta RF ot 25/03/2020 no. 206; Ukaz Prezidenta RF ot 02/04/2020 no. 239; Ukaz Prezidenta RF ot 28/04/2020 no. 294), the right to work was limited to prevent congestion in public transport and workplaces, but the state shifted responsibility for payment for these days onto employers.

As recalled by one of the interviewees, the company where he was employed refused to comply with the state's restrictions and continued remote work of its employees, thus adhering to the rule of fair remuneration, which would otherwise be violated. Such activities of the company revealed flaws in state restrictions as employees were still forced to work to continue the firm's operation. Its decision can be explained by economic expediency; however, this still did not save the interviewee from being fired.

Nonadherence to the principles of social distancing in institutions where detained citizens were held

At various levels of state administration authorities, Russian citizens encountered a clear breach of the regulations requiring the observance of the principle of social distancing.

This problem gained importance when, following the rules applicable during the pandemic and in compliance with all the binding requirements (masks, gloves), Russian citizens decided to take to the streets as a reaction to the Russian authorities' flagrant violation of the law. What came as an opportunity to test the state authorities' observance of the pandemic rules were diverse actions organised by members of the Libertarian Party of Russia and the Moscow-based all-Russian association "Civil Society" aimed at presenting police brutality and the commonly experienced injustice. "Russian Lives Matter", similar to the slogan "Black Lives Matter" in the United States, has become the motto of a Russian social movement that opposes the authorities' practices against citizens.

The direct reason for organising a "Russians Lives Matter" demonstration in Moscow was the murder of a 27-year-old resident of Yekaterinburg, Vladimir Taushkanov, by members of the Rosgvardia (Lukmanov & Guselnikov, 2020). Because mass events had been banned (Postanovleniye Glavnogo gosudarstvennogo sanitarnogo vracha Rossiyskoy Federatsii ot 13.03.2020 no. 6; Ukaz Mera Moskvy ot 05.03.2020 no. 12-UM, 2020), one-person pickets were organised in compliance with all the pandemic restrictions. To maximise the reach, Moscow activists shared on Twitter an appeal #RussianLivesMatter (https://twitter.com/hashtag/Russianlivesmatter?f=live). The response to these civic actions was numerous arrests of the protesters ("V Moskve desyatki", 2020).

Lusine Minasian, who protested in a one-person picket on 2 June 2020, was alarmed by the fact that the forces controlled by *siloviki* did not comply with the pandemic laws while detaining protesters in the streets. After the detainees were placed in police cars, the required social distance was not respected. While one-person pickets do not threaten others, putting individuals in a tiny space without minimum precautionary measures does (Zvorykina & Putresha, 2020).

The international group for the defence of human rights "AGORA", addressed the issue of protests during the pandemic in its report *Apology of the Protest: Disinfection of a Protest* (AGORA, n.d.), pointing to several important aspects. Firstly, some restrictions were intended to neutralise peaceful civil protests and not to protect citizens against the coronavirus. The legal basis for such actions of the authorities was the restrictions introduced under Article 20.2 (regarding violation of the established order of organising meetings, rallies, demonstrations, processions, or pickets) of the Code of the Russian Federation on Administrative Offences. Secondly, although gatherings, marches, and pickets cannot be legally prohibited even in the conditions of the declared high alert state, during the pandemic in Russia such forms of protest were actually regarded as a violation of the self-isolation rules. After lifting the quarantine restrictions, the authorities, in turn, began to consider these forms of protest a threat to the health and sanitary-epidemiological well-being of the population. Thirdly, the fight against the coronavirus is still used to pressure and illegally detain picketing activists. What serves this purpose are relevant provisions of the Code of the Russian Federation on Administrative Offences: the aforementioned Article 20.2 and Article 20.6.1 regarding non-compliance with the rules of conduct in emergency situations or the threat of their occurrence. Their application depends on a reasonably arbitrary approach: they can be applied separately and jointly to the protesters. Respective regulations in individual subjects of the RF accompany the provisions of the Code. In practice, most cases are treated as a violation of Article 20.6.1 of the Code of the Russian Federation on Administrative Offences. The lawyers of "AGORA" concluded that "in Russia, the current practice of using the laws regulating social and political life in the time of a pandemic shows that certain measures and restrictions have nothing to do with the actual fight against the spread of the disease, but are aimed at quenching and neutralising peaceful civil protest" (AGORA, n.d.).

Fines for violating the self-isolation rules imposed by state institutions

Another example of violating civil rights in the RF during the pandemic is fines imposed on citizens for violating self-isolation or quarantine restrictions.

Every person who had contact with somebody ill with COVID-19 or had a positive test result was obliged to remain at home in self-isolation. Moreover, they were required to download the "Social monitoring" application. In time, those people started to receive notifications about fines imposed on them by the system during their stay in isolation or after they were removed from the register of COVID-19-infected individuals run by *Rospotrebnadzor* (Russian Federal Service for Surveillance on Consumer Rights Protection and Human Well-being). Feeling unjustly punished, the citizens and their lawyers sought assistance from relevant state institutions. The number of improperly fined people quickly turned out to be very high. According to official data, at the end of May 2020, around 30% of users of this application received fines totalling over 216 million rubles (Lyauv & Kodachigov, 2020).

Analysts note that monitoring patients with COVID-19 and their temporary isolation is part of the system of controlling the spread of the infection, which affects the right to personal liberty and integrity, and resembles a restriction such as a house arrest. Therefore, the state must carefully select appropriate measures to implement these types of control. Following public outrage, the chairman of Russia's Presidential Human Rights Council, Valery Fadeev, stated that due to serious issues with the Social Monitoring application, its use could not be considered an appropriate measure to contain the spread of the disease. Thus, all fines levied on Muscovites were to be cancelled as when they were imposed; these citizens were either staying at home as recommended or had already been released from isolation. According to official data, from 19 May to 22 May, the capital's courts registered more than 1.8 thousand complaints from Moscow residents about the alleged violation of Article 3.18.1 of the Moscow Code of Administrative Offences (Starikova et al., 2020).

Decrease in sales of goods

The restrictions introduced by the central authorities and the RF subjects were aimed at limiting the transmission of the SARS-CoV-2 virus. However, in private companies' cases, the enterprise owners' business rights have been violated. It resulted from a failure to respect the balance between entrepreneurs' and society's interests.

During the pandemic, small and medium-sized business activity has been regulated not only by the aforementioned presidential decrees on additional paid days off for employees, which were to be covered by employers. The second legal regulation was the Decree of the Mayor of Moscow on 5 March 2020, "On the introduction of high alert state" (Ukaz Mera Moskvy ot 05.03.2020 no. 12-UM, 2020). These documents constituted the legal basis for closing the retail space, which, under the guise of counteracting COVID-19, made it possible to interfere directly with the sphere of ownership. In this way, certain types of economic activity were limited.

According to entrepreneurs, government measures to counter the spread of the infection have limited the right to business freedom and property rights. On the one hand, these measures aimed at preventing large gatherings of people, but on the other hand, the high alert state and the paid days off were introduced. The authorities' failure to observe the principle of balance between the interests of entrepreneurs and the interests of society made business owners bear the responsibility for the operation of their companies during the COVID-19 pandemic. In practice, while government support measures turned out to be beneficial for employees, they were insufficient for employers. In fact, the state escaped its obligation to fully compensate entrepreneurs for the damage caused by the pandemic.

Small and medium-sized enterprises were granted preferential loans of six minimum gross remunerations per employee. However, the assigned funds were exhausted within just three months. While this financial support had little influence on the further operation of companies, for an individual employee, 12,130 rubles was a substantial amount (Postanovleniye Pravitelstva RF ot 12.05.2020 no. 657).

What came as the greatest disappointment was the employees' attitude; they immediately demanded that their employers adopt the solutions introduced by state authorities in response to the pandemic. An example is the mentioned presidential decrees on the additional 35 paid days off. Business owners could not implement this new regulation as they struggled to meet their employees' social expectations and run their businesses during the progressing lockdown. The way private enterprises operate in the pandemic conditions can be summarised by a warning that if the authorities impose any further restrictions, either the economy will die (in this situation, entrepreneurs may close down their businesses to avoid increasing their debt burden) or the government will no longer rule (Zvorykina & Putresha, 2020).

Changing general hospitals into specialist healthcare facilities for patients with symptoms of SARS-CoV-2 infection

In combating the effects of the coronavirus spread, the authorities were forced to provide an appropriate number of medical facilities where the citizens with COVID-19 would be hospitalised. Due to the increasing number of patients with severe symptoms, most hospitals became specialist facilities. While nobody questioned the need to take such action, there was widespread concern over the method of financing medical personnel and the management of specialist healthcare institutions.

The pandemic has been a time of increased workload for healthcare staff and personnel. Although there have been instances of adequate logistical preparation of hospitals where patients with COVID-19 were treated, certain cases have proved the failure of regional authorities to fulfil that particular task. Thus, the state, aware that doctors were most exposed to the infection, introduced several measures to protect people's lives. Medical staff have often emphasised the need for protective equipment; they also spoke of preventive measures, periodic testing, and rules to minimise the risk of spreading infection. Therefore, to effectively support the efforts of medical staff and personnel, the authorities have allocated additional funds for the above measures.

Providing financial security for medical staff was an urgent issue for policymakers. President Putin promised state support for healthcare staff and social institutions at a conference. He announced that special funds from the state budget were allocated for this purpose and instructed the government, the Ministry of Health, the Ministry of Labour, and the regional authorities to monitor the calculation of all additional payments. He said, "Absolutely everything should be transparent and clear: to whom, for what the money goes". All information on the acts regulating these issues should be communicated to society and explained in detail, and the feedback should be structured ("Putin provodit soveshchaniye", 2020).

Other equally important issues that the president addressed were:

1 The decree signed on 6 May 2020 on compulsory life and health insurance for medical staff "who from the very beginning participated in the fight against the pandemic and suffered damage to health" (Ukaz Prezidenta RF ot 6.05.2020 no. 313);
2 The decree on the use of e-prescriptions signed on 17 March 2020 (Ukaz Prezidenta RF ot 17.03.2020 no. 187).

Following the president's statement, the government and the authorities in individual RF subjects began implementing the policy. The Council of Ministers of the Russian Federation issued two regulations which referred to "special working conditions and the stress this situation creates" in dealing with coronavirus patients and those who are at risk; it also mentioned rewarding "the particularly important work of assisting citizens diagnosed with the new COVID-19 infection".

Problems with implementing the support policy for healthcare staff and personnel became evident with the first information about the failure of individual state authorities to fulfil the tasks assigned to them by the Council of Ministers. One such case was issues with payments to medical staff in Ryazan Oblast ("V Ryazani ne khvatilo", 2020). The scale of the problem was by no means small and started to touch many regions. This was evidenced by information provided to journalists by anonymous healthcare workers and actions such as personal letters to Putin, collective complaints, strikes, and hunger strikes. As emphasised by Andrey Konoval, the Inter-regional Trade Union of Health Workers "Deystviye" co-founder, these rather laxly drafted legal acts show an evident inequality. Some employees are paid double for the same job, while others are not at all, and other medical workers receive only a part of their due wages. All of this is due to the ambiguous language of government regulations, which allows regional health departments to limit the number of health professionals who can apply for additional payments. This approach shows the willingness to save budget funds, which is unacceptable when life and the right to life are at stake (Yasenitskaya et al., 2020).

However, in many cases, there have been no issues with financial support for healthcare workers or the logistics of managing specialist facilities. The economic benefits promised by the state have been paid, personal protective equipment has always been available, and hospital regulations have been formulated clearly and transparently, with a shift schedule and clean and red zones distinctly marked. In addition, the state has adopted and implemented social obligations in the field of additional material support and additional years of service counted towards retirement (increased seniority).

Summarising their study on the violation of human rights by the state during the coronavirus pandemic, Ekaterina Zvorykina and Valentina Putresha concluded that civil rights and freedoms had been violated to varying degrees. In some cases, the restrictive measures did not affect individuals; in others – they created serious problems. While the state has fulfilled its obligations concerning the right to life, there were often instances of using inadequate or excessively restrictive preventive measures. The latter is particularly evident in limiting the possibility of organising one-person pickets. Moreover, the government has not chosen to introduce a state of emergency, thus avoiding its obligation to pay full compensation for the pandemic damage.

"It is not clear what lessons the state will learn from the COVID-19 pandemic: it can analyse its mistakes in restricting rights and freedoms so as not to repeat them and become more responsible. Or it can use the threat of the spread of the infection to restrict rights and freedoms in cases where it is not required at all" (Zvorykina & Putresha, 2020).

Human and civil rights – the dream and declarations of the earliest Soviet dissidents such as Andrei Sakharov – continue to arouse widespread dissatisfaction among the rulers of the Russian state to this day. The primacy of the state over the individual is still a rule in Russian politics, although not written down anywhere. Over the many years of the USSR and then the RF, they have been a salt in the eye of decision-makers. Systematically tightening the law while expanding the executive powers of the force structures in the conditions of both the pandemic crisis and before, it found its legal justification, which did not arouse concern among the Russian public except for groups of so-called right-wingers who did not agree with the omnipotence of the state. The COVID-19 pandemic, although it drew attention to the compliance and circumvention of the law by individual people, groups, unfortunately did not result in an expansion of public control over compliance with the provisions in this aspect.

#MYVMESTE (#WEARETOGETHER) initiative

The citizens of the RF participate in grassroots civic activity within numerous non-governmental, non-commercial organisations. During the COVID-19 pandemic, the entities that promote grassroots mutual assistance in society deserve particular attention.

One such organisation, with a corporation-like structure, is the All-Russian Public Movement of Medical Volunteers "Volontery-Mediki" (RPMMV). It was established in 2013 by the activists of the project Sklif Volunteers; in 2016, it gained the status of an all-Russian civic organisation, and in 2018 joined the group of socially oriented non-commercial organisations SO NKO.

With the support of the Ministry of Health of the FR, 85 regional branches of the Movement were opened, gathering over 83,000 members. About 4 million Russians receive help and support from medical volunteers every year. Over 5,000 medical, educational, public, and other organisations from the entire RF are partners of the RPMMV (Volontery-mediki, n.d.).

Following the declared mission of "reviving the traditions of charity and providing help to the practical healthcare" (Volontery-mediki, n.d.), the founders listed the goals, tasks, and activities for the volunteers united in the movement as given in Table 11.1.

Table 11.1 Goals, tasks, and activities of volunteers from the RPMMV "Volontery Mediki"

Goals and tasks	*Activity*
Development of volunteering in healthcare	Assisting personnel in medical institutions
Educating the population on health matters	First aid training
Raising the prestige of healthcare professions	Assisting at sports and other mass events
Increasing the human resources available for healthcare	Involvement in preventive activities
Fostering patriotism and active citizenship among Russians	Promoting donations of blood and bone marrow
	Promoting healthy lifestyle
	Providing vocational guidance at schools

Source: own research based on Volontery-mediki (n.d.)

With such guidelines, it was unsurprising that the volunteers have assisted people in need during the COVID-19 pandemic. Aware of the immense scale of society's needs, the All-Russian Public Movement of Medical Volunteers members initiated a large-scale project, "All-Russian Mutual Aid Initiative #MYVMESTE". The plan from 29 September 2020 to 1 September 2021 includes volunteer activity in several fields (Table 11.2).

Table 11.2 Projects included in the #MYVMESTE initiative

Project	*Description*	*Number of volunteers involved*
Help in the delivery of food and medicines	Volunteers aid seniors in quarantine or unable to go outside. All volunteers receive training and necessary personal protection means.	Over 10,000
Help at medical institutions (for volunteers with medical training and students of medicine)	Help in patient care, monitoring vital signs, working with documentation and admitting patients.	5,322
Help at medical institutions (for volunteers without medical training)	Help in patient care, monitoring vital signs, working with documentation and admitting patients.	1,807
Psychological help (for volunteers 16+ with training in psychology)	Trained volunteers provide phone or online help in three-hour shifts, available 24/7	1,126
Help at call-centres (for all volunteers)	Volunteers call individuals treated on an outpatient basis, using specially developed scripts to dynamically monitor their health and send a doctor on a home visit if needed. The volunteers also answer citizens' questions regarding coronavirus infection and relay test results.	2,019
Volunteer drivers (with cars)	Volunteers drive doctors and other health workers, which approximately doubles the number of home visits.	524

Source: own research based on DOBRO (n.d.); volunteer numbers for 24 May 2021

The #MYVMESTE initiative has been introduced in the whole RF territory. Among the numerous partner institutions, there are national as well as foreign entities. Their involvement is a testament to the awareness of the needs that must be satisfied during the pandemic. To meet the expectations of the decision-makers, the largest corporations – both private Russian enterprises and foreign businesses operating in Russia – actively participated in the mutual aid initiative (Table 11.3).

Table 11.3 Involvement of corporate institutions in the #MYVMESTE initiative

Institution	*Contribution*
Johnson & Johnson	Over 30 tonnes of personal hygiene products and cosmetics
Coca-Cola	24,675 L of water delivered to Moscow hospitals; providing drinks for volunteers in 12 regions of the country; Moscow Coca-Cola factory used its 3D printing capabilities to make personal protection means for volunteers
Garage Café at Moscow Museum of Modern Art	860 lunches delivered to hospitals daily
AB InBev-Efes	35,000 L of sanitisers delivered to hospitals. 45 tonnes of bread kvass delivered to Moscow hospitals
Mr. Food Company, Creative Kitchen	Three balanced meals delivered daily for healthcare workers (860 meals per week)
Dunkin Donuts	Several hundred doughnut packs sent to hospitals and volunteer centres.
MEGA Teplyi Stan	Break-room food delivered to Moscow hospitals.
Nestlé	Over 20 tonnes of food delivered for Moscow and St. Petersburg hospitals, including coffee and coffee machines
Kraft Heinz	Over 300 tonnes of products given for charity purposes in several oblasts
Danone	Over 80 tonnes of products delivered to different regions of the Russian Federation
Bio Food Lab; Take a Bitey	Over 20 tonnes of fruit bars and milk donated to charities
HARIBO Konfety OOO	Over 80 tonnes of products donated to charities
PhosAgro Group of Companies	Equipment and protection gear worth over 1 billion rubles delivered to medical institutions. Fundraising actions among employees
#ironmed20	Masks, protective suits, and energy-boosting food made and delivered for personnel working with COVID-19 patients
Inter RAO Group	Over 97 million rubles
PIK GROUP	35 million rubles
Russian Railways	Over 200 million rubles
SUEK JSC	5 million rubles
Rosseti, Public Joint Stock Company (PJSC ROSSETI)	5 million rubles
TikTok Company	25 million rubles
RUSNANO Group	31 million rubles
The State Atomic Energy Corporation ROSATOM	Over 180 million rubles

(*Continued*)

Table 11.3 (Continued)

Institution	*Contribution*
State Space Corporation ROSCOSMOS	Over 10 million rubles
Galamart Goods and Shops	10,000 sets of non-food necessities donated in 38 regions to seniors and multi-children families
Amway	Over 1,000 sets of personal hygiene products donated to state hospitals
UNITED CONFECTIONERS Holding Co.	Over 70,000 boxes of chocolates given to WWII veterans all over Russia
"Chistaya liniya" OOO	Several thousand boxes of ice cream delivered to Moscow coronavirus hospitals
TRANSKAPITALBANK TKB	1 million rubles for purchasing personal protection means
XIAOLONG GROUP	100,000 three-layer non-medical masks donated to volunteers.

Source: own research based on DOBRO (n.d.); data for 24 May 2021.

The role of the mutual aid project implemented in the RF under the #МЫВМЕСТЕ banner can be seen in the results presented below:

- 6,122,342 recipients of direct aid
- 1.81 billion rubles collected through the website
- 9,747 domestic, foreign, state (Russian) and private partners
- 188,092 volunteers
- 30 million personal protective equipment donated (#MYVMESTE, n.d.).

The initiative would not have reached such a scale without the active support of the state. However, the awareness of assisting those in need has become the primary determinant of grassroots social activity of the citizens of the RF. In this way, empathy has begun to return to social awareness, and people have realised that providing voluntary help to others is one of the values that shape every society and nation.

The RPMMV "Volontery-Mediki" aid has also translated into promoting a new form of social activity, commonly perceived as a manifestation of responsibility for oneself and one's neighbours. During the coronavirus pandemic, the status of volunteering rose, further improved by many campaigns promoting this lifestyle, such as the Volunteer Day organised on 4–5 December 2020 as part of the Online-marathon #МЫВМЕСТЕ ("Na onlayn-marafone", 2020). President Putin also spoke about the value of volunteerism, emphasising the commitment of volunteers in all areas of life, their invaluable role in the fight against COVID-19 and the selfless desire to assist others: "I sincerely congratulate millions on this celebration, millions of Russian citizens whom I have not mentioned and who do good deeds for the benefit of others, who show the whole society an example of enormous moral strength" ("V Den' volontera", 2020).

The president then spoke online with the finalists of the "Volunteer Russia 2020" competition and volunteers from all over the country participating in the live meeting from their homes, workplaces, hospitals, and the headquarters of the #МЫВМЕСТЕ initiative. Emphasising that "Russia is a country of opportunities", Putin committed himself to promoting this form of civic activity. He also said that the volunteers become one of the leading forces in the fight against the coronavirus pandemic. He noted that in 2020, over 15 million volunteers from the whole Federation took part in various projects of social importance and that the society had changed during the pandemic: "This year we thought a lot – we started to value life more, treat our relatives, friends, people living and working nearby with more care and attention". In his opinion, people stopped being ashamed of doing good deeds. He also emphasised Russian businesses' responsibility and social maturity during the pandemic (Zamakhina, 2020).

The phenomenon of voluntary action in every country is profitable. It is a confirmation of the maturity of citizens and the groups they form to actively participate in the social, economic, and political life of the country. Because it is independent, created entirely from below, it instils fear among those in power in an authoritarian state. The lack of control is something that constitutes, or is interpreted as, a real threat to dictatorship. Unable to pass this movement, which is proliferating in the era of the COVID-19 pandemic, Putin has initiated the celebration of a volunteer holiday every 5 December, as is the case worldwide (International Volunteer Day 5 December). The opportunity to empower citizens and recognise their commitment to grassroots social activism was missed with the start of the aggression against Ukraine. Once it is over, will it help to rebuild society and the state? There is hope for this.

The support of business for the society: the Russian Union of Industrialists and Entrepreneurs

Considering the extraordinary financial and organisational challenges that businesses face due to the COVID-19 pandemic and actions undertaken to mitigate it, it should be noted that private enterprises, particularly those small and medium-sized, have limited resources to join the fight; during the pandemic, their priority is to survive and adapt. In turn, larger businesses can actively participate in this combat, support citizens, and diminish the negative economic consequences.

There are several critical directions of business activities aimed at combating the pandemic threat:

1 To support and protect their employees, companies have undertaken a variety of measures.

   a Wherever possible, employees work from home.
   b Employees with children work from home as kindergartens and schools are closed. Different options are considered in case of duties that cannot be performed off-site.

c Employees' health is monitored, and personal protection means (masks, disinfectants) are provided.
d Business trips, meetings, and events are cancelled; continuous production is adjusted to minimise the concentration of employees.
e Companies pay employees one-time support. For example, Severstal designated 500 million rubles for all its employees except the top 100 managers ("Aleksey Mordashov", 2020);
f Many companies pay 100% salary to employees on sick leave due to respiratory illnesses.

2 The Russian Direct Investment Fund (RDIF), Russia's Sovereign Fund, the Russian Union of Industrialists and Entrepreneurs (RSPP), Yandex, and Mail.ru Group announced creating an alliance to fight COVID-19. Leading Russian clinics and analytical laboratory chains will cooperate with the project. The main goal is to ensure fast testing of the population for coronavirus using the best technologies available. The alliance will also ensure industrial safety and the undisturbed operation of the largest Russian enterprises (Lisitsyna et al., 2020).
3 Businesses offer money and infrastructure for developing medicines, producing goods highly demanded during the pandemic and solving other problems. For example:

a AFK Sistema PAO announced investment of ca. 1 billion rubles to counteract the coronavirus spread in Russia. The funds will be used to develop testing systems for detecting infection, changing the designation of clinical hospitals to research COVID-19, hospitalisation and treatment of coronavirus patients, and production of protection means. Sistema also contributes to mitigating socioeconomic results of anti-pandemic measures by developing remote service channels and providing free online services. As new initiatives appear, the investments will increase ("AFK 'Sistema'", 2020).
b Norilsk Nickel announced giving an additional 10.5 billion rubles for actions combating the COVID-19 pandemic. Ten stationary and five mobile testing laboratories would be placed in the Norilsk Industrial District and the Kola Peninsula. The number of beds in the infectious diseases ward in the municipal hospital in Norilsk increased from 45 to 100. If the course of the pandemic follows pessimistic predictions, this number can be quickly raised to 1,000 (Pavlova, 2020). Norilsk Nickel had previously announced assigning 1 billion rubles for medical protection in cities in the Norilsk area (Ivanov, 2020), which included a purchase of about 30 ventilators. The Vladimir Potanin Foundation assigned 1 billion rubles to support funds helping citizens not covered by social protection. Non-profit organisations can receive up to 1 million rubles to keep their employees and adjust to new work models (Silko, 2020).
c The gold-mining company PJSC Polyus and the Far East and Arctic Development Fund have begun to finance measures to counter the coronavirus spread in the Far East. The target amount of the dedicated fund is 1 billion rubles. As the first instalment, Polyus and the Development Fund would transfer

250 million rubles to implement anti-epidemiological measures. The part will support the Magadan area and Yakutia in purchasing personal protection means and medical equipment; the remaining money will support all Far Eastern Federal District subjects. Further, 750 million rubles would be obtained from other non-state sources. Large companies with investments or industrial assets in the macroregion have been invited to join the programme ("Uchrezhdeniye fonda", 2020). Polyus also announced that 45 ventilators would be delivered to hospitals in the area of the company's operations.

d Oleg Deripaska financed the construction of three specialised clinics to combat the coronavirus pandemic ("V Irkutskoy oblasti," 2020). En+ Group promised to deliver 800,000 medical masks free of charge to the Irkutsk Oblast Ministry of Health ("En+ Group", 2020). United Company RUSAL initiated a volunteer movement supporting retired employees over 70 who remain in self-isolation. Until July 2020, they received free monthly sets of basic necessities delivered by volunteers from the corporation. Furthermore, RUSAL's charity fund, the Centre for Social Programmes, has opened a helpline where retired company employees can ask for assistance ("Vremia pomagat'", 2020).

4 Trading companies specialising in essential products and goods have adapted to working during the lockdown. To promote online purchases and attract customers used to traditional shops, many firms offer various discounts for delivery, increase expenditures on advertising online shopping, and introduce new regulations to protect the health of the buyers and couriers (contactless payment at delivery, refusal to carry purchases into the apartment). However, despite the active promotion of online purchases, shops have remained open after introducing additional measures regarding disinfection and distancing. Specific solutions include:

a Protection of particularly vulnerable groups – a priority time slot reserved only for pensioners (Billa and Magnit); free delivery for pensioners (Perekrestok).

b Additional cleaning and extended distance – increased frequency of cleaning and disinfection of surfaces in the shop, providing hand sanitisers, organisation of preventive actions (OBI). Special floor markings reminded to maintain distance (Lenta, Magnit, Detskiy mir).

c Voluntary closures of shop chains or branches.

5 The banking sector

a Banks voluntarily limited the number of offices. VTB Bank introduced continued servicing of expired cards to minimise the need to visit its branches.

b Credit holidays and opportunities for debt restructuring for natural and legal people afflicted by the pandemic were introduced by VTB Bank, Public Joint-Stock Company Promsvyazbank PJSC, Alfa Bank JSC, Credit Bank of Moscow, Commercial bank "Absolut Bank" (PAO), Bank DOM.RF (Joint-stock company), Public Joint-Stock Company MTS Bank (Milyukova & Petukhova, 2020).

The involvement of the business sector of both private and state-owned enterprises, as well as Russian and foreign corporations, provided another example of non-state-controlled activity. The scale of the problems faced by entrepreneurs themselves, as well as their employees, and the awareness of giving support to those in need determined the actions of the second sector. They very often bailed out state institutions. They thus bore witness to their effectiveness and efficiency, which gave the rulers the impetus to redefine the goals of the expansionist policy, the tenets of which lay at the heart of the projected strategy of "collecting Russian lands" in the 21st century.

Conclusions

Due to the experiences of the pandemic, the value and significance of grassroots citizens' activity – a voluntary form of self-organisation of society members – have been noticed by decision-makers and ordinary citizens alike. Volunteering has risen significantly as it has been the primary way of providing genuine assistance to many people in need. It has also brought about the renaissance of the concept of mutual help, giving a new meaning to the lives of both the helpers and the helped.

As the SARS-CoV-2 virus spread through Russia, it became clear that the civil society, so far marginalised, is good not only for propaganda purposes in foreign relations. The usefulness of the non-governmental, non-commercial sector was finally confirmed during the pandemic-related crisis when these organisations, which have been developing human capital from the start, laid the foundations for dynamically developing philanthropy. The increasing lack of security experienced during the pandemic motivated the citizens to act. The growing tendency to help each other in need, personal obligations notwithstanding, has been observed among individual citizens and their commercial and non-commercial organisations, in the media, in state and private institutions and entities, and in business corporations.

In the difficult circumstances of the fight against coronavirus spread, the relations between society and the state have undergone significant transformations, and the events of 2020 have become an essential inspiration to develop the public-state dialogue. A partnership model has been adopted to address the most socially sensitive issues, and civil society structures have become actively involved in developing and tuning state solutions. New ideas, experiences, resources, and points of view are becoming increasingly valuable for the state facing the challenge of the COVID-19 pandemic and its socioeconomic effects.

In its summary of the 2020 events, the Civic Chamber of the RF emphasised the grassroots activation of citizens, which took various forms. Over 118 million volunteers in the country have participated in the fight against the coronavirus by supporting senior citizens and disabled people living on their own, as well as orphans and veterans. The volunteers delivered food, medicines, and necessities to all needy people and assisted with household chores. Over 9,000 partner organisations have joined the initiative. The collected donations from companies and individuals amounted to over 1.8 billion rubles, which translated into providing charitable support to ca. 3.5 million persons in the entire country; for many of the recipients, this was a very significant help.

Regional civic chambers were also actively involved in this work by coordinating the volunteers' assistance, informing the authorities about areas of growing tensions related to the imposed restrictions, and monitoring whether local state entities provided the centrally promised support. Due to the efforts of regional civic chambers, helplines were set up to organise volunteers' work for citizens, to assist in maintaining the self-isolation system and purchasing personal protection measures, and to provide information and legal advice for citizens, health workers, and non-profit organisations. As regards the increased demand for personal protection means, non-profit organisations supported the Civic Chamber of the RF in sewing masks from fabrics purchased by non-governmental organisations as a donation for medical institutions (Obshchestvennaya palata RF, 2020).

As noted by the Civic Chamber's spokesperson Lidya Mikheeva, during 2020, the citizens showed unusual activity in solving acute social problems and other wide-range issues. Thus, it can be said with certainty that citizens and civic organisations have become outright participants in implementing national-scale projects. The society has demonstrated solidarity and has become a reliable partner for the government in solving the most severe social problems and developing state solutions ("Opublikovan doklad", 2020).

The grassroots activity of the RF citizens also received support from the state. Aware of the economic, social, and health issues afflicting the nation, the authorities allocated significant resources (predominantly monetary) to minimise the effects of the pandemic-related crisis. Following numerous conversations with representatives of different professional and social groups, the non-commercial sector organisations strove to present the nation's state to the decision-makers as precisely as possible. This work was appreciated by president Putin: during a meeting with the representatives of the Russian third sector, he highlighted the contribution of this sector's entities in this field.

Social participation has been reborn during the crisis caused by the threat of the SARS-CoV-2 virus, thus redefining relations between the first sector, represented by the state entities, the second sector, represented by the world of business, and the third sector, whose foundations are the non-commercial, non-governmental organisations. The consequences of this change in the internal policy cannot be predicted at present. However, one thing is certain: there is no return to the previous model of state entities' omnipotence concerning citizens, particularly to commercial and non-commercial organisations.

Questions about the relevance of grassroots social activism among Russian citizens as a response to the state's deepening peri-pandemic crisis take on particular significance after 24 February 2022, when the RF launched an belligerent, unprovoked aggression against its neighbour Ukraine. From one unfinished pandemic crisis, Russia fell into a second, much more fraught long-term crisis – a peri-war crisis. While the invasion was an intention planned years in advance, which the Russian state, against common sense and social, economic, and political realities, had been preparing for since 2005, the coronavirus pandemic triggered waves of activity that Russian decision-makers found difficult to control. Unfortunately, in both cases, human lives do not matter. The potential for human involvement activated and revealed during the pandemic was not used when Russia conducted its so-called special military operation. The question is – was it not wasted? There is no clear answer to this question, for it is now in a state of petrification. Once the turmoil of war is over, the time will come for its awakening and revival, with the hope of building a better, more stable future.

Contrary to expectations, civil society has not been strengthened in spite of widespread bottom-up organised social activity by various political actors. Activated bottom-up created by individual citizens and their groups, private enterprises, cultural institutions, philanthropic activities did not have the chance to bear abundant fruit, on the contrary. The potential generated was used in the most cynical way by Russian decision-makers to realise their goals of imperial expansion. It cannot escape notice that it was interpreted as a real threat to Putinist stability. The so-called special military operation became the salvation from this oppression, for in this way, the rulers rid the country of its most mobile and therefore uncontrollable "human factor" for a long time. After the trauma of the pandemic, it became important for every society to rebuild its self-esteem, to rebuild its life. It was at this point that the rapid, successful "march to the West" was intended by those in power to restore a sense of normality to Russian citizens. How egregious a mistake this was, both citizens and those in power found out quite quickly.

i The threat of the spread of the COVID-19 virus was not an imaginary phenomenon, but a real one, affecting all people without exception. Hence, the restrictions imposed by governments on their own citizens were understandable to most of them, although this does not mean that they did not cause dissatisfaction. Authoritarian states such as Russia, in this particular case of a pandemic, were in no way able to use the tightened laws to empower decision-makers further. Instead, the decisive factor here turned out to be fear for themselves, their loved ones or, in the longer term, the launching of a series of actions of a destructive nature for the state and society. Thus, the period of the COVID-19 pandemic was not, in this case, used to strengthen the *vertikala vlasti*; rather, it provided an opportunity for top state officials to retreat to the so-called rear. Handing the baton of state management to lower-level officials was done deliberately. It was, however, a temporary retreat from the field, for it made it possible to "inventorise" specific citizens, those social groups or formations and legal entities that could be harnessed to implement one's own plans or, failing that, effectively neutralised. However, in order for this goal to be achieved, groups of new Kremlin ideologues led by Timofey Sergeev, Viktoria Nikiforova, Lyudmila Chertkova, and Lyubov Stepushova have been working since 2014 to prepare the appropriate ground (A. Jach, 2023, pp. 125, 139–142).

ii An important question arises – to what extent will top-down inspired institutional social activism translate into the development of grassroots civic activism? Although the state has supported the voluntary movement and promoted its ideas in society, it has realised from the outset that it is the voluntary movement that poses the greatest threat to authoritarian rule. Controlled by no one, growing and expanding on a hitherto unknown scale, it could not go unnoticed by the Kremlin. Hence, the decision to establish the holiday "Volunteer Day" offered an opportunity to skilfully redirect citizens' attention away from state-wide problems towards those closest to them – the satisfaction of basic needs. Unfortunately, as a result of the start of the invasion of Ukraine on 24 February 2022, just like other grassroots activities shaping civil society, the volunteer movement also lost its *raison d'être*. In today's Russia as a police state, after two years of open warfare, no one is thinking about helping other citizens; everyone is looking only at themselves, focused on not getting caught up in the state's war machine themselves. "Touching the system" now takes place on at least two levels: (1) mobilisation and being sent to the front; (2) a criminal trial based on the new tightened provisions of the Criminal Code of the Russian Federation, as a result of which one loses not only one's job, one's social position, one's property but also one's freedom for many years and, ultimately, one's life. The Russian state is not only fighting an enemy personified by Ukraine and the West supporting it but also fighting its own citizens.

iii Before the outbreak of full-scale war in 2022, there was a real opportunity for support for civic engagement from the business world to strengthen the social structures of grassroots activism; the experience of private sector involvement in solving the problems caused by the SARS COVID-19 pandemic only confirmed the causality of the second sector. For Russian policymakers, the vitality of the business world has created the hope that there is ample opportunity to use the assumptions of the corporatist structure in Russia's imperial expansion plans. Already, the decision-makers recourse to this sector was intended to create optimal conditions for support for any action on the part of both state and private entrepreneurs. This was in line with previous assumptions about the omnipotence of the state sector over the other two in Russia itself but also about the passivity of international structures towards Russia's policy. For the dominant motto of the Western world for many years was business as usual. A reset in relations between the West and Russia was perceived by the latter as a weakness, hence the shock of Russian decision-makers at the strong reactions following the aggression against Ukraine. The *casus* of support for militaristic policies from the Russian business world was not confirmed. To make matters worse, additional sanctions have been launched against individuals in Putin's entourage, as well as against businesses that are in any way complicit or co-financing the hostilities in Ukraine. The situation in the Russian state has started to deteriorate, and nothing heralds any improvement in the near future.

Can this experience of grassroots social activism, including volunteering, offer any hope for the future of Russian citizens? The answer is yes, but this will be possible on the condition not only that the war ends but also that the mentality of Russian society is rebuilt and, at the state level, that the founding myth of imperial Russia – the idea of Moscow the Third Rome – is deconstructed. Only a de-imperialisation of the Russian state and society carried out from below, with external support, can bring about the desired peace, but also create a lasting foundation for building a world without wars in the future.

Bibliography

#MYVMESTE [Project website]. (n.d.). Available at https://мывместе.рф/

AFK "Sistema" investirovala 1 mlrd rubley v bor'bu s koronavirusom [AFK "Sistema" invested 1 bn rubles in fight against coronavirus]. (2020, April 2). *Vedomosti*. Retrieved from https://www.vedomosti.ru/business/news/2020/04/02/826874-sistema-investirov-ala-mlrd (2020, April 8).

AGORA. (n.d.). Doklad Apologii protesta: Dezinfektsiya protesta [A report of the Apology of the Protest: Disinfection of a protest]. Retrieved from https://www.agora.legal/fs/a_delo2doc/203_file__.pdf (2022, April 8).

Aleksey Mordashov prinyal resheniye o dopolnitel'noy vyplate okolo 500 mln rub. sotrudnikam "Severstali" [Aleksey Mordashov decided to pay additional 500 million rubles to Severstal employees]. (2020, April 6). *Severstal*. https://www.severstal.com/rus/media/news/document40799.phtml

Baranyuk, Y. (2020, March 16). "Masok ne nosim, Ioann i Bogoroditsa zashchishchayut". V Kazanskom sobore Sankt-Peterburga tseluyut moshchi i virusa ne boyatsya ["We do not wear masks, John and the Mother of God protect". In the Kazan Cathedral of St. Petersburg people kiss the relics and are not afraid of the virus]. *Current Time TV*. Retrieved from https://www.currenttime.tv/a/covid-russia-believers/30491417.html (2022, April 8).

DOBRO. (n.d.). #MYVMESTE [a mutual aid initiative] [targeted project description]. *DOBRO*. Retrieved from https://dobro.ru/project/31720 (2022, April 8).

En+ Group peredast Minzdravu Irkutskoy oblasti 800 tysyach meditsinskikh masok [En+ Group will donate 800 thousand medical masks to the Ministry of Health of Irkutsk Oblast]. (2020, April 3). *En+ Group*. Retrieved from https://enplusgroup.com/ru/media/news/esg/en-group-peredast-minzdravu-irkutskoy-oblasti-800-tysyach-meditsinskikh-masok/ (2022, April 8).

Garlicki, J. (2016). Partycypacja polityczna [Political participation]. In W. Sokół, & M. Żmigrodzki (Eds.), *Encyklopedia politologii: Pojęcia, teorie i metody [The Encyclopaedia of politology: Concepts, Theories and methods]* (pp. 457–460). Wolters Kluwer Polska.

Grudtsyna, Y., & Petrov, S. M. (2012). Vlast' i grazhdanskoye obshchestvo v Rossii: vzaimodeystviyei protivorechiye [Power and Civil Society in Russia: Interaction and Contradiction]. *Administrativnoye i munitsipal'noye pravo*, *1*(49), 21.

Ivanov, A. (2020, April 2). (Vladimr Potanin: Yesli ya khotel komu-to pomogat', to seychas samoye vremya [Vladimir Potanin: If I ever wanted to help someone, now is the time]. *Komsomolskaya Pravda*. Retrieved from https://www.kp.ru/daily/27112/4190163/ (2022, April 8).

Jach, A. (2019). *Pozarządowy sektor niekomercyjny w Rosji w latach 2000–2018. Osobliwości funkcjonowania [The non-governmental, non-commercial sector in Russia in 2000–2018: Peculiarities of functioning]*. Wydawnictwo Księgarnia Akademicka. https://doi.org/10.12797/9788381380829

Kaźmierczak, T. (2011). Partycypacja Publiczna. Pojęcie, ramy teoretyczne [Public participation: Definition and theory]. In A. Olech (Ed.), *Partycypacja publiczna. O uczestnictwie obywateli w życiu wspólnoty lokalnej [Public participation: On citizens' participation in the life of a local community]* (pp. 83–99). Fundacja Instytut Spraw Publicznych.

"Kino Okko", "Cinema Park", "Formula Kino" v Moskve budut prodavat' po 50 biletov na seans ["Kino Okko", "Cinema Park", "Formula Kino" in Moscow will sell 50 tickets per show]. (2020, 16 March). *TASS*. Retrieved from https://tass.ru/kultura/7996767 (2022, April 8).

Kodeks, R. F. *ob administrativnikh pravonarusheniyah ot 30.12.2001 N 195-ФЗ (ред. от 30.04.2021, с изм. от 17.05.2021)* [Code of the Russian Federation on Administrative Offenses of 30 December 2001 no. 195-F3 (redaction of 30 April 2021, with changes of 17 May 2021)]. (2001). Available at http://www.consultant.ru/document/cons_doc_LAW_34661/

Kondratyeva, Y. (2020, March 18). Koronavirus vyrabotayet v rossiyanakh grazhdanskoye obshchestvo [Coronavirus will develop civil society in Russians]. *Vzglad*. Retrieved from https://vz.ru/society/2020/3/18/1029547.html (2022, April 8).
Kuznetsov, V. (2020, June 3). Chto ostayetsya v istorii. Teatr Nikolaya Kolyady ob'yavil o zakrytii. [What goes down in history. Nikolay Kolyada theatre announced closure]. *Rossiyskaya Gazeta*, *120* (8174). Retrieved from https://rg.ru/2020/06/03/reg-urfo/teatr-nikolaia-koliady-obiavil-o-zakrytii.html (2022, April 8).
Lisitsyna, M., Skrynnikova, A., & Balashova, A. (2020, March 19). "Yandex" i Mail.ru Group voshli v alyans po bor'be s koronavirusom ["Yandex" and Mail.ru became allied in fight against coronavirus]. *RBC*. Retrieved from https://www.rbc.ru/society/19/03/2020/5e739b6a9a7947e123155bb1 (2022, April 8).
Lukmanov, A., & Guselnikov, A. (2020, June 2). Muzhchina, ubityy v Yekaterinburge Rosgvardiyey, był brokerom [The man killed in Yekaterinburg by Rosgvaidiya was a broker]. *URA.Ru*. Retrieved from https://ura.news/news/1052434657 (2022, April 8).
Lyauv, B., & Kodachigov, V. (2020, May 20). Pol'zovatelyam «Sotsialnogo monitoringa» vypisali shtrafov boleye chem na 200 mln rubley [Fines for the users of "Social monitoring" exceed 200 million rubles]. *Vedomosti*. Retrieved from https://www.vedomosti.ru/technology/articles/2020/05/20/830668-sotsialnii-monitorng (2022, April 8).
Milyukova, Y., & Petukhova, L. (2020, March 23). Banki dadut postradavshim ot koronavirusa kreditnyye kanikuly [Banks will give coronavirus victims credit holidays]. *Forbes*. Retrieved from https://www.forbes.ru/finansy-i-investicii/395795-banki-dadut-postradavshim-ot-koronavirusa-kreditnye-kanikuly (2022, April 8).
Na onlayn-marafone #MYVMESTE otprazdnovali Den' volontera [#MYVMESTE celebrated the Volunteer Day at an online marathon]. (2020, December 5). *#MYVMESTE*. Retrieved from https://мывместе.рф/news/tpost/perphjsrm1-na-onlain-marafone-mivmeste-otprazdnoval (2022, April 8).
Obshchestvennaya palata RF [Civic Chamber of the RF] (2020). Doklad OP RF o sostoyanii grazhdanskogo obshchestva za 2020 God [report of the civic chamber of the RF on the state of the civil society for 2020]. Obshchestvennaya palata Rossiyskoy Federatsii.
Opublikovan doklad OP RF o sostoyanii grazhdanskogo obshchestva za 2020 god [The report of the Civic Chamber of the RF on the state of the civil society for 2020 has been published]. (2020, December 23). *RAPSI*. Retrieved from http://rapsinews.ru/human_rights_protection_news/20201223/306615460.html (2022, April 8).
Pavlova, O. (2020, 14 April). "Nornikel' "profinansiruyet sozdaniye laboratoriy dlya vyyavleniya COVID-2019 [Norilsk Nickel will finance the creation of laboratories to detect COVID-19]. *Kommersant*. Retrieved from https://www.kommersant.ru/doc/4321506 (2022, April 8).
Postanovleniye Glavnogo gosudarstvennogo sanitarnogo vracha Rossiyskoy Federatsii ot 13.03.2020 no. 6 "O dopolnitel'nykh merakh po snizheniyu riskov rasprostraneniya COVID-2019" [Resolution of the Chief State Sanitary Doctor of the Russian Federation of 13 March 2020 "On additional measures to reduce the risks of the spread of COVID-2019"]. (2020). Retrieved from http://publication.pravo.gov.ru/Document/View/0001202003170005 (2022, April 8).
Postanovleniye Pravitelstva RF ot 12.05.2020 no. 657 "O vnesenii izmeneniy v perechen' otrasley rossiyskoy ekonomiki, v naibolshey stepeni postradavshikh v usloviyakh ukhudsheniya situatsii v rezultate rasprostraneniya novoy koronavirusnoy infektsii" [Resolution of the Government of the RF of 12 May 2020 no. 657 "On Amendments to the List of Industries of the Russian Economy Most Affected by the Deterioration of the Situation as a Result of the Spread of the New Coronavirus Infection"]. Retrieved from http://publication.pravo.gov.ru/Document/View/0001202005130041 (2022, April 8).
Potok k moshcham Ioanna Krestitelya v Peterburge oslab iz-za koronavirusa [The Crowds to See the Relics of John the Baptist in St Petersburg Have Thinned Due to Coronavirus]. (2020, March 17). *RIA NOVOSTI*. Retrieved from https://ria.ru/20200317/1568753215.html (2022, April 8).

Putin provodit soveshchaniye po doplatam medrabotnikam [Putin holds a meeting on additional payments to health workers] [Broadcast]. (2020, May 19). *Russia Today*. Retrieved from https://www.youtube.com/watch?v=kHsJB9I5yN4&t=9s (2022, April 8).

Silko, G. (2020, 29 March). Rossiyskiye milliardery vstupili v bor'bu [Russian billionaires joined the fight]. *Kommersant*. Retrieved from https://www.kommersant.ru/doc/4307948 (2022, April 8).

Starikova, M., Voronov, A., & Rozhkova, Y. (2020, May 26). SPCH ishchet vykhod iz prilozheniya. Moskvichi massovo osparivayut shtrafy, vypisannye s pomoshchyu "Sotsialnogo monitoringa" [Human Rights Council seeks a way to abandon the application. Massive numbers of Muscovites challenge fines issued with the help of "Social monitoring"]. *Kommersant*. Retrieved from https://www.kommersant.ru/doc/4356500 (2022, April 8).

Troyanskaya, T. (Host). (2020, June 27). *Osoboye mneniye SPB. Boris Vishnevskiy* [Individual opinion from St. Petersburg. Boris Vishnevskiy] [Radio broadcast transcript]. Retrieved from https://echo.msk.ru/programs/personalno/2682957-echo/ (2022, April 8).

Uchrezhdeniye fonda po bor'be s COVID-19 na Dalnemvostoke ob'yemom 1 mlrd rubley [Establishment of a fund to fight COVID-19 in the Far East in the amount of 1 bn rubles]. (2020, March 26). *Polyus*. Retrieved from https://polyus.com/ru/media/press-releases/establishment-of-a-covid-19-fund/ (2022, April 8).

Ukaz Mera Moskvy ot 05.03.2020 no. 12-UM "O vvedenii rezhima povyshennoy gotovnosti" [Decree of the Mayor of Moscow of 5 March 2020 no. 12-UM "On the introduction of high alert state"]. (2020). Retrieved from https://www.sobyanin.ru/static/pdf/ukaz-12-um-23-03.pdf (2022, April 8).

Ukaz Prezidenta RF ot 17.03.2020 no. 187 "O roznichnoy torgovle lekarstvennymi preparatami dlya meditsinskogo primeneniya" [Decree of the President of the Russian Federation of 17 March 2020 no. 187 "On retail trade in medicinal products for medical use"]. (2020). Retrieved from http://www.consultant.ru/document/cons_doc_LAW_347818/ (2022, April 8).

Ukaz Prezidenta RF ot 25.03.2020 no. 206 "Ob ob'yavlenii v Rossiyskoy Federatsii nerabochikh dney" [Decree of the President of the RF of 25 March 2020 no. 206 "On announcement of non-working days in the Russian Federation"]. (2020). Retrieved from http://www.consultant.ru/document/cons_doc_LAW_348485/ (2022, April 8).

Ukaz Prezidenta RF ot 02.04.2020 no. 239 "O merakh po obespecheniyu sanitarno-epidemiologicheskogo blagopoluchiya naseleniya na territorii Rossiyskoy Federatsii v svyazi s rasprostraneniyem novoy koronavirusnoy infektsii (COVID-19)" [Decree of the President of the RF of 2 April 2020 "On measures to ensure sanitary and epidemiological well-being of the population on the territory of the Russian Federation in connection with the spread of the new coronavirus infection (COVID-19)"]. (2020). Retrieved from http://www.consultant.ru/document/cons_doc_LAW_349217/ (2022, April 8).

Ukaz Prezidenta RF ot 28.04.2020 no. 294 "O prodlenii deystviya mer po obespecheniyu sanitarno-epidemiologicheskogo blagopoluchiya naseleniya na territorii Rossiyskoy Federatsii v svyazi s rasprostraneniyem novoy koronavirusnoy infektsii (COVID-19)" [Decree of the President of the RF of 2 April 2020 "On the extension of measures to ensure sanitary and epidemiological well-being of the population on the territory of the Russian Federation in connection with the spread of the new coronavirus infection (COVID-19)"]. (2020). Retrieved from http://publication.pravo.gov.ru/Document/View/0001202004290001 (2022, April 8).

Ukaz Prezidenta RF ot 6.05.2020 no. 313 "O predostavlenii dopolnitel'nykh strakhovykh garantiy otdel'nym kategoriyam meditsinskikh rabotnikov" [Decree of the President of the Russian Federation of 6 May 2020 N 313 "On the provision of additional insurance guarantees to certain categories of medical workers" (2020). Retrieved from http://kremlin.ru/acts/news/63306 (2022, April 8).

V Den' volontera obsudili budushcheye Obshcherossiyskoy aktsii vzaimopomoshchi #MYVMESTE [On Volunteer Day, the future of the #MYVMESTE All-Russian Mutual Aid Action was discussed]. (2020, 15 December). *#MYVMESTE*. Retrieved from https://

мывместе.рф/news/tpost/38yb3ttf51-v-den-volontera-obsudili-buduschee-obsch (2022, April 8).

V Irkutskoy oblasti postroyat tri infektsionnyye kliniki na den'gi Deripaski [In Irkutsk Oblast three infectious diseases clinics will be built with Deripaska's money]. (2020, March 31). *RBC*. Retrieved from https://www.rbc.ru/rbcfreenews/5e82f8709a79472bc977b132 (2022, April 8).

V Moskve desyatki chelovek zaderzhany na piketakh protiv politseyskogo nasiliya [In Moscow dozens of people detained at pickets against police violence]. (2020, June 3). *19RUS*. Retrieved from https://19rus.info/index.php/vlast-i-politika/item/129064-v-moskve-desyatki-chelovek-zaderzhany-na-piketakh-protiv-politsejskogo-nasiliya?template=ia2020&is_preview=on (2022, April 8).

V Ryazani ne khvatilo deneg na vyplatu medikam, rabotayushchim s patsiyentami s COVID-19 [In Ryazan there was not enough money to pay doctors working with COVID-19 patients]. (2020, 6 August). *Novaya Gazeta*. Retrieved from https://novgazrzn.ru/novosti/13817.html (2022, April 8).

Volontery-mediki. (n.d.). O nas [About us]. *Vserossiyskoye obshchestvennoye dvizheniye dobrovol'tsev v sfere zdravookhraneniya "Volontery-mediki"*. Retrieved from https://волонтеры-медики.рф/o-nas/ (2022, April 8).

Vremia pomagat' [Time to help]. (2020, April 3). *Tsentr sotsyalnykh programm RUSAL*. Retrieved from https://fcsp.ru/press/news/191020/ (2022, April 8).

WHO. (2020, December 1). Rekomendatsii dlya naseleniya v otnoshenii infektsii, vyzvannoy novym koronavirusom (COVID-19) [Coronavirus disease (COVID-19) advice for the public]. Retrieved from https://www.who.int/ru/emergencies/diseases/novel-coronavirus-2019/advice-for-public (2022, April 8).

Yasenitskaya, A., Zurman, O., & Konstantinova, A. (2020, May 15). "My tak i ne ponyali, chto eto bylo". Chto proiskhodit s nadbavkami k zarplatam medikov, o kotorykh govoril prezident ["We never actually knew what it was". What is happening with the supplements to doctors' salaries mentioned by the president]. *Mediazona*. Retrieved from https://zona.media/article/2020/05/15/pay-covid-19 (2022, April 8).

Zamakhina, T. (2020, December 6). Volonter v bede ne brosit [A volunteer won't abandon you in trouble]. *Rossiyskaya Gazeta*. Retrieved from https://rg.ru/2020/12/06/vladimir-putin-poblagodaril-volonterov.html (2022, April 8).

Zvorykina, E., & Putresha, V. (2020, November 26). Kak koronavirus narushil prava cheloveka v Rossii [How the coronavirus violated human rights in Russia]. *Institut prava i publichnoy politiki*. Retrieved from https://academia.ilpp.ru/kak-koronavirus-narushil-prava-tcheloveka-v-rossii/?fbclid=IwAR1Za5QB19A5xNqv9I_F882r8cFzKIa4BKRPsy7khHOGZ4b55XuzB_wjgZ8 (2022, April 8).

Conclusions

Lessons for the Future from the COVID-19 Pandemic

Jędrzej Skrzypczak and Oscar Pérez de la Fuente

The question posed in the title of this book as to whether the 2020–2023 years and thus the period of the COVID-19 pandemic had changed the world seems rhetorical. Nevertheless, another doubt arises – how this tragic global experience has indeed changed the world?

The crisis referred to as the COVID-19 pandemic was caused by the SARS-CoV-2 pathogen. Although the aphorism that history is the teacher of life has been very popular since antiquity, the fate of the world, countries, and society convinces us that, unfortunately, humanity does not learn diligently enough from its mistakes. Although the end of the pandemic has only recently been declared, this does not mean the virus has been eradicated. Moreover, further waves of this pathogen or others with similar "potential" to SARS-CoV-2 cannot be ruled out. It seems that, as humanity, we have a specific gene of repression and forgetfulness, which allows us to quickly erase from memory, including social memory, various traumatic experiences, and events.

Such was undoubtedly the deadly toll of this coronavirus. Hence, it should be postulated that at the very least, scientific reflection should tirelessly call for appropriate conclusions to be drawn and, consequently, for the necessary social, political, and organisational reforms to be made so that, should further threats of this kind arise, we can act better, or at least try to save as many lives as possible effectively. We hope that this book is part of this trend.

The end of the pandemic should prompt us to take stock. It is only now that reliable conclusions and findings can be formulated. Only now are things that were concealed during this phenomenon coming to light. Hence, it is only in the recent period that trustworthy reports have been produced which indicate appropriate recommendations (Montserrat, 2023; Sachs et al., 2022; McCaul's Final Report, 2023). The Club Madrid Report can doubtlessly be included in this group (Club de Madrid, 2021). The authors of this volume wish to join this direction from a human rights point of view and, based on their research, propose recommendations and suggestions on what to do if similar challenges to humanity arise. That this will happen; none of us has any doubt. The only question is whether the source of such a new global non-human threat will be another pathogen, a climatic threat, or other factors or phenomena.

The aftermath of the pandemic proved to be an unprecedented and dramatic experience on a truly global scale that shook most societies, countries, and international

DOI: 10.4324/9781003482710-13

organisations, as well as ordinary human beings. While the resulting medical, financial, and social crises can be set right in the future, no one or nothing will positively repair the trauma of those who lived through the passing of their loved ones dying alone, often suffocating. It will also be challenging to heal the psychological harm of children separated from their peers.

At the beginning of the pandemic, when the first cases of coronavirus infection occurred in China and then quite rapidly in many parts of the globe, basically no one knew how dangerous this pathogen could be to the health and life of the global population, how to protect against the virus successfully, and finally how to effectively treat infected individuals. It will be recalled that at the time, we, as humankind, did not have access to vaccines to defend against infection or to medication for those affected. The only form of limiting the spread of the coronavirus was the ordering and implementation of lockdowns, in other words, the remedy known for centuries in the event of an epidemic, that is quarantine. This usually resulted in serious negative consequences in practically all spheres of life on a social and individual level. It nearly halted the functioning of economies worldwide and in all their aspects, from production, especially the provision of all services, to transport. The operation of many social, political, and human activity spheres was frozen. The structures and institutions of the state and democracy, education, and entertainment were functionally discontinued. No state or society was prepared for such a situation, even though many had been warned of such a threat for years. For example, according to an audit conducted by the Supreme Chamber of Control (i.e. the national audit institution) in Poland and a report prepared on this basis and published in 2023, when the first case of the SARS-CoV-2 coronavirus was detected in the country in March 2020 – the organs and institutions of the state, medical entities, and services were quite unprepared for the outbreak, even though, in theory, plans to combat epidemics had been known for a long while (NIK, 2023). Life brutally verified these arrangements. Moreover, policymakers should have been aware as early as the end of 2019 when there were reports of the emergence of the epidemic and how to combat it in the PRC. Nonetheless, they failed to react appropriately to the seriousness of the situation at the time.

The only secure activity sphere in this period turned out to be cyberspace. The entities and individuals operating efficiently in this domain have proved to be the biggest winners of this crisis. Most countries then decided that public life institutions and procedures must be transferred to the parallel digital world. This required time and appropriate legal procedures. Due to constitutional considerations, this was often not possible. Moreover, the passage of time worked against it in this case. For example, because of the pandemic threat, it was impossible to convene procedural bodies to make the applied legal changes.

Many democracies have dealt with this challenge by further strengthening citizens' trust in the institutions of the democratic rule of law. Unfortunately, in many cases, this applies to some of the countries regarded as democracies; it appeared that the enormity of the challenge posed by successive waves of pandemics had outstripped the capacity of policymakers (Club de Madrid, 2021).

The global management of the COVID-19 pandemic by the United Nations (UN) and the World Health Organisation (WHO) has been criticised despite the enormous efforts made by these institutions to combat the contagion, as mentioned in the introduction. These criticisms relate to issues such as the timeliness of the response to the threat, the transparency of the decisions taken, and the fairness and effectiveness of the reaction. The WHO and the UN were deprecated for their delayed answer to the declaration of COVID-19 as a public health emergency of international concern (PHEIC) and then as a pandemic. Critics argued that a faster response could have led to more effective early action to contain the virus worldwide. Initial communication with governments and the public about the severity of the pathogen was also disapproved of, potentially leading to an underestimation of its impact in the early stages. The WHO was criticised for relying on data from member states that could have been more accurate and up to date. This reliance was cited as potentially hindering a more effective early global reaction. Concerns were also raised about the WHO's relationship with China, particularly its over-reliance on assurances from the Chinese government early in the outbreak. This may have contributed to a delay in taking the necessary action to contain the epidemic in the PRC. The vaccine distribution strategy, known as COVAX, was also reprobated. The main objections were that high-income countries secured large quantities of vaccine doses directly from manufacturers, delaying the product availability in low- and middle-income countries. Similar allegations were made about the distribution arrangements for other resources, such as personal protective equipment and testing. Many countries faced shortages that affected their ability to manage the pandemic effectively. The WHO was also faulted for changing its guiding principles on issues such as mask use and airborne transmission of the virus. These changes may need clarification from the public and decision-makers. Guidelines and recommendations were sometimes perceived as insufficiently adapted to specific country contexts, particularly for countries with different health infrastructure capacities. Similarly, the UN and the WHO faced funding and political support challenges, affecting their ability to respond effectively. The latter organisation, in particular, has been subject to political pressures that may have influenced its actions and statements. Criticism of both institutions' response to the COVID-19 pandemic highlights the complexity of managing a global health crisis. Issues such as timeliness, transparency, equitable access to resources and adaptability of policies play a crucial role in the effectiveness of the worldwide response. This provides valuable lessons for future health crises and highlights the need for reforms in global health governance, improved emergency preparedness and a more equitable international health system. There are certainly lessons to be learnt for the future. The worldwide management of similar crises needs to be adjusted (Fidler, 2020; The Economic Times, 2021; UN, 2023b).

This crisis undoubtedly called for unusual, immediate solutions, regulations, and a decisive response to limit the spread of the disease and ensure the sanitation of populations. The dramatic health situation often made it relatively easy to justify even the most restrictive solutions and constraints. However, it was often a convenient pretext for the introduction of oppressive monitoring of individuals and entire communities and the violation of human rights – such as political, social, and cultural rights (especially freedom of expression) – surveillance of citizens, invasion of privacy, restriction of movement, forced taking up of specific jobs, and many other human rights and the opportunity to make vast fortunes using extraordinary public purchasing procedures. Instead of resorting to the solutions in the constitutions, for example in Poland, the authorities did not declare a constitutional state of natural emergency. Instead, through the special Act on COVID, they amended the law based on which even more far-reaching restrictions, prohibitions, and orders were imposed (NIK, 2023). This was motivated by considerations of political gamesmanship.

To be specific, due to the presidential elections scheduled for May 2020, the introduction of a state of emergency, the only solution provided for such extraordinary circumstances in the Constitution of the Republic of Poland was avoided at all costs, as it would automatically postpone the election date to a later time. It was expected that the complex economic and social situation during this period would result in a decline in the future popularity of the incumbent president running for re-election. Therefore, attempts were made, by any means necessary, to conduct the presidential elections in the so-called "envelope" voting, that is postal voting by all electorate, when the existing President still enjoyed relatively high public support. Let us add that neither the binding electoral law in Poland nor her Constitution provided for voting in such a mode. Appropriate preparations were made at that time, although not even a new law was passed allowing such a procedure to be carried out. The printing of electoral cards was ordered, and an agreement was reached with the postal operator. However, none of the decision-makers cared about whether it could infect many people with the virus through the delivered voting envelopes. Not to mention the equality of constituents' votes (in the country, a certain group of residents do not have mailboxes). During an election meeting, one of the leaders of the then ruling political party publicly claimed that the danger of coronavirus infection was over. It was undoubtedly a clear example of the cynical use of legal institutions and the bending of constitutional rules to achieve own political goals of the ruling party leaders. Due to the obstruction of voting in the Upper House of the Polish Parliament of a special Act providing the basis for conducting elections in this mode, the poll was not held. All this cost the state budget, and therefore Polish taxpayers, approximately EUR 15 million.

Declaring a state of emergency would have meant that the elections would have had to be postponed until further notice. At the same time, it was expected that a pandemic could undermine confidence and, thus, public support for the existing authorities. There were also quite a few cases of the state of the pandemic being used for corrupt activities and to make huge fortunes. For example, the so-called "respirator scandal" had a significant public impact in Poland (Khan, 2023). It concerned the decision of the Polish Ministry of Health to immediately purchase medical ventilators at the beginning of the pandemic to secure the needs of emerging temporary hospitals. Vast sums of public money were used to buy such equipment from an entrepreneur previously active in another industry, who offered to supply the scarce devices. It turned out that only some of them were delivered, and most were unusable and at inflated prices. As the Supreme Audit Office's inspection showed, mechanisms to ensure the proper spending of public funds were abolished urgently, with the result that the Prime Minister's Office and the Ministry of Health misspent almost EUR 20 million on incomplete, inoperable, or substandard ventilators. The same happened with the hasty purchase of gloves and protective masks. At first, political decision-makers even boasted that they had managed to import more (e.g. in Poland, the prime minister held a press conference against a window-dressing background of the transport aircraft loaded with such goods). After some time, it turned out that the goods did not meet the required quality and hygiene standards. All this under the pretext of fighting a pandemic (NIK, 2023).

Human rights, civil, political, economic, and social rights were constantly tested to save lives and health. It was not only in authoritarian states that there were various temptations to pursue private interests and political and legal actions in non-transparent ways under the pretext of fighting a pandemic. Most tragically, according to the World Health Organisation, as of 5 July 2023, close to 800 million individuals have struggled with the virus, often with adverse permanent medical consequences, and nearly 7 million have died from SARS-CoV-2 worldwide (WHO, 2023). Of course, it is difficult to conclusively determine whether better policy decisions, crisis management, and more efficient and honest spending of public resources could have saved any of the victims of this disease.

Now that the end of the pandemic has been officially declared, it is time to present the first conclusions and recommendations for the future. Although we will undoubtedly be dealing with the effects of the viral surge for years to come, the accurate scale of this misfortune will become apparent in a few years.

As the COVID-19 pandemic seems to suggest, it is necessary to remodel the notion of human rights towards a concept of rights understood as human needs. Traditionally, it has been argued that human rights are primarily for protecting human dignity through legal norms. In this view, human rights are defined as privileges enjoyed by all human beings, regardless of race, gender, nationality, ethnicity, language, religion, or any other status (UN, 2023a). In a slightly different approach, human rights are defined as "the inherent values of a human being deriving from the inherent personal dignity of every human being, socially conditioned, characterised by equality, inalienability, temporal permanence, subject, object and territorial universality" (Orzeszyna K., & Skwarzyński M., et al., 2023). However, at the end of the 20th century, in connection with the process of globalisation, the need to search for a new axiological basis for the concept of human rights began to be recognised. It was increasingly argued that the European human rights protection system was not universally accepted. One such alternative view is the concept of human needs as a basis for considering the content of individual human rights. This is because needs are the motive for an individual's activity aimed at its satisfaction, regardless of the political, economic, or social system. (Sitek, 2016). It is argued that "the ideas of human rights and basic human needs are closely linked. Human rights – those that apply to every person because they are human beings – can be seen as rights to meet or be able to meet basic human needs. These needs form the basis of human rights./…/Fundamental human needs are anything that people need to be able to achieve a level of functioning that meets a given ethical concept of an acceptable minimum; such concepts include, for example, human dignity or the avoidance of serious harm. Needs derived from these concepts typically include, in particular, a basic level of physical and mental health" (Gasper, 2005). Behind human rights are thus "freedoms and needs so fundamental that their denial threatens human dignity itself" (Goldewijk & de Gaay, 1999, p. 117; Hamilton, 2003; Penz, 1991). Following on from the concepts above, based on the experience of the COVID-19 pandemic, it is necessary to give an entirely new position and meaning to the right to health as a need to ensure adequate levels of physical and mental well-being (Montserrat, 2023). These are the conclusions of Marianne Séverin and Hannah Muzee's findings based on the experience of the COVID-19 pandemic on the African continent, among others. It should, therefore, be emphasised that the right to health consists not only of the question of access to healthcare and its quality but also of equality in access to medical services, which was extremely important in the context of the order of access to vaccines for COVID-19. Indeed, this crisis has also shown how important it is for individuals and entire societies to have universal, equitable healthcare, and social protection systems covering all community members equally and non-discriminately. As J. Skrzypczak and T. Maksymiuk demonstrate in their chapter, it should also be underlined how essential it is to ensure the personnel resources of such systems, such as an adequate supply of medical professionals.

Last but not least, such a right to health should also include access to drinking water, which, in the context of climate change, may prove to be a fundamental problem and a strategic resource not only in Africa. Furthermore, the right to health, so understood, should also consist of the provision of adequate sanitation, proper food, housing, safe work and environmental conditions, medical education, and even gender equality. However, in the African context, all these components of the right to health are violated due to state mismanagement and poverty, and the COVID-19 pandemic revealed the dire situation in many corners of the globe and many continents.

The period highlighted many hitherto unseen flaws and shortcomings of political systems. The pandemic has shown that the resilience of democracies to the threat of authoritarian and populist tendencies in the face of a crisis is unfortunately not guaranteed anywhere in the world. As Joanna Rak and Roman Backer point out in their chapter, during the COVID-19 pandemic, civil liberties were significantly curtailed in many cases. This was not always done to fight the pandemic but to achieve specific partisan goals of a particular body in power, political party, or interest group. Drawing on the example of Poland, the authors point out that from the point of view of legislative technique, such restrictive regulations were introduced within the framework of ordinary law. However, it was possible to declare a state of emergency by invoking the norms contained in the Constitution. The latter would have allowed for the imposition of legal restrictions but, at the same time, would have forced the ruling party to provide certain constraints and to act in a particular mode, subject to deferred control. For example, if the state of emergency provided for in the Constitution were to be imposed, this would have postponed the presidential election by at least three months. The logic of party interest and convenience won out over the rule of law. Citizens were deprived of the possibility to convene public assemblies and could not freely oppose unconstitutional changes to electoral law or regulations on other sensitive issues. For example, on this occasion, the ruling party tried to tighten the abortion law without public debate, even though the problem was highly controversial. In this way, the intention was to avoid mass protests that would probably have occurred under normal circumstances.

This pandemic has also demonstrated the importance of procedures to monitor compliance with constitutional guarantees and the rule of law, with effective oversight by democratically elected parliaments and independent courts (Club de Madrid, 2021). As Oscar Pérez de la Fuente points out, the concept of democracy must be closely linked to accountability, where those in power are held liable and responsible for their actions in government. This has diverse mechanisms and levels. The quality of democracy depends largely on the effective exercise of accountability, with its elements and different types, over those in power.

It is undoubtedly necessary to consider reforms of many institutions of democratic states under the rule of law to improve the capacity to deal with such crises (Club de Madrid, 2021). J. Skrzypczak and T. Maksymiuk show that healthcare systems were more effective in providing medical staff when solidarity principles could be invoked than in countries where compulsory labour was introduced. Globally, one observes different approaches by individual countries to providing strategic medical staff resources in the fight against epidemics. Sometimes, one acts through appeals and entreaties to ethical obligations, resorting only to such soft measures and persuasion. Still, other countries, such as Poland, use hard legal instruments and state coercion. Polish solutions involving the introduction of forced labour have proved highly ineffective and, at the same time, highly controversial from a human rights perspective.

Any planned reforms of institutional arrangements should be based on and serve to build social trust, capital, and solidarity and strengthen civil society (Club de Madrid, 2021). As Anna Jach shows, the experience of the pandemic has meant that the value and importance of grassroots civic activity – a voluntary form of self-organisation by members of society – has been recognised by decision-makers and ordinary citizens. The profile of volunteering has also risen considerably, becoming the leading way to provide real help to many in need. Coming forward has also brought about a renaissance in the concept of mutual aid, giving new meaning to the lives of both the helpers and the helped. With the spread of the SARS-CoV-2 virus, it has become apparent even in Russia that civil society, hitherto marginalised, is suitable not only for propaganda purposes in foreign relations. The usefulness of the non-governmental, not-for-profit sector was finally confirmed during the pandemic crisis, when these organisations, which had been developing human capital from the start, laid the foundations for booming philanthropy. Growing insecurity during the period motivated citizens to act. Regardless of personal commitments, a growing willingness to assist each other in times of need was observed among citizens and their commercial and non-commercial organisations, in the media, in state and private institutions and entities, and in business corporations.

In the difficult circumstances of combating the spread of the coronavirus, the relationship between the public and the state was significantly transformed, and the events of 2020 became an essential inspiration for the development of public-state dialogue. A partnership model in addressing the most socially sensitive issues has been adopted, and civil society structures have been actively involved in developing and adapting state solutions. It can, therefore, be said with certainty that citizens and civil society organisations have become direct participants in implementing projects on a national scale. Society has demonstrated solidarity and become a reliable partner for the government in solving the most severe social problems and developing state solutions.

It is also necessary to call for full transparency in political decision-making based on consultation with parliament, opposition parties, and social actors. Ensuring a robust civil society with confidence in policymakers and competent and transparent advisory and control structures is essential. In democratic systems built on specific values of civil society, it is crucial, especially in this type of crisis management, to guarantee the respect of these principles by public officials, taking into account the rules of transparency, equality, and respect for human dignity. It is utterly unacceptable to forgo the legal responsibility of public officials under the pretext of fighting an extraordinary threat and acting in a state of emergency (Club de Madrid, 2021).

Furthermore, every crisis puts representatives of all kinds of minorities at a disadvantage. Therefore, it is critical to guarantee adequate rights to the various minorities during such times of concern (Ibid.).

As Oscar Pérez de la Fuente points out, states of emergency of all kinds are part of the democratic *raison d'etre*. The rationale for this institution stems from the fact that in exceptional situations, it is necessary to temporarily restrict certain rights to protect the proper functioning of the rule of law. These states have previously been regulated by the Organic Law, which determines who can suspend their rights, how, when, and for how long. This is a guarantee provided by law that, in justified cases, certain rights may be temporarily limited using a pre-established procedure.

The experience of the COVID-19 pandemic convinces us that it is also necessary to put in place appropriate plans for the state's emergency management in situations of global emergency, incorporating flexible but transparent crisis control principles (Club de Madrid, 2021). As Oscar Pérez de la Fuente points out in his chapter, the pandemic challenged different societies, especially democratic ones, in this respect. In many countries, the right to move has been curtailed, and work patterns have been changed from face-to-face to online due to mandatory confinement at home. There should also be public debates on whether and to what extent legal paternalism is justified in similar emergencies, which boiled down to whether the state can force its citizens to wear masks or vaccinate.

Strategies for implementing the indispensable emergency procedures also need to be developed. The example of the quarantine perfectly illustrated this dilemma. Using the example of the Czech Republic, Maciej Skrzypek analyses and demonstrates the effectiveness of the various models used for such a restriction of civil liberties. This is an interesting example: the Czech response to the coronavirus crisis significantly shifted from smart quarantine to strict blockade. Interestingly, despite adopting more stringent measures in the second phase, the pandemic worsened in September 2020. Of course, one cannot conclude that more rigorous quarantine forms are counterproductive. However, the issue was something else. During the "first wave" of the pandemic in the Czech Republic, anti-pandemic measures had parliamentary legitimacy. In contrast, during the "second wave", the dramatic situation and one of the worst outcomes in Europe led to a lack of confidence in the pandemic policy and government decisions. At the beginning of 2021, the lack of trust in Prime Minister Babiš's policy forced the Prime Minister to apologise for the conditions and promise to save public health. However, the statement did not change anything in civic governance.

The COVID-19 pandemic demonstrated, as never before, that digital technologies based on internet communication can become a strategic resource for states to function and meet the primordial needs of society in almost every sphere (Club de Madrid, 2021).

It is also imperative to advocate creating state policies based on facts and evidence rather than conspiracy theories.

However, in this type of emergency, the spread of "infodemia", understood as a flood of disinformation, can be as dangerous to human health and safety as the pandemic. As J. Skrzypczak and K. Duda show in their chapter, it is essential to counter disinformation as a toxic driving force of the secondary effects of a pandemic, which can increase the risk of conflict, violence, human rights violations, and mass atrocities. The fundamental question, however, is how to combat such a phenomenon. The simplest solution, used in many non-democratic countries but downright unacceptable from a human rights perspective, is either to shut down social media altogether or to introduce draconian penalties. It is much more challenging to deal with infodemia through painstaking, patient and usually very costly outreach and education. As it seems, however, the COVID-19 crisis has shown how vital education is not only in the realm of media and digital skills. When vaccines for the coronavirus were developed in record time as the only virtual panacea in the fight against the disease, and it seemed that the COVID-19 outburst would finally crush all sorts of flat-earthers, including adherents of anti-vaccine movements, it paradoxically turned out that these movements were strengthened. Even their arguments were taken up by some populist political actors. This is another unpleasant experience of the pandemic era.

As never before, so-called medical populism has developed, that is such political or social behaviour and strategies of downplaying the dangerous effects of a disease, proposing easy solutions to the crisis or scientifically unproven treatments, raising pseudo-scientific objections to medical knowledge to demonstrate assumed populist theses.

This crisis, like perhaps none before, has shown once again how vital, reliable, and responsible journalism and media are for a democratic system, as well as for media education, information awareness, and digital skills. These can all be counted among the strategic resources of states today. Nevertheless, the COVID-19 pandemic has shown how essential access to information is to the authoritative and fact-based functioning of the media. Ensuring transparent access to reliable information about the pandemic in many countries was critical for preventing the spread of disinformation, as J. Skrzypczak and K. Duda demonstrate in their chapter. In this context, the authors call for the creation of adequate safeguards in access to information in crisis and emergencies and, secondly, the provision of appropriate communication models between governments and citizens based on honesty, integrity, and empathy.

As Wojciech Adamczyk points out, the COVID-19 pandemic has also left its mark on the media market and the freedom of action of journalists. Some phenomena described can be seen as catalysts for change, accelerating specific transformative processes in how editors and reporters operate (remote working and the hybrid formula of editorial work). Other processes, such as the inevitable downsizing, the demise of many traditional media editorial offices or the relatively severe reduction in the reach or frequency of their publications, represent a painful experience for the media environment. In some ways, the pandemic benefitted the online media, which adapted very well to operating under the sanitary conditions of COVID-19 and profited from the high demand for information about the coronavirus. However, the disease has also been used by the governments of many countries to attempt to limit media pluralism in terms of content, information sources, and content providers, with a detrimental effect on the level of freedom of expression. In many countries described, official political power has imposed states of emergency, introduced rushed regulations, restricted access to information to cover up its mistakes and omissions, and even harassed reporters who have been critical of these actions. The journalistic community in these countries should pressure the authorities to roll back the transitional provisions and bad practices against the independent media once the pandemic is over.

However, this will not always be possible. As Vladyslav Zinichenko shows using the examples of Belarus and Ukraine, there were significant media freedom violations in many countries during the COVID-19 onslaught. For instance, Belarusian journalists were often fined for attempting to report on the pandemic, and it should be noted that they were not afraid to publish the truth under conditions of total censorship. On the other hand, Ukrainian reporters may have lost their jobs due to funding cuts or attempts to take away their jobs.

Mass vaccination also appears to be an essential and effective way to protect the public. Unfortunately, the voluntary inoculation system is ineffective in combatting the COVID-19 pandemic because not enough people are vaccinated. The compulsory approach becomes the only method to encourage more individuals to be inoculated. However, opponents of COVID-19 vaccination have put forward many arguments against the procedure. Many of them are irrational, and only two require consideration from a human rights perspective. The first is that inoculation is a kind of medical experiment, and the second is that obligatory vaccination violates human dignity related to personal freedom and the right to protect private life. Both arguments are wrong. The most popular BioNtech-Pfizer vaccine has been tested, proven, and approved for use by medical product control authorities in the European Union, the United States, and other Western countries. Compulsory inoculation is also justified for public health protection, a widely accepted reason to justify human rights and freedoms restrictions.

On the one hand, the COVID-19 pandemic has shown how vital state-financed support and public assistance in crises are for most areas of modern states, such as healthcare, the economy, and culture. Hence, at a time of prosperous state revenues, it is necessary to call for a reduction in public debt. It is also mandatory to promote responsibility in using crisis-support funds. On the other hand, effective methods to combat corruption and exclude impunity for political decision-makers are also required. Oscar Pérez de la Fuente argues that the pandemic may have fostered corruption due to several factors. Firstly, the rapid development of the phenomenon and the associated economic downturn led to fierce competition for essential resources. Secondly, governments quickly mobilised public funds (for healthcare and financial stability) on an unprecedented scale, creating opportunities for easy money, including outright corruption. Thirdly, politicians, civil servants, and health professionals enjoy considerable discretion in the allocation of resources. The loss of transparency and weakened supervision and enforcement have exacerbated issues of corruption and fraud, and public measures against these crimes have not kept pace with the unfolding crisis. In the case of the COVID-19 pandemic, huge uncertainty and discretion in decision-making affected the vast majority of the population. In addition to these factors that could increase corruption, horizontal accountability diminished during this period.

Furthermore, parliamentary activity was suspended during the state of emergency, thus limiting horizontal accountability and the right to political participation. Additionally, as shown in a chapter, African government officials squandered donor funds from international organisations such as the World Bank and the International Monetary Fund, which were supposed to help reduce the social burden during lockdowns, modernise health facilities, and accelerate the population's vaccination. Funds raised from extensive aid efforts in many countries worldwide to support the socioeconomic situation during the pandemic in African countries did not reach those who most deserved them. As a matter of fact, they were diverted by officials to build their private empires. As some cases on the African continent show, the COVID-19 upsurge created a massive opportunity from the outset to "exploit poor supervision and insufficient transparency to divert funds away from people in their hour of greatest need". South Africa and Uganda are two categorical examples where "COVID entrepreneurs" have emerged to benefit at the expense of the masses they are supposed to serve.

Additionally, business corporations should also be postulated and encouraged to bear social responsibility in response to crises.

Finally, the COVID-19 pandemic demonstrated the importance of international cooperation mechanisms based on transparency and solidarity. At the same time, inclusion in the elaboration and decision-making process of global NGO networks should be called for. As Alexander Sugurov points out, there is an opportunity to use Gorbachev's renewed "new political thinking" as an alternative to the non-interventionism doctrine in world politics after the pandemic. In terms of scale, the period can be compared to the Chornobyl disaster in 1986. The shock caused by how information about the accident had been concealed was considered one of the main factors in the emergence of "new political thinking" in the Soviet Union. This approach proposed reconstructing the world system with respect for universal human values instead of force and ideological antagonisms. Similarly, an analogous distress was experienced worldwide due to Chinese efforts to hide information about the new coronavirus. As an application of renewed "new thinking", possible directions for reform of the UN Security Council that would strengthen its effectiveness as a global exercising authority structure are also being considered.

The COVID spell was a real opportunity to assess the quality of governance, legal systems, crisis management models, the strategic reserves of states, and the accountability principles of decision-makers in virtually every corner of the globe. The inferences we present in this book are not optimistic. Although some seem to suggest that non-democratic states have coped better than those traditionally categorised as democracies in the fight against the pathogen, the conclusions drawn from the authors' research of the individual chapters convince us that this thesis is wrong. Firstly, it is essential to ask what it means to "cope better with a pandemic". How is this to be measured? By the number of deaths, public confidence, or yet another indicator? Simple data showing the number of deaths in this context cannot be considered reliable; the number of victims of SARS-CoV-2 depended not only on the efficiency and severity of the implementation of restrictive restrictions such as quarantine, movement bans, and orders to wear masks. It was undoubtedly a product of the health and condition of later virus victims. While some restrictions on civil rights and freedoms were necessary, not all human rights can be sacrificed to fight a pandemic. There is also a social-political life after it is over.

Moreover, lost trust in policymakers after such a traumatic experience cannot be rebuilt quickly. Besides, perhaps acting in an emergency and extreme situation has shown that some countries regarded as democracies do not meet these criteria. In the post-COVID era, there is an even more vital need to ensure that those in power can be held accountable for their decisions. This also applies to exceptional and urgent circumstances. Only then can it be hoped that democracies will become stronger and the lessons from the COVID pandemic will be well learnt?

Bibliography

Club de Madrid. (2021). *Democracy & emergencies. Lessons from the COVID-19 pandemic for democratic resilience. Final report of the Global Commission on Democracy and Emergencies*, December 2021. https://clubmadrid.org/wp-content/uploads/2022/04/ClubdeMadrid_resumen_ingles_DIGITAL.pdf

Fidler, D. P. (2020). *The World Health Organization and Pandemic Politics. The good, the bad, and an ugly future for global health.* https://www.thinkglobalhealth.org/article/world-health-organization-and-pandemic-politics

Gasper, D. (2005). Needs and human rights. In R. Smith, & C. Anker (Eds.), *The essentials of human rights* (pp. 269–272). Hodder & Stoughton.

Goldewijk, B. K., & de Gaay, F. B. (1999). Goldewijk, B.K. & B. de Gaay Fortman (Eds.), *Where needs meet rights*. WCC Publications,

Hamilton, L. (2003). *The political philosophy of needs*. Cambridge University Press.

Khan, A. (2023). *Political turmoil and corruption scandals: Dissecting Poland's 'Respirator Affair'*. https://bnn.network/politics/political-turmoil-and-corruption-scandals-dissecting-polands-respirator-affair/
McCaul's Final Report. (2023*). The origins of the global pandemic, including the roles of the CCP & WHO.* https://foreignaffairs.house.gov/finalcovid-19pandemicoriginsreport/#
Montserrat, D. (2023). *Special Committee on the COVID-19 pandemic: Lessons learned and recommendations for the future.* https://www.europarl.europa.eu/doceo/document/A-9-2023-0217_EN.html
NIK. (2023). *Ineffective management of the COVID-19 pandemic in Poland - Press conference at NIK.* https://www.nik.gov.pl/en/news/ineffective-management-of-the-covid-19-pandemic-in-poland-press-conference-at-nik.html
Orzeszyna, K., Skwarzyński, M., & Tabaszewski, R. (2023). *International Human Rights Law, Warszawa.*
Penz, P. (1991). The priority of basic needs. In K. Aman (Ed.), *Ethical principles for development: Needs, capacities or rights* (pp. 35–73). Montclair State University.
Sachs, J. D. et al. (2022, September 14). The lancet commission on lessons for the future from the COVID-19 pandemic. *The Lancet, 400*(10359). https://www.thelancet.com/journals/lancet/article/PIIS0140-6736(22)01585-9/fulltext
Sitek, M. (2016). *Prawa (potrzeby) człowieka w ponowoczesności, C.H.* Beck.
The Economic Times. (2021). *WHO's pandemic response: From criticism to Nobel?* https://economictimes.indiatimes.com/news/international/world-news/whos-pandemic-response-from-criticism-to-nobel/articleshow/81443977.cms?from=mdr
UN. (2023a). *Human rights.* https://www.un.org/en/global-issues/human-rights)
UN. (2023b). *High-level political forum, 1ST and 2ND meetings (AM & PM), 10 July, Impact of pandemic, worldwide crises must be overcome to achieve sustainable development goals, speakers stress, as high-level political forum opens.* HTTPS://PRESS.UN.ORG/EN/2023/ECOSOC7134.DOC.HTM
WHO. (2023). *World Health Organisation, overview.* https://covid19.who.int

Index

FSC
www.fsc.org
MIX
Papier | Fördert gute Waldnutzung
FSC® C083411

Kolibri 360 GmbH
Ferdinand-Jühlke-Straße 7
99095 Erfurt, Deutschland
produktsicherheit@kolibri360.de